REWARD MANAGEMENT

REWARD
MANAGEMENT

Michael Rose

KoganPage

LONDON PHILADELPHIA NEW DELHI

First published in Great Britain and the United States in 2014 by Kogan Page Limited

Reprinted 2014 (twice)

2nd Floor, 45 Gee Street	1518 Walnut Street, Suite 1100	4737/23 Ansari Road
London EC1V 3RS	Philadelphia PA 19102	Daryaganj
United Kingdom	USA	New Delhi 110002
www.koganpage.com		India

© Michael Rose, 2014

The right of Michael Rose to be identified as the author of this work has been asserted by him in accordance with the Copyright, Designs and Patents Act 1988.

ISBN   978 0 7494 6980 1
E-ISBN   978 0 7494 6981 8

British Library Cataloguing-in-Publication Data

A CIP record for this book is available from the British Library.

CIP data is available
Library of Congress Control Number: 2013047713

Typeset by Graphicraft Limited, Hong Kong
Printed and bound by 4edge Limited, Essex, UK

CONTENTS

ACKNOWLEDGEMENTS

I would firstly like to thank all the people who gave their time to provide information for the case studies on their organizations that add so much value to this book: Neal Blackshire of McDonald's, Margaret Brierley of Shropshire Council, Kim Brosnan of *Which?*, Dermot Coutier of Kingfisher plc, Tim Fevyer of Specsavers, Ann Govier of Marks and Spencer plc, Tony Peers of The National Theatre, Stewart Pyke of HSBC, Kerry Smith of The Royal Horticultural Society and Kate Worral of Guideposts Trust. Charles Cotton, Reward Adviser at the Chartered Institute of Personnel and Development (CIPD) was very helpful in making suggestions on possible case studies and relevant research.

Thanks to my three partners in RCP, Evan Davidge, Sylvia Doyle and Chris Wilson, who reviewed the first draft of the book and gave very helpful comments. Also to Phil Lurie who provided some valuable comments. Finally, thanks to Chris Blundell, employment tax partner at MHA MacIntyre Hudson, for reviewing the tax chapter.

ABOUT THE AUTHOR

Michael Rose has been an independent reward consultant through his company Rewards Consulting Limited (**www.rewardsconsulting.co.uk**) since 2009. He is also a partner at Reward Consulting Partners LLP. He is based in London and works with a range of organizations to help them develop reward strategies to meet their particular aims and culture.

Michael's most recent corporate role was Director of Reward for Aon Limited covering 16,000 people in the UK and EMEA. His other major corporate roles have been Head of Reward Management for TSB Bank plc; Human Resources Manager, European Insurance Operations, NZI Insurance, and Compensation Manager, Abbey Life Assurance.

Michael also has a decade's experience as a reward consultant, with KPMG and Arthur Andersen where he worked with clients across all sectors and in many countries on reward and broader HR projects.

Michael has an MA in Human Resource Management, is a Companion of the CIPD, an Associate of the Chartered Insurance Institute (CII) and a Fellow of the RSA. He was Vice President Reward for the CIPD, 2006–2008 and was voted Compensation and Benefits Professional of the year for 2009 by *Employee Benefits* magazine.

Michael is often quoted in the press and has appeared on radio and television. He has spoken at conferences around the world and has published over 25 articles on reward and HR issues. Michael's first book, *Recognising Performance*, was published by the CIPD in 2001 and reprinted in 2003. His second book, *A Guide to Non-cash Reward*, was published by Kogan Page in February 2011.

Introduction

Do you get the best value from what your organization spends on reward? Reward (pay, benefits etc) is important. It can be as much as 75 per cent of the costs of an organization and all reward carries messages – intentional or not. So you need to get it right to deliver value and carry the right messages to help engage people in your organization. This book tries to help you do this.

The book is in two parts. Part One (Chapters 1 to 7) covers the fundamentals of reward management – reward strategy and how you develop it, communicating reward and tax issues. Part Two (Chapters 8 to 13) is about reward in practice and covers each of the main parts of reward, from grade structures to long-term plans.

Across both parts of the book I have tried to achieve the right balance between theory and practice. My approach to reward management is fundamentally pragmatic: we need to get things right in the situations we find. But I also strongly believe in the importance of getting the strategy right, drawing where relevant from theories and research. I have included an appendix that summarizes many of the theories that are relevant to reward management. Used in the right way these can be very helpful to provide some evidence for the strategies we may develop.

My knowledge and experience in reward management has been built up over a good many years as a practitioner and consultant in a huge range of different situations. Whilst I cannot hope to make the reader into a reward expert just by reading this book, I have shared my views on what I see as important in reward management. I have also given more time to those aspects of reward that people, in my experience, find most challenging. I cover what I see as the most important parts of reward but, inevitably in a book this size, some things will only be covered briefly.

Reward is now more complex than ever with greater choices. For example, the 2013 CIPD Reward Management survey listed a total of 71 different benefits provided by participants. I have tried to rationalize the huge range of reward components the reward practitioner is faced with and how they fit together. I have summarized some of the key issues that I expand on in the book in the table below:

TABLE I.1

Reward	Issues to cover
Basic pay	Position in the external market, internal equity, rationale for pay reviews, grade structures, salary structures
Variable pay	Will a bonus help or hinder? What would it cover? How different for different groups of people? Use recognition as an alternative? Long-term and/or short-term bonus?
Benefits	What's the rationale? How much choice? Tax efficient?

Throughout the book I have given brief examples of practice to help explain a particular point. In some cases they are things I have been involved in.

For a number of the chapters, I have written up one or two case studies to help bring to life some aspects of what the chapter covers. They are examples of good practice that worked for the organization in the case. However, I advocate *best fit* rather than *best practice* so I am not suggesting that each case study is best practice that should be followed by everyone but I believe that they are all helpful and have some interesting learning points.

The case studies reflect the position at the time of writing in late summer 2013. However, circumstances change in organizations so some of the case studies are likely to have been overtaken by events and may not reflect the organization's detailed practice now.

I have also provided a few short exercises and close each chapter with a few questions that the reader can ask about their own organization.

PART I

THE FUNDAMENTALS OF REWARD MANAGEMENT

Reward and reward strategy

The first part of this book is about reward strategy. I try to demystify it and give examples of what reward strategy is, and perhaps more important, explain what I mean by taking a strategic position on reward. It is all about maximizing value from reward through ensuring it aligns with the business (or organizational) strategy. This is real, practical and firmly organizationally focused.

In this first chapter I define what I mean by reward and reward strategy along with some associated terms and ideas. To start us off I need to deal with a few terms so you can see how I am using them in the rest of the book:

Reward

Definitions

- **Reward** – which is what this book is about. I will use the word to mean the total of all of the financially valuable related elements received by employees in an organization.

- **Remuneration** – means the same as 'reward'. It is commonly used in the context of the 'Remuneration Committee', which oversees the remuneration of senior executives and sometimes remuneration policy.

- **Compensation** – this is commonly used in the US and refers to pay and bonus. In larger US organizations, the two functions of compensation and benefits (referring to pension and healthcare in the US) are often separated.

- **Benefits** – are the non-cash parts of reward that are provided by the employer either to all employees or differentiated by level.

'Remuneration' and 'Reward' are interchangeable whilst 'Compensation' and 'Benefits' are a part of reward or remuneration. I have sometimes seen a job title such as Reward and Remuneration Manager, which makes no sense as it is a tautology.

- **Total Reward** – has started to be used to mean both reward plus a range of other non-reward items such as training and development. I do not think that this is helpful. My preference is to use 'Reward' or 'Total Reward' interchangeably and use a quite different phrase to capture the other things that in total make up the employee experience, such as the 'employee deal'.

- **Recognition** – is also sometimes used as in 'Reward and Recognition'. As I show in Chapter 9, recognition is very different from reward.

If you do want to take a broader definition of total reward then this may be helpful. Vartiainen *et al* (2008) suggest that rewards are all of the monetary, non-monetary and psychological payments that an organization provides for its employees in exchange for the work they perform. They go on to define reward as an outcome one receives from others for doing one's job, and they see three types of reward:

- Financial rewards – are all the monetary payments an employee receives. Financial rewards derive their motivating potential from their exchange function: money can be exchanged for desirable outcomes, eg goods and services.

- Material rewards – have an indirect identifiable monetary value, implying a cost for the organization although the employee cannot exchange the reward for its monetary value, eg training opportunities and presents.

- Psychological rewards – are the supportive and positively evaluated outcomes of the professional interpersonal relationships an employee develops with their supervisor, colleagues and/or clients eg compliments and recognition.

Elements of reward

Reward can be broken into the four parts illustrated in Figure 1.1, which should also help explain the relationships between the terms discussed above.

Figure 1.1 implies the relative size of the four components, but of course this will vary considerably by corporate structure, sector, employee group and reward strategy.

FIGURE 1.1   The four components of reward

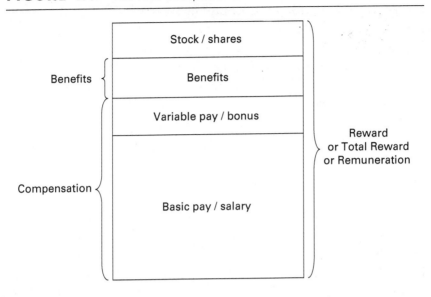

Basic pay/salary

Basic pay (also referred to as base pay) is the contractual salary and may include allowances that are paid regularly and are, in effect, salary. Basic pay is dealt with in Chapters 8 and 9. For the vast majority of people, basic pay will always be the largest part of their reward. The two main exceptions are:

- senior executives whose reward may incorporate a large potential annual bonus and very significant share plans; and

- sales people or traders whose bonus and commission potential may be much greater than their salary.

Variable pay/bonus

Variable pay can come in many shapes and sizes, but mostly means some form of bonus. Unlike salary which is a fixed cost, variable pay is just that, variable – its payment will be contingent on something and so it may or may not be paid. If it is fixed, like a guaranteed bonus, I would consider this is the same as salary just dressed up as something else by using a different name. Bonus is discussed in Chapter 10.

Benefits

Benefits are not cash and will include tangible things like company cars, insured benefits like life assurance or medical insurance, pensions and some terms and conditions such as holidays. Whilst I have classified shares as a separate element of reward, primarily because for executives their value can be very large, they may be considered part of the benefit package. The range of benefits (covered in Chapter 13) will vary between sectors and, often, by seniority. Interestingly, the proportion of cost devoted to benefits can be highest in the UK public sector due to the pension arrangements. In public sector defined benefit (DB) pension plans still dominate whilst they are now extremely rare in the private sector where some form of defined contribution (DC) plan is more common. The cost of a DB pension plan is normally very considerably higher than a DC plan.

Stock/shares

Share plans, by definition, will only be available within private sector companies with shares. Shares are mostly available for the more senior employees, but some companies have 'all employee share' plans that allow everyone in the business to become a shareholder, usually by buying shares within a tax approved plan. The types of share plan will vary considerably and are heavily dependent on the relevant tax legislation. Shares are dealt with in Chapter 12.

The whole should be greater than the sum of the parts

Effective reward management is about both the individual elements of reward and the total cost and value. The different parts of reward may be for different purposes but they all cost money to provide, so the organization needs to look at the total as well as the separate elements. There will be some choices about where to spend the organization's money to best effect in the balance between the different parts of reward. For example, fixed basic pay could be lower but with a high potential bonus or profit share. Or more could be spent on tax-efficient benefits that deliver good value to employees than fully taxable salary.

What is important is that the options and the impact of these choices are considered carefully taking a strategic approach and the rationale is clearly explained to employees. It was common in the past, and persists in many organizations today, that the different elements of reward were managed separately and sometimes in a piecemeal fashion. For example, cars were managed by fleet management, pensions by the pension's department and so on. Whilst this might have been administratively efficient, overlooking the total value proposition to employees would lose the value to the organization of their total spend on reward. I discuss how this can be helped by effective communications in Chapter 6.

Cost of reward

It is a surprise to some organizations quite how much they spend on the total cost of reward and in particular the proportional cost of the various elements. For example, I have worked with an organization where the cost of the DB pension for just 15 per cent of their employees cost half of the total amount spent on all benefits for the whole company. As you might expect, they did something about this inequitable spend.

A valuable way of considering the total cost of reward is as a proportion of all of the costs of an organization (property, technology, power, insurance, interest etc). Reward can be anything from 5 per cent to 75 per cent of total costs. At one end there is the service sector which has little capital employed and where reward is likely to be more than 70 per cent of total costs. At the other extreme, in a sector such as oil and gas, which uses a huge amount of capital, the total cost of reward can be less than 5 per cent of all costs. Whilst employment costs will be of interest to all finance directors and leaders of organizations, where it is by far the most significant cost, it should be given particular attention.

I believe that it can be very helpful to show the total costs of reward as a percentage of the total costs of the organization plus the costs of the different categories of reward. You can illustrate these for your own organization as pie charts. This information can attract the attention of key stakeholders, who may never before have considered reward in these terms. It can lead to questions and valuable discussion on the role of reward in the organization.

Reward strategy

Definition

Valuable insights can come from unexpected sources. For example, in *Alice's Adventures in Wonderland* by Lewis Carroll, Alice asks the Cheshire cat which way she ought to go. But when asked where she wants to get to, Alice says that she doesn't care much. In which case, says the cat, 'Then it doesn't matter which way you go.'

The point for us is pretty obvious. We need to have a sense of direction to enable us to develop reward strategies that are relevant, meaningful and will help the organization. A sense of direction also helps us filter the opportunities that we come across which are likely to support or hinder our progress.

Armstrong and Murlis (2004) note the importance of direction as an element in a reward strategy: 'Reward strategy determines the **direction** in which reward management innovations and developments should go to **support the business strategy,** how they should be **integrated,** the **priority** that should be given to initiatives and the **pace** at which they should be implemented'.

Duncan Brown (2001) says that '... reward strategy is ultimately a way of thinking that you can apply to any reward issue arising in your organization, to see how you can create value from it'.

Three other unattributed definitions of reward strategy I have come across are:

- 'The incorporation of business issues into decisions on reward policies'.
- 'An integrating approach, linking company strategy, employee behaviours and outcomes'.
- 'A means of ensuring that reward systems actively help businesses to go where they need to'.

The shorthand definition of reward strategy that I use is:

> Reward strategy is an approach to reward based on a set of coherent principles in support of the organization's aims.

A fundamental element of reward strategy reflected in all of these definitions is to support the organization. That is not to say that reward strategy should be only reactive. But the approach taken needs to reflect the culture and aims of the organization. In some cases it can help to drive change. Certainly as part of the HR strategy getting reward 'right' can help deliver solutions that help drive strategy. But you do need to understand the aims and values of the business. A survey of business leaders concluded '... HR must develop a deep understanding of the business – in the same way, and using the same 'language', as other managers. The measures it proposes must be tied to business outcomes: the impact on customer service, the reduction in costs, the support of a specific new growth area, the increase in staff loyalty and so on.' (KPMG, 2012a)

Armstrong and Murlis (2004) say that reward strategy

'... clarifies what the organization wants to do in the longer term to develop and implement reward policies, practices and processes that will further the achievement of its business goals. It is a declaration of intent, which establishes priorities for developing and acting on reward plans that can be aligned to business and HR strategies and to the needs of people in the organization.'

Based on the examples in this part of the book, you can define what reward strategy means for your own organization. But whatever definition you decide on, it is important to see reward strategy squarely in the context of the organization's business strategy and HR strategy.

Prevalence

It is perhaps surprising that few organizations have a reward strategy. This reflects my experience of the lack of a strategic approach to reward. According to the CIPD 2010 Reward Management survey (the last year they collected this data), only 35 per cent of participant organizations had a written reward strategy. As you can see from Table 1.1 this had not increased very much over the previous couple of years despite participants' stated intentions.

TABLE 1.1   Prevalence of reward strategy in organizations

	2008	2009	2010
Participants with a reward strategy (%)	33	26	35
Participants planning to introduce a reward strategy (%)	23	24	31

Best fit

There is a paradox in that product development, marketing and sales are greeted with plaudits when coming up with a new product, process or approach to market. It is the new that can beat the competitors in this fast-changing world. But when HR come up with a new idea it can often be greeted with the question, 'What do our competitors do?' This reaction, of course, does not acknowledge the uniqueness of the particular organization's culture.

Whilst we must reward people to ensure that we can compete effectively in the appropriate employment markets, the way we do so should reflect our particular organization. It is the culture and values that define the brand and reward should reflect these, not blindly follow the market. So I strongly advocate an approach of 'best fit' not 'best practice'. Not 'me tooism' but, 'What will work for us?' Whilst there will be some issues on legal compliance which need to be followed, in general 'best practice' is an invalid concept. Certainly look at what others are doing, but develop the reward strategy that is right for you, not some other larger organization down the road with a different history and culture.

A recent survey of World at Work members (Workspan, 2012) found that whilst two-thirds of respondents agreed or strongly agreed that 'Our compensation function is focused on creating unique/tailored compensation solutions for our business', 42 per cent said that there needed to be a greater focus on this for the future.

You should also guard against following the latest fad that seems to be doing the rounds. But rather, evaluate its fit for your organization based on evidence. This can be particularly sensitive when it is the chief executive who makes the suggestion as something they have come across that they think you should have in your organization.

Other terms

Reward strategy may be the overall approach you take, but there are other related terms that we should touch on. I do not think we need to agonize over which term means exactly what, rather use the terms in the way that works best for your organization. But I give here my suggestions on how the following terms may be used:

- **Reward Philosophy** – (also Reward Principles) the description of the beliefs of reward and how it should operate within the organization. It may be linked to the organization's values. It is overarching and is used to broadly frame the reward strategy. In Chapter 5 I discuss how you can develop this and give some examples.

- **Reward Framework** – the broad overview of the related and possibly interlinked elements of reward. May be diagrammatic to illustrate how the pieces of reward fit together.

- **Reward Policy** – the detailed policies on specific elements of reward which give the flexibility, discretion and limits. Typically, this will cover the main 'rules' about reward and may be part of the terms and conditions of employment.

- **Reward Procedure** – the detailed procedure and processes that explain what exactly has to be done by different people to enable an element of reward to change or be introduced, typically giving work flow of forms, authorization levels etc. For example, annual pay review process or absence procedure.

Timing

The nature of reward is that much of it runs on an annual cycle such as: financial year, annual pay review, annual bonus and annual renewal of insurance policies. This means that if you miss making a change at the right time in the cycle, you may have to wait another whole year. Often you need to take a long-term view and, based on the sense of direction, may need to make changes over two or three years. This is not just a practical issue, but may be needed to carry the key stakeholders with you.

Of course, whilst the strategy might move you neatly in a particular direction and at an ideal pace, both are likely to be influenced by internal and external factors (discussed in Chapter 4). These can and are likely to throw you off course. That is just the real world we live in. It must not, however, put you off developing a reward strategy. It is the reward strategy that will help you determine the best approach in light of the inevitable changes along the way.

It is the totality of what we do that is important and all of the elements of reward carry messages. But the strategy is made real by making things happen. So whilst the reward strategy should give you the direction and general approach, it is the aggregation of the things that are done that move the organization on.

How you make reward strategy come to life is a central theme of the rest of this book.

Summary

Whilst there are different terms used to define reward and reward strategy, you need to get this clear and consistent for your own organization. Whether you develop something you call a reward strategy, philosophy or framework, you should have what works best in your organization, provides some framework within which reward changes can be made and helps give a sense of direction.

Questions

- What terms will you use to describe reward?
- How will you establish your definition of reward strategy?
- Would it be of value to analyse the total costs of reward as a percentage of the organization's overall costs?
- Would it be helpful to see the cost of each category of reward?

Why reward is important and how it can make an impact

02

In this chapter I look at how reward can make an impact within the organization. In Chapter 3 I then address the issue of the role of reward in motivation; the age-old question of, 'does money motivate?'

Symbolic messages in reward

Reward carries strong messages. If you want to see what an organization values, look at what it pays for, not what it says. Words are cheap and it is easy to make statements about what is important in an organization. However, if you say one thing, but pay for something quite different you can guess which message will have the greater effect on what people will actually do.

That is not to say you should pay for everything; far from it. But if you are to take a strategic approach to reward, you need to consider very carefully the alignment between what the reward system is saying and what the stated culture, values and aims of the business are. As Tyson (1995) says, 'Monetary rewards may not motivate in the long term, but they certainly symbolize the value corporations attach to specific behaviours – for example rewarding long service, interpreted as loyalty, or rewarding performance above other attributes.'

Let's take a couple of examples – long-service awards and sales bonuses.

Long-service awards

It is fairly common for employers to use some form of long-service award. Typically, they provide a gift or cash and some degree of celebration to acknowledge a period of service with the employer. Long-service awards have been around for a very long time. Go to a local museum and you are likely to find a piece of silverware engraved with a date in the 19th century awarded to an employee by some company or institution for 25 years-plus service.

As I mention in Chapter 7, Her Majesty's Revenue & Customs (HMRC) has a specific tax concession to allow certain long-service awards (for at least 20 years) to be made tax free. The concession was introduced in the mid-1970s when a career with a single employer was still the norm.

But whilst such awards are still very common, we need to question their fit in a modern organization in this fast-moving, technology-driven society where many of the largest companies in the world are only a few years old. Young people joining the job market would mostly be horrified at the idea of staying 40 years with the same employer. Jobs for life are dead, and have been for many years. Values in organizations are around effectiveness, commitment, engagement, challenge etc. How many organizations recognize long service as a core value? Almost none.

The value may not be high, but the message of a long-service award is clear: we value long service. Of higher cost and carrying similar messages are service-related benefits such as holiday and defined benefit pension plans. There are some professions – mostly in the public sector – where long service is valued highly. So if you really do value long service for itself, fine; it may be appropriate to use awards to recognize it. But most organizations do not. So I suggest that long-service awards are, for the most part, a throwback to a bygone age where they were simply milestones in a 40-year career. If really thought through, they are unlikely to reflect the values of most organizations, so they carry the wrong message. Therefore, most organizations should review if their long-service awards should be part of their reward strategy.

Sales bonuses

The role of bonuses is covered in Chapter 10. But it is helpful to use this example here to illustrate the point on messaging. It is no surprise that sales bonuses or commissions are generally designed to increase sales. If a bonus works well as an incentive, the recipient is likely to try to achieve the result that the bonus is incentivizing. If valued by the recipient the incentive value of the bonus is likely to be the key driver of behaviours in pursuance of the incentive.

But as we know, over recent years there have been very many examples, primarily in financial services, of mis-selling. Typically, this has been due to sales being made to people for whom the service or product is unsuitable. A good deal of this has been blamed on the role of incentive bonuses. This should not come as a surprise as the reward carries a strong message.

In many cases the company will have given training and guidelines on the suitability of what is being sold. But the bonus plan does not discriminate – a sale is a sale and the bonus gets paid. So whilst the company may, somewhat naively, believe that the sales people's behaviour will be modified by what is taught or said, the simple sales message carried by the bonus is too strong. If you want to use financial incentives you need to incentivize the right things.

The rhetoric reality gap

The two examples above illustrate the same point – you should examine carefully what message each element of reward is carrying and ensure it is what you want. If it is not, where there is a rhetoric reality gap, change it. You have to make sure that the desired message and the reward are aligned.

You can find these sorts of conflicts between the messages that the reward system carries and the desired or stated aims or values everywhere. Here are some more examples in Table 2.1. Are any of these familiar?

TABLE 2.1   Rhetoric and reality gaps in reward

Rhetoric	Reality
We pay for performance	Only as a tiny % of total cash
We are customer focused	We incentivize sales
Contribution to team success is key	Pay reviews are based on individual objectives
We value contribution and performance	We have service-based benefits and pensions
We push down decision making to all	There is no choice in any parts of reward

Supporting values and culture

As we have seen in the last section, there can be significant gaps between what the organization wants and what it pays for. Mostly this is unwitting as no one has done the work to look for the gaps. Sometimes it is on the naive assumption that no one will spot the obvious conflict. But people normally do and it can destroy trust.

As reward can be so powerful in delivering messages it can help support the values of the organization. Where an organization has stated values, they should be a pivotal reference point in aligning the reward strategy. Many organizations take a values-based approach. The HSBC case study in Chapter 11 is an excellent example where HSBC has used recognition to support its values.

Reward can help support values in a number of ways, for example:

- the way in which incentives and other variable pay systems work;
- the factors that are taken into account in annual pay reviews;
- the range and flexibility available in the benefit programmes;
- the way in which reward is communicated;
- the way in which changes to reward programmes are undertaken – eg open and involving people.

Having real values that are lived by the leadership and not just paid lip service will be hugely helpful in reviewing and designing reward. You can keep using the question, 'How does this support our values?' However, a problem with values is that they can just become part of the rhetoric.

Here is what seems to be a well thought out set of values that was developed by a very large global business and appeared in its 1998 Annual Report (McLean and Elkind, 2004). They are short, simple and well written. As a reward director, I would be happy to be able to test out what our reward and performance management programmes were doing against these values. They also help in thinking how we would go about developing new programmes and how we should communicate reward. What do you think?

Respect: We treat others as we would like to be treated ourselves. We do not tolerate abusive or disrespectful treatment. Ruthlessness, callousness, and arrogance don't belong here.

Integrity: We work with customers and prospects openly, honestly, and sincerely. When we say we will do something, we will do it; when we say we cannot or will not do something, then we won't do it.

Communications: We have an obligation to communicate. Here, we take the time to talk with one another… and to listen. We believe that information is meant to move and that information moves people.

Excellence: We are satisfied with nothing less than the very best in everything we do. We will continue to raise the bar for everyone. The great fun here will be for all of us to discover just how good we can really be.

We may be able to agree on this as the sort of value set that could be used by Reward and HR to reflect the desired behaviours and culture and permeate everything HR do and the way managers and leaders act. There is only one problem – they didn't. The company we are talking about here is Enron. In 2001 it became the most famous corporate collapse leading to the largest bankruptcy case in US history. The global accountancy firm Arthur Andersen also collapsed in its wake. Many of the leaders were jailed for fraud. If only they had lived their stated values.

Let me be clear, I am a strong believer in the importance of values. I am simply a critic of the sort of rhetoric–reality gap that can, and often does, exist. If the leaders do not live the values, there is little we can do with reward to counter that.

Culture and values are strongly linked. Current thinking about the way organizations should work has changed significantly over recent years and this has had a strong effect on the desired culture. This in turn has impacted on the HR Management model and, as part of that, the impact that reward can have to reflect and help drive the changes.

Figure 2.1 (Deloitte, 2013) suggests the contrast between the more traditional approach and associated HR thinking, with the emerging trends.

FIGURE 2.1   Traditional and emerging trends influencing HR

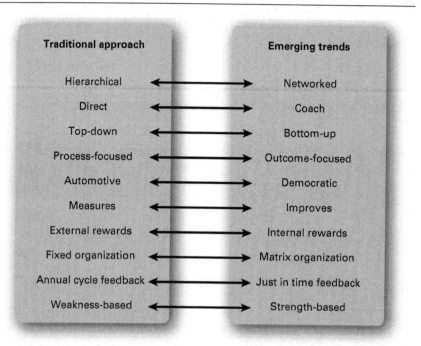

The extent to which an organization may be moving culturally from the left to the right box will require changes in the reward systems to ensure they are carrying consistent messages.

Alignment with organization strategy

In Chapter 1 I suggested that a definition of reward strategy will have some reference to supporting the organization's strategy. My definition of reward strategy is: an approach to reward based on a set of coherent principles in support of the organization's aims. As I have suggested, reward can carry strong messages about what is important and so can be important in reinforcing or supporting the organization's aims and values. As part of an integrated HR strategy, reward can help drive business strategy not just support it, but at the least it should be aligned and supportive.

Peter Cheese, chief executive of the Chartered Institute of Personnel and Development, says that HR needs to understand the business and the business strategy, particularly the value drivers. He believes that HR needs to be clear how it can best impact on those things that drive value based on real insights driven by better data analysis. (quoted in *Employee Benefits* magazine, 26 November 2012)

It follows, of course, that you need to know the aims of the organization to ensure that reward supports them. This is no different to any other aspect of HR. But in the real world it is not always clear what the aims and values of an organization are. They can also change, sometimes quite fast. So you may be operating in something of a vacuum. The question, then, is how can you target reward if you do not know what you are aiming at? You still need to create some sort of framework within which to develop your reward strategy.

Normally there are at least annual targets or goals you can look at. You need to get close to the business to see what is important. You can work with others in HR to establish the sort of 'people proposition' that is needed. Ultimately, in the absence of a clear set of values and aims, you need to use judgement to consider what seems to be the right thing to do based on the information you do have.

Alignment with HR strategy

Although reward is seen as one of the most 'technical' HR disciplines, it will fail badly if not embedded as part of a holistic approach to HR. It is always the totality of what we do to change things in an organization that makes a difference. So we need to be clear that we are providing, 'joined-up HR'. Whilst there will be differences between the different parts of HR, there needs to be co-ordination and co-operation and the messages that the different HR programmes carry need to be aligned.

These links between organizational, HR and reward strategy are reflected in Figure 2.2 taken from my last book: *A Guide to Non-cash Reward*.

In particular, I see a strong connection between reward and learning and development or talent management. As shown in Figure 2.2, I see that neither recognition nor performance management sit comfortably in one function or the other, but need strong input from both. Although not illustrated, there will be equally important connections with the people who deal with resourcing – to ensure reasonable salary levels and benefits. So

FIGURE 2.2 Holistic HR links

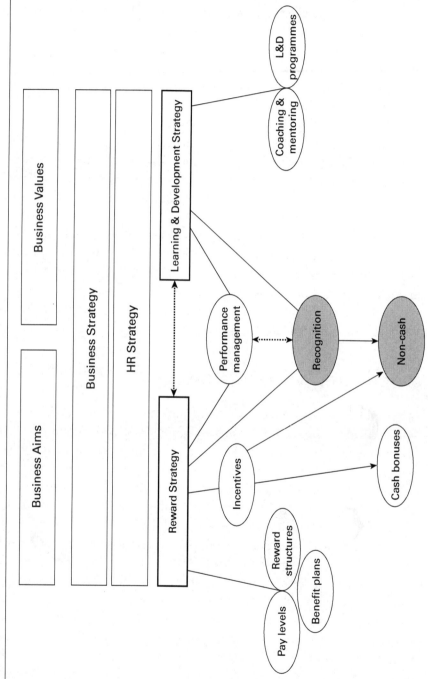

reward can have an impact in supporting delivering the broader HR strategy by being aligned with it and carrying the right messages.

Role in change management

Because reward carries strong messages, it has an important role to play in change management. I have said that reward should help support the organization's aims and values. When these change, the relevant reward elements must also change to ensure that they align with the new world.

Clearly, if an organization is restructuring or has to operate in a new way the reward system must reflect these changes and not the old model. If the reward system is not aligned, it will simply be a barrier to change, rather than an enabler.

> I worked with the division of a company that had moved from the prime unit being individuals to team working. There was now significant dependency between the members of the team to support each other to achieve success. As you might imagine, this was quite a significant change for the people involved. There was a bonus plan in place, covering about 40 per cent of the employees based on individual objectives. This needed immediate attention as it would have led to selfish rather than team behaviours and undermined the new working model.
>
> We ended up buying out the bonuses and introducing team recognition to applaud the success of teams.

It is always vital to review variable pay plans in times of change to ensure that they reflect the changes being made. It may also be important to look at the pay review system and how, if at all, it links with performance management and other measures.

Measuring the impact

Introduction

Measuring the impact of any HR initiative can be difficult because you are dealing with a large number of independent variables. The nature of what you are measuring is inherently difficult as you cannot easily control the environment and the other variables. Whilst you may be able to show a positive correlation between an intervention and a behavioural variable it is often impossible to prove causality.

Nevertheless, if you are going to take a strategic approach to reward, you need to determine at the start what a successful outcome will look like from the changes you make. So you need to consider how to assess whether an intervention has had the effect intended. It may be that you will have to deduce a relationship between the intervention and some measurable changes. Two other issues to look out for:

- The third variable problem. For example, it may not be the particular initiative that is of itself having an impact, but that management are showing interest in the people affected (Hawthorn effect).

- There is also the linking variable issue. This is where the impact is not directly from the initiative to the result, but there is an intermediate, linking variable. For example, a change to reward may give a cost saving. But it might be that the change in reward has meant that people had to reorganize themselves to work in a different way which led to the cost saving.

When you set up the planned change it is good practice to establish what success will look like ie what would be different if the change had its intended impact. It may involve one of the measures I have mentioned here or something else.

So a word of warning – ensure that what it is you are going to measure is value added and not just chosen because it is easy to measure. For example, I discourage counting the number of recognition events on its own as a measure of the success of a recognition programme. Rather use employee attitude surveys to track the effect.

Below, I give some ideas to consider. None is perfect because of the inherent problems I have mentioned.

Employee surveys

My view is that the most effective and realistic measure is changes in employee survey results. Many organizations use some sort of employee attitude or engagement survey. The trend nowadays is to use shorter more frequent surveys rather than the very large and costly two-yearly surveys that were common. Many surveys (for example Gallup Q12) do not directly cover reward. There may be questions you can add to existing regular surveys that you can use to monitor views on aspects of reward over time.

It is now very cheap and simple to run online surveys using excellent tools such as Survey Monkey. Therefore, to complement existing surveys, you can easily run short surveys on a specific reward topic and track results. I have done this before and after introducing flexible benefits and could show a significant increase in awareness of the benefits provided after flex was implemented, which was one of the aims.

A UK FTSE 100 business saw from its engagement survey that people did not feel valued and recognized. It introduced a whole range of recognition-related initiatives and saw the recognition score increase substantially over the next three years.

Exit interviews

Exit interviews are where people who are leaving the company are asked about their views. They need to be well structured, but I have always found them a valuable source of data. My experience of running them, when I was an HR generalist many years ago, was that people were generally open and honest and actually wanted to tell you what was wrong. The problem is often that the information obtained is not disseminated to the relevant functions. But capturing reward-related data from exit interviews can be a valuable qualitative source of views.

A word of warning, though, on exit interview data. It is common to find that when people leave an employer they move to a new organization for a larger salary. Whilst the salary may be higher you need to check, if you can, the other elements of reward as there may be some trade-offs that have been made. But more important is that the larger salary may be due to the new job being bigger – ie a promotion. Also, salary is rarely the key factor in deciding to leave. So just because the new salary is larger do not conclude that this was the motivation to leave. It is almost always something else. For example, it may be that the career development process within your organization needs improving rather than salary at any particular level.

Staff turnover

Changes in (voluntary) staff turnover may be of some interest as an indicator of the impact of particular programmes, but it will be difficult to show any causality using an overall figure. However, turnover broken down by other factors such as length of service may be a little more valuable. For example, higher turnover in the first year is most likely to suggest a problem in the recruitment and selection process. You may be able to track turnover by salary for different levels in the organization to see if there are any obvious trends that show. This may provide some information that can indicate the likely impact of a reward initiative, but it can be stronger if turnover rates are considered alongside exit interview data.

Pilots

Large organizations can sometimes pilot an initiative. This can be difficult in smaller organizations and may also depend on the structure. But a well-designed pilot study can be used to investigate the effect of a reward change.

A retail pub group piloted the impact of a points-based incentive and recognition programme with a group of their pubs; they also used a control group. Compared with the control group, the average change in the pilot group was an increase in sales of 3 per cent and an increase in profit of 9 per cent. The customer care score – measured using customer surveys – increased by 7 per cent. Based on this successful pilot the new programme was rolled out to the rest of the group (Rose, 2001).

Costs

It may be that the result is pretty easy to measure if it is simply that you are looking for a reduction in cost. Whilst never completely simple, in most cases you can see if you made the financial saving or not. It can be problematic where you are reviewing a cost saving with a changing population. In which case you may need to look at cost per head or rework the data to show the initial costs for the same population after the reward change.

There is, of course, the question of whether cost saving is the right aim on its own. You should consider the impact of cost saving on other areas of value, such as engagement. As a single measure cost saving may be easy to measure but may be too crude, when you should perhaps be looking for value.

Aon Hewitt (2012) found that higher performing organizations were more likely to define and measure success through a range of employee value and return on investment indicators in addition to budget and cost management. Whereas the lower performing organizations were more likely to use cost as a measure. This is shown in Table 2.2.

TABLE 2.2   Percentage of companies using the following to measure the success of total rewards programmes

	Higher performing companies	Lower performing companies	Difference
Employee engagement	69	55	+14
Higher employee satisfaction with programmes	45	30	+15
Moulding of total rewards spend against key business objectives	43	30	+13
Business leaders use programmes to motivate and retain talent	37	27	+10
Rate of cost increase	33	48	−15

Summary

Reward implicitly carries messages about what is important in the organization, so it should be aligned with everything else you are saying explicitly. Reward needs to be an integrated part of your HR strategy in support of your business strategy. If well designed, reward can help you make change, but it can also hinder progress if it is not aligned properly.

When you are planning to make changes in reward, think through what you would want to be different if the change was a success. Be realistic and look for those things that are indicators of value added even if difficult to measure, rather than things that are easy to measure.

Questions

- To what extent do your current rewards support your values?
- What are the reward-related rhetoric and reality gaps in your organization?
- What can you do about any gaps you list?
- Where is reward adding value to the HR strategy and where can alignment be improved?
- What sources of data do you have that can be used to help track the impact of changes in reward?

Relationship between motivation and reward

03

In Chapter 2 I emphasized the importance of reward in carrying messages. That is, reward has a strong symbolic effect. The question that is frequently asked, is, does money motivate? In terms of reward this really means incentives, bonuses and performance-related pay.

The most common reference made when the role of reward as a motivator is raised is that Hertzberg said money is a hygiene factor (see Appendix). That is something that can cause damage if removed, but does not act as a motivator like achievement and recognition. But even with Hertzberg it is not quite that simple. Because Hertzberg also said, '...money thus earned as a direct reward for outstanding individual performance is a reinforcement of the motivators of recognition and achievement. It is not hygiene as is money given in across-the-board wage increases' (1968).

Intrinsic and extrinsic motivation

Introduction

Fundamental to an understanding of the role of reward in motivation are the concepts of intrinsic and extrinsic motivation.

- Intrinsic motivation is the internal satisfaction the individual has from doing the work. This is about basic job satisfaction; someone taking pride in their work. It builds self-esteem and feelings of competence and self-determination.

- Extrinsic motivation is the behaviour that results from factors external to the individual such as reward and punishment. Any form of financial incentive (eg bonuses, performance-related pay) is, by definition, an extrinsic motivator.

I suggest that the evidence demonstrates that intrinsic motivation is more powerful and sustained than extrinsic motivation that can be short term and lead to unexpected negative consequences. But beliefs held within organizations that reflect McGregor's Theory X (see Appendix) do not necessarily reflect this.

Beliefs

Many managers in the US and UK have deeply held assumptions about the role of incentive pay in motivation. This can be because money is the only 'currency' used by some organizations to thank people; giving the message that it is only cash that demonstrates your worth (Nelson, 1996). In other words these managers promote a self-fulfilling prophecy so that employees learn to expect cash as the only true form of thanks.

If a child is deprived of love by its parents but receives only toys then although it may crave the love, it ends up demanding more toys – the currency that the parent uses. The parallel with reward is clear – what is really needed is genuine appreciation and understanding by managers of employees. However, as with children – toys are better than nothing (La Motta, 1995).

Daniel Pink (2010) believes that using extrinsic motivators such as pay are ineffective, and he cites significant research to support his view. But he goes on to say, 'On both sides of the Atlantic, the gap between what science is learning and what business is doing is wide.'

According to the Institute of Leadership and Management (2003) some 94 per cent of organizations offer an annual financial incentive to UK staff. However, they are shown to have little or no effect on commitment and performance for all but 13 per cent of staff.

Nelson (1996) suggests if you only use money to thank people, then money becomes a psychological exchange for enduring a miserable job with no other appreciation.

Kohn (1993), a well-known critic of financial incentives, believes that 'Incentives, a version of what psychologists call extrinsic motivators, do not alter the attitudes that underlie our behaviours. They do not create an enduring commitment to any value or action. Rather, incentives merely – and temporarily – change what we do.'

Research by Jacquart and Armstrong (2013) found that higher pay for executives fails to promote better performance. Instead, it undermines executives' intrinsic motivation, inhibits their learning, leads them to ignore other stakeholders, and discourages them from considering the long-term effects of their decisions on stakeholders. In particular, the research found that it is not possible to relate incentive payments to executives' actions in an effective manner. Incentives also encourage unethical behaviour. The research concluded that organizations would benefit from using validated methods to hire top executives, reduce compensation, eliminate incentive schemes, and strengthen stockholder governance related to the hiring and compensation of executives.

The particular strategy you employ will be influenced by the belief system on the role of reward. Figure 3.1 illustrates the nature of the continuum of beliefs. Where you sit on the continuum will affect the reward policies you employ and how you see their relationship with other factors that engage people at work.

FIGURE 3.1   Reward: continuum of beliefs

We believe that reward's role on performance and behaviour is...

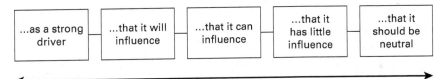

My view is that, for the most part, somewhere from the middle to the right in this model is a realistic position to take. Although reward can have a direct and significant effect in the short term it is unlikely to be a sustained source of motivation. As Pink (2013) says, 'Money matters a heck of a lot, yet people can think about the work more if they are not thinking about the money.'

The impact on intrinsic motivation by an extrinsic approach

If you put money against an outcome or behaviour there is a danger that the recipients may see it as changing the nature of the relationship from trust and self-determination to one of manipulation. That is their underlying intrinsic motivation becomes cancelled out by the external action. The relationship then can be more instrumented rather than one of partnership.

Adrian Furnham, professor of psychology at University College London, illustrates this through the story of the writer who was disturbed by children playing in the park right by his office window. His solution was to go out and say to the children how much he enjoyed them playing there and gave them £1 each. He did this for a couple more days, but on the next day he told them that he was not going to pay them anymore. Their reaction was that in that case they were going to play somewhere else.

Impact on more complex roles and tasks

There is evidence suggesting that financial incentives may have a negative impact on creativity and may limit rather than improve problem solving. Glucksberg took groups of participants and told them that he was going to time them to see how quickly they could solve a particular problem (the candle problem – to attach a candle to the wall without it dripping wax on the floor, given a candle, a box of tacks and some matches) (Pink, 2010). He divided the participants into two groups.

- He told one group that he was going to time them to determine how long it typically took people to solve this type of problem.
- He offered the second group $5 (£3.30) if they were in the 25 per cent that solved the problem the fastest. In addition, the person who was the fastest of all would get $20.00.

On average, it took the second group, which was offered the cash incentive, three and a half minutes longer to solve the problem than it took the first group.

Glucksberg repeated the experiment, except this time, he presented not a box with tacks in it, but an empty box with the tack on the table beside it. In other words, he made the problem easier because once the box was not being used as a container it took less mental flexibility to be able to assign it a different function. This time, the group that was being incentivized finished the task a lot faster than the other group.

The conclusion that may be drawn from these findings is that extrinsic rewards may work well for tasks with a simple set of rules and a clear aim. But rewards may narrow our focus and concentrate the mind. But for the real candle problem – the one with the thumb tacks in the box – you don't want tunnel vision: you want to be able to see what is on the periphery; you want to be looking around; you want to expand your possibilities. Pink concludes that as long as the task involved only mechanical skill, bonuses worked as they would be expected: the higher the pay, the better the performance. But once the task called for 'even rudimentary cognitive skill', a larger reward 'led to poorer performance'.

Incentives

Expectancy theory (see Appendix) tells us that people will undertake an action if they see that the action will lead to an outcome that they value. So if you give a big financial incentive that the participants want, they are likely to do what you ask. Exactly that and no more. One of many dangers is that this can and does lead to cutting corners and even unethical behaviour; who cares as long as you achieve the goal? In the longer term this is likely to lead to more problems as the corporate brand is tainted and can even be destroyed completely – consider Enron and Arthur Andersen.

Even if you support using financial incentives, you need to take account of the potential cumulative effect they may have. This is because recipients of incentive schemes may well adjust their efforts to optimize the return they get via the incentive.

But where the belief is that incentives strongly motivate it can lead to asking the wrong question on reward. The question I am sometimes asked as a consultant is:

'How should we design our incentive plans so that we get the behaviour we want?'

I would reframe the question as:

'How can we best get the behaviours we want and what part can reward play in helping us achieve this?'

One of the dangers of giving too much emphasis on incentives is that you can end up believing that they can manage for you. They can't. It is the context that is critical – so getting everything else right (effective management, clear aims, feedback, recognition etc) is likely to be more impactful than an incentive.

PwC (2011) conducted a survey of 100 senior executives that looked at the balance for individuals between intrinsic and extrinsic motivation. They correlated responses on goal-setting and work preferences. They found that goal-setting was important for motivation, regardless of whether people were intrinsically or extrinsically motivated. The process of identifying and setting challenging goals is in itself motivating for many, regardless of whether money is attached to the outcome. They conclude, 'So incentives do not replace management.'

Even where cash is dominant there may be other motivators at work. I once worked in a life assurance company where the sales people were on commission only, with no salary. On the face of it this suggests a motivation environment based entirely on the extrinsic value of money. But it was not as simple as that. In addition to the cash commission, the company employed a whole range of non-cash awards, prizes and incentives. There was the million dollar roundtable, the chairman's club, the regional awards and the annual conventions in luxury locations abroad. There was a degree of exclusivity about the prizes. Only a relatively small number would achieve them to be feted by the executives of the company. These very desirable things enabled the successful sales people to demonstrate their success in a way that cash alone could not. Achieving these different non-cash awards was all about getting recognition and esteem from others.

Retention effect

Reward can be used to help retain people. This is discussed in Chapter 12. There is little doubt that a substantial sum of money (say 75 per cent of salary) payable at a date in the fairly near future (say two years) is likely to retain the individual if everything else is ok. But unless the payment is due very soon, it will not retain someone who is completely disengaged.

The PwC (2011) survey found that respondents would take a pay cut of around 50 per cent to do their ideal job; 25 per cent would take a pay cut of 70 per cent or more. Only 5 per cent of respondents would not take any pay cut for their ideal job.

Pay that is well below the market level is likely to lead to more people leaving, so getting salaries close to the market may reduce turnover. But once pay is at around the market level the marginal impact on retention for further increases in salary will have a smaller impact than for those well below the market. So as long as pay is around the market median all the other things about working for the organization will have a greater impact on retention. But pay well below the market is more likely to have an impact on retention.

Reward or other factors in motivation

Survey data

Work on engagement has found that reward is relatively low down the list of what engages people. Here are three examples from significant surveys.

The global strategy consultancy McKinsey (2009) found that

- praise from immediate manager;
- leadership attention eg 1:1 conversations;
- chance to lead projects or task force.

was equal to or more effective in motivating people than:

- cash bonuses;
- increased base pay;
- stock or stock options.

Mercer (2011) found that the top three factors influencing motivation and engagement at work were:

- being treated with respect;
- work–life balance;
- the type of work that you do.

Base pay came sixth and incentive pay/bonus was last. This was the same relationship for almost every country surveyed.

The Civil Service People Survey (2012) in the UK had 300,000 participants. It found that over the past four surveys, analysis has shown consistently that the strongest influences on levels of engagement were:

- perceptions of leadership and managing change;
- what work people do; and
- the quality of managers.

It concluded that focusing action on these areas is likely to have the biggest impact in terms of improving engagement. Pay and benefits came fourth or fifth in each of the surveys 2009–2012.

In this fast-moving world we need to be clear about what is important to people in the organization and use our valuable resources on that, not on something we may think that they want. Towers Watson (2010) found that employers across the world did not recognize the value to employees of three factors that were important to them:

- convenient work location;
- holiday/paid time off; and
- flexible schedule.

Each of these factors relates to the employees' use of time, which is of growing importance. Time is a very valuable commodity and employees will make employment decisions influenced by the flexibility of time as well as reward and other aspects of working for the organization. Overemphasis on any one part of the employee proposition, such as reward, is likely to be unsuccessful in the long term.

Millennial generation

The Millennial generation, those born between 1980 and 1995, will make up 50 per cent of the workforce by 2020. PwC (2013) found that the Millennial generation of workers would choose workplace flexibility, work–life balance and the opportunity for overseas assignments over financial rewards.

The survey also found that millennials are more likely to stay in a job if they feel supported and appreciated, are part of a cohesive team and have greater flexibility over where and how much they work. This contrasts with the non-millennial generation, who place greater importance on pay and development opportunities.

Unlike past generations who were willing to work beyond their contracted hours in the hope of rising to higher-paying positions later on, millennials are largely unwilling to give up a good work–life balance. This generation of workers is not convinced that such early career sacrifices are worth the potential later rewards.

The report concludes that many companies will have to completely rethink how they attract and reward their workers, or risking losing the best talent to companies that adapt to meet their needs.

Technology has made huge impact on productivity and the speed of change. Social media and open information will continue to put pressure on organizations that can no longer control their employee brand. The Millennium generation is plugged into networks in a way that was unheard of only a few years ago. They want transparency and clarity and will see through rhetoric. This puts even more emphasis on the need for a strategic aligned approach to reward and requires greater involvement of people in the organization in the changes you plan.

Pay equity

One aspect of reward that can act as a demotivator relates to employees' perception of inequity in reward (see equity theory in the Appendix). Of more importance than the individual's absolute level of reward is the perception of their reward relative to others. So the extent to which employees see their pay as unfair or inequitable is likely to be a greater demotivator than their perception of their pay against the external market.

The Ultimatum game originated in 1982 and is played between two subjects. One person is given an amount of money – typically around $10 – and told that he must offer a share of it to the other person. If the other person accepts the offer they both keep their share. But if the other person rejects the offer, then neither of them receive any money. A purely rational response would be for the responder to accept whatever was offered. After all it is the only way the responder will get anything. But our innate sense of fairness means that where the offer is low it will often get rejected.

Researchers have replicated the Ultimatum game many times and in many locations. A meta-analysis of 37 papers with 75 results found that on average 16 per cent of the offers are rejected. On average the proposer offers 40 per cent of the pie to the responder. The rejection rate is higher for smaller shares offered. The analysis also found differences in behaviour of responders (and not of proposers) across geographical regions (Oosterbeek et al, 2003).

Research shows that monkeys can react very negatively if they see that their treatment is unfair compared with others. In an experiment, pairs of capuchin monkeys were trained to hand the experimenter a rock in exchange for cucumber. This was fine until the monkey in the adjoining cage was rewarded with grapes. At this point the first monkey rejected the cucumber. You can see the result on youtube.com at the following address: **http://www.youtube.com/watch?v=HL45pVdsRvE**

Analysis of some of the differences between the best performing employers and the average companies (Workspan, 2013) showed that the best employers excelled in 10 specific drivers of engagement compared with average companies. One of the 10 was 'paying fairly' where the best companies clearly put more emphasis.

Research by Kenexa (2013) indicates that employees who believe they are fairly paid are more engaged, less likely to quit, experience less stress at work, feel healthier physically and psychologically and are more satisfied with their personal life.

Research by PwC (2011) also shows the power of perceived fairness in pay as a potential demotivator as shown below.

Respondents were asked to say which of the two characters would be more motivated in this scenario.

Jean and Jacques leave business school. Jean is offered a job to join the management team of company A at a salary of £600,000. Jacques is offered a job at company B for £700,000. Subsequently, Jean discovers that the average pay in the management team at company A is £500,000, whereas Jacques finds out that at company B the average is £800,000.

Over 60 per cent said Jean would be more motivated and only 17 per cent said Jacques.

This research illustrates the point of perception of fairness and is in line with what I have found to be the reality within organizations where I have worked. As humans we do seem to be hard-wired to look out for what we see as unfairness. This is important and means that we must take care to ensure that, as far as we can, our reward systems are fair, unbiased and non-discriminatory and we explain clearly to employees what fairness means. It is not that everyone is paid the same, but that the underlying basis for reward is fair in relation to what we are asking people to do. Like many other countries, in the UK, we also have equal pay legislation. Fairness is likely to be an important part of a reward strategy.

Reward policy

It is not uncommon to find statements about the role of reward such as, 'Reward in XYZ Co is to recruit, retain and motivate our employees.' My view is that this sort of glib statement is pretty well worthless. Firstly, reward can only ever help with some of these three aims; it is unlikely to be the most significant. Secondly, only some parts of reward can help with some of these.

However, it is helpful to think about which parts of reward might help achieve each of the three elements: recruit, retain, motivate. It will vary by level and role, but here are my thoughts on this:

TABLE 3.1   Possible role of parts of reward

Aim	Part of reward that might help
Recruit	Basic salary, guaranteed first-year bonus, flexible benefits
Retain	Share plan or other financial retention, flexible benefits
Motivate	Recognition, clear and open reward system, bonus

You may wish to review how you see these operating in your own organization. But whatever the case, in building a reward policy or reward strategy you need to be realistic. You need to determine what overall reward can help achieve as well as what each element may be able to support. There is no point in setting unrealistic expectations of what reward can deliver as you just set yourself up to fail.

As illustrated in Figure 3.1, an organization may choose to use reward very proactively to seek to influence behaviour and outcomes. But at the other extreme you may decide that reward is not an important motivator and so try to ensure that reward is neutral. This may be thought of as to take pay off the table and use the important things to motivate and engage people.

Summary

Reward can signal very clearly what the organization considers to be important. Financial incentives can positively increase performance on relatively simple tasks over the short term. But overall very great care needs to be taken in using reward as a motivator.

On balance I believe that often too great an emphasis is put on the role of reward as an extrinsic motivator at the cost of a deeper understanding of how to get an environment that seeks to have intrinsically motivated, engaged people. That is not to say it has no role, but for reward to have impact in motivation it has to operate in a context where it is only one part of the motivation mix.

Questions

- What is the dominant attitude on the impact of reward in your organization against the range in Figure 3.1 on page 31? What does this mean in the way in which you manage reward?

- What is the balance between intrinsic and extrinsic motivation in your organization?

- What does equitable mean in relation to reward in your organization?

- What do each part of reward do in relation to recruit, retain and motivate or engage?

04

How reward fits together

Influences on reward strategy

One of the practical issues to take into account in developing a reward strategy is the range of influences there will be on it. Whilst the specifics will vary with place and time, the nature of the issues will always need to be monitored and considered. There are two categories of influence: external and internal.

External influences

Because these will differ from one country to another, they are particularly important to consider when developing an approach to reward internationally. These differences will limit the opportunity to have a common reward package in all countries. Rather, you need to think about what should be the same and what must be different. For example, there is no point in trying to operate a share plan in a country where its legislation means that a recipient would have to pay tax when the plan was granted, maybe three years before any value would be available. I suggest that there are six areas of external influence that can impact reward strategy, which I discuss below.

Legislation

Legislation will always have a significant impact. Minimum levels of obligation that an employer has to its employees will be reflected in employment laws. For example, in the UK and many other countries, there is minimum wage legislation. Although not in law, but of growing impact in the UK is the concept of a minimum living wage, which at the time of writing is about 25 per cent higher than the minimum wage. There are a minimum number of paid holidays, maximum hours, maternity and paternity leave etc.

Changes to pension legislation have been very frequent and have had a significant impact, particularly amongst higher paid employees. Employers are now providing cash allowances in lieu of pension contributions for those employees who have reached the new caps and wish to become a deferred member of the pension scheme. This is but one example of the sort of change that will impact on reward.

Taxation

An employer can only operate within the tax system that exists at the time, but which inevitably changes all the time. It is not for the employer to change salaries etc if the tax rate increases, although employees may ask for this. But similarly the employer will not ask employees to take a pay cut if tax rates drop. It is important to be clear what your position is on changes to taxation.

Whilst many organizations will think it reasonable to arrange reward to help employees legitimately reduce their tax, this should not be their prime concern. But there can be value to both parties if the employer is able to restructure pay to deliver more to employees at a lower cost to the employer.

Some benefits are not taxable and so an employer may well wish to look at delivering more value by directing spend to such benefits. But they do change. For example, in the UK company-provided cars used to be taxed pretty lightly and were a common benefit for managers. But for some years tax on cars has been increasing, so that a taxable car allowance, typically paid monthly through payroll, has become much more common. However, in some countries cars are still not heavily taxed and so remain an important benefit. Taxation is covered in Chapter 7.

Social system

This is primarily about what is provided by the state and what is provided by the employer. The most common benefits where this is relevant are healthcare and pension, but there are other issues in some countries such as childcare. There are significant differences internationally in the balance between provision by the state and the employer. Ultimately, they have to be paid for, either out of taxation including payroll taxes if mostly provided by the state, or by the employer (and employee) out of profits and salary.

In some countries the bulk of pension is provided by the state, so it is uncommon to have any private sector pensions; similarly, with private healthcare.

Market sector

The external competition for staff may mean that there are certain elements of reward that the majority of employers operating in the sector are likely to offer. For example, profit share, bonuses and all-employee share plans are common in the financial services sector. Sectors such as oil and gas typically have very comprehensive benefit packages as the cost is low compared with the other costs of the business.

Market pay movement

An organization does not operate in a vacuum, and so it is sensible to be clear about your position on basic pay changes in light of pay movement in the relevant market or markets. It is generally not appropriate simply to follow pay movement without considering your overall pay levels. I cover this in Chapter 9.

Business sector

There are different norms by sector – private, public, not-for-profit and charity. For example, there are fewer bonuses outside the private sector. By definition, share plans are only available in the private sector. The public sector tends to have more long-term and service-based reward components such as incremental pay spines and defined benefit pensions.

Internal influences

I suggest that there are five main areas of internal influence as discussed below.

Values of the organization

In Chapter 2 I have already covered the importance of values to help frame the reward strategy. They should strongly influence the HR and reward strategies.

Structure and size of the organization

The structure is likely to influence how similar the approach to reward will be across the organization as a whole. For example, an organization in one business segment on one site is more likely to have a consistent approach to reward than a multinational highly decentralized business operating in many markets. Commonly, the more decentralized, the broader the range of reward practices.

Smaller organizations are likely to have fewer benefits, as their cost can be disproportionately expensive. Larger organizations, simply by virtue of their size, can develop a broader and more comprehensive range of programmes than smaller businesses. Certain benefits such as private medical insurance are also more common in larger organizations.

Organizational change

Change is constant; all organizations change all the time. The types of change are many and varied but may have an impact on reward strategy: eg restructuring, acquisitions, disposals, mergers, new products and services.

Profitability

To the extent that the organization is aiming to make a profit, the level of profitability is likely to influence pay levels and in particular, bonuses. The organization's ability to pay based on its finances may be a stated component of its position on reward. Of course even if it is not a profit-making organization it will still need to take a view on how it will state its position on the relationship between whatever financial measures are relevant and its pay policy.

Industrial relations (employee representation)

Where a union is recognized it is likely that the company will need to negotiate pay reviews, changes to terms and conditions and changes to its pay systems. This is likely to be a significant influence on the organization's position on reward.

Summary

These internal and external factors will all influence the approach to reward, what programmes you provide and how they fit together. Whilst the spend may be similar from place to place the 'shape' of the total reward provided may well differ according to the external factor present at the time. Your reward strategy will need to be able to take these sort of internal and external changes into account.

Trade-offs between different parts of reward

Total cost

All of the elements of reward cost the organization money to provide and, as suggested in Chapter 1, it can be valuable to capture all of this to engage with the decision makers in the organization. But it is also important to be able to show the total value of reward to employees. I discuss this in more detail in Chapter 6.

In Chapter 1 I gave the four elements of reward: basic pay, variable pay (bonuses), benefits, share plans. Reward can carry messages and may have a role to some degree in helping recruit, retain and engage people in the organization. I have said that it is important to both deal effectively with each part of reward as well as keep a perspective on the whole spend on reward.

Trade-offs

To maximize the value and impact of reward you need to think about the opportunities for trade-offs between different elements. By this I mean that from the total reward spend you may wish to reallocate costs to different elements of reward but for a similar overall cost. This strategic approach means that you need to understand what each part is currently for, how much it costs and how well it is understood. You need to keep abreast of the external and internal factors that may impact your reward strategy. You also need to keep up to date on products, offerings and research that might provide opportunities for change.

A flexible benefits plan, covered in Chapter 13, is designed to allow employees to choose, within limits, the benefits that will suit them best. They trade off one benefit against another and cash to optimize value for themselves, whilst remaining cost neutral for the employer. So flexible benefits can provide a platform within which new benefits can be provided but with the cost controlled.

In addition to a flexible benefits scheme, you should consider what other trade-off there might be that can add value as priorities change or opportunities present themselves. For any change you would need to check the contractual position and take great care about how you made the change, communications etc. Here are a few examples:

- Consolidating into salary – allowances or small annual payments such as a Christmas bonus that are outdated and no longer serve a purpose or are being provided to only a small number of people may be consolidated into salary, normally best at the time of the annual pay review.

- Benefits as part of a pay review – whilst the pay review is normally just about increases to salary, consider new tax-effective benefits that might be introduced in lieu of some of a pay increase. For example, this may be helpful when moving from a hierarchical benefits system when you wish to equalize benefits across an organization.

- Benefit changes – as new benefit products come into the market or changes are made to more effectively managing benefit costs you may want to introduce a new benefit and reduce or discontinue an existing benefit.

- Bonus and recognition – you may consider allocating a small part of the bonus spend on a recognition programme.

- Shares and salary – you may consider adding an all-employee share plan in one year in place of the pay review.

- Salary and bonus – you can introduce a variable pay plan or cash profit share in place of a salary review.

The main point I want to make is that the 'shape' of total reward should not be considered to be fixed but may be changed over time as the internal and external environment changes. You need to think about how you can leverage best value out of the total spend by potentially changing the reward mix.

The role of the reward professional

Before we look at the practical application for each of the main areas of reward, I want to cover how I see the role of the reward professional in delivering reward strategy.

Being good with spreadsheets just doesn't cut it anymore. I know that being an effective reward professional has always been more than that. But in the past, the reward people were the nerds of the HR world: they were comfortable with compa ratios and pivot tables, regression analysis and quartiles, but you wouldn't want a beer with them. So what's changed?

I believe that reward people now need to work in a different way and need new skills and behaviours. I suggest that there are now six aspects of reward management that are needed to deliver effective reward strategy. Some reflect points that I have already made in this chapter:

1 **Take a long-term perspective but with short-term actions** – this is a balancing act. Firstly, you need to know where you are going – the organizational strategy etc. Without that, you have problems. And if it doesn't exist then you need to set the agenda and map out the future. But we operate in the real world so you need to be flexible. Typically, you can only move in steps that are achievable. Of course at the same time internal and external events happen that will impact on what you are doing. The check is that you need to look at these things in the context of the direction of travel.

2 **Recognize holistic HR** – whilst we need more specialists in HR, we also need to join up the dots. Reward professionals need to look outside their specialism to understand the links with other parts of HR. There is always a danger that you see a problem only within the terms of your specialism. But there is rarely a single solution, even if you can define the problem. Therefore, you must work with other specialists such as Learning and Development and Resourcing to maximize value.

3 **Use a consulting approach** – to get a sensible solution you need to understand the context: the issues, attitudes, aims etc. So ask lots of questions. The best are simple questions. What is this for? Why do they do that? What is the real aim of this? Too quickly we slip into the solutions without understanding the context and trying to define the problem. A consulting approach does just that. A good example is designing a bonus plan. You never start at the design; you start by understanding the context and exactly what success looks like. The design may be fairly straightforward once these are clear.

4 **More emphasis on change management and less on reward design** – whilst getting the design right is important, we do need to understand that a lot of what we do is as much art as science. There may be a number of reward solutions that can be effective; it will partly depend on the context of the organization within which the programme is meant to operate. But what is crucial, always, is the way in which it is communicated and implemented. We must take that into account in the design. So I am arguing that we need to shift the balance to more understanding of change management and

communications than simply technical reward. A vital element is knowing how best to manage stakeholders. You need to understand what is important to your key decision makers in particular, and present the benefits to the organization not the features of the design. You need to know how to 'sell' best fit business-focused solutions based on evidence to your leadership or you will fail.

5 **Meld the academic with the practical** – we often need to challenge assumptions about the role of reward. So make sure you can use relevant academic research to support your argument. For example, Vroom's expectancy theory (see Appendix) is very helpful in discussing bonuses. You must be selective in what you draw on for your audience; this isn't about making you look smart, but helping the organization get the best solution. So read up on relevant motivation theories and don't be afraid to use them. My experience is that, used sparingly, many managers can find them engaging and challenging.

6 **Manage external relationships** – the world gets even more complex as it gets smaller. So even as specialists we are likely to need some external help and advice from time to time. Therefore, you need to understand how to manage external advisers to ensure your organization gets good value. Ensure you understand the fee structure, be very clear on the scope of the project. Divide it into discrete phases with clear deliverables. But also remember that you should stick to what you said you'd do. It only costs you money if you don't.

Summary

Whilst I recommend that organizations should have a reward strategy, there will be a stream of internal and external factors that will influence what you can do and also provide new opportunities. The sense of direction that you have should not change materially by these influences.

You should monitor the external and internal environment to ensure you understand the opportunities that are available. You should also look for trade-offs between different parts of reward to help maximize their value.

The reward professional needs a new set of skills and behaviours to be able to operate effectively and make impact.

Questions

- What are the main external factors that impact reward in your organization?

- What are the main internal factors that impact reward in your organization?

- Can you get better value and impact by trading off one part of reward with another?

- How do you measure up to the six elements of reward management I suggest are now important? Do you need to do anything to improve in any?

How to get started with a reward strategy

05

So far in this part of the book I have discussed a number of aspects of what I see as the fundamentals of reward strategy. I now turn to how you get started. The issues covered apply to reward as a whole. You may wish to come back to this chapter after having gone through Part II, which looks at each of the elements of reward in some detail.

An approach to developing a reward strategy

Key requirements

CIPD (2005) research suggests that there are five key requirements in developing an effective and tailored reward strategy:

1 Clear reward goals and priorities derived from the business strategy and its requirements.

2 A strong organizational fit of reward policies and practices with the structure and design of the organization.

3 Alignment of the reward practices with each other in a total-reward approach and with the other HR programmes in the organization.

4 Aligning with and involving employees in the development and delivery of the reward strategy.

5 Treating the reward strategy development as a process of continuous improvement and interaction between principles and practices.

This is a helpful model that we should take into account as we consider reward strategy in the organization. A prerequisite is a clear understanding of the relevant organizational issues, business aims and culture, other HR programmes etc. You cannot start to develop a reward strategy or framework without this in-depth knowledge. So here is one place to start. You need the answers to these questions:

- What are the main aims of the organization over the next few years?
- What are the main priorities?
- What are the big business challenges that may restrict the organization's ability to meet its aims?
- What is the current culture and the desired culture of the organization?
- What are the values of the organization and how well are they lived?
- How does decision making work here?
- How does the 'people proposition' need to change to help meet the organization's aspirations?
- What is the HR strategy and what is the role of reward?

Clarity of reward issues

I have often found that reward programmes exist because of historical rather than strategic reasons. Whilst the business strategy and aims may have changed, some reward programmes have just been left. These are the sort of comment you find: 'I don't know when this was introduced; it was here when I joined nine years ago', or 'It was introduced by the founders and we have never reviewed it.'

There may still be a fit, but it is vital to question what is there, particularly if it has been unchanged for some years. Based on an understanding of the business strategy, aims, culture etc, to help develop a reward strategy it is valuable to challenge the organization by asking some very simple questions such as:

- What are each of the different elements of reward for?
- What messages do our reward programmes carry?
- Are the messages they carry in conflict with our aims or values?
- Are the messages they carry in conflict with those carried by other HR programmes?
- How cost effective are our reward programmes?
- What is the perceived value of reward programmes in the eyes of employees?

● What should be the same, and what can be different? (particularly useful for international organizations)

You need to make sure that you get the full answer, not what may have grown up as company folklore. So probe to get the real answers. This might require some survey or analysis of existing data. If you can drive down to a clear answer to each of these questions, you will have a solid foundation on which to build your reward strategy.

Developing a reward framework

When you are clear on what the organization wants to achieve, its values, and what people think about what reward is doing, you can move on to develop a simple Reward Philosophy or Framework. What I mean by this is a simple statement giving some of the organization's beliefs and principles on reward, such as:

● reward compared with other things about working in the organization;

● what internal equity means;

● market position;

● the organization's ability to pay/profitability;

● the relationship between base pay and variable pay;

● position on benefits;

● recognition and reward.

This can be covered in less than a full page, although some organizations may use two or three pages. Going through the process of drafting a reward philosophy will act as a catalyst in raising questions that need to be agreed and will typically start to get stakeholders to think more strategically about reward.

I suggest doing an initial draft and then discuss it with the key stakeholders – senior management, board etc. You can adjust the paper in light of the discussion. You may also wish to take the draft out to consult with other employees in the organization. In my experience, this is likely to give a better result and it also starts to engage the people who will be impacted by any changes.

One way to engage your stakeholders is to use a reward gap analysis tool such as that shown as Figure 5.1, adapted from Brown (2001).

FIGURE 5.1   Reward gap analysis tool

X = current   O = desired

Left statement	Current (X) / Desired (O)	Right statement
Our pay approach strongly reinforces the actions results and competencies that support our strategy for business success	O → X	Our pay approach essentially operates in isolation from business requirements
Our pay approach emphasizes internal equity and consistency	O ← X	Our pay approach emphasizes external market competitiveness
We pay high against the market	OX	We pay low against the market
We pay very much for the job and its defined requirement	X → O	We pay for the person and their contribution
We pay for results/outputs, the 'whats'	X ← O	We pay for how results are achieved, the behaviours and competencies
Our pay arrangements are highly structured and controlled	XO	Our pay arrangements are flexible and loosely managed
Our pay issues are determined largely by HR	XO	Our pay arrangements are determined largely by line management
We maintain high levels of openness and understanding of our pay system	O ← X	Our pay information is largely secret and not understood
Our pay and reward system is strongly merit-based	O → X	Our pay and reward system is hierarchical, legacy and status-based
We put emphasis on cash reward	X → O	We put emphasis on non-cash rewards
We maintain a harmonized, consistent pay structure for all staff	O ← X	Our pay structure varies for different types/groups of staff
We reward performance through an organization-wide bonus and/or incentive plan	O	We reward performance through individual and team bonus/incentive plans
Our benefits are mainly legacy based and fixed	X → O	Our benefits can flexibly meet HR/business and employee requirements
We use cash to recognize people who display the right behaviours and do a good job	O	We use different ways to recognize people who display the right behaviours and do a good job

Start with the blank schedule and meet with your stakeholders to agree where you are currently and what is your desired position. Figure 5.1 shows an example where the current and desired have been completed. This can help you both develop the reward framework and also start to set an agenda for change.

You should review all of the comments made during the consultation and then get final sign-off as appropriate. An agreed version will provide a framework in which a reward strategy can be developed to support the cultural, values, guiding principles and aims of the organization. Once finalized, I recommend that it is communicated throughout the organization using your normal channels. This then sets the reward framework within which you can make changes. You can refer back to it in communications as you make changes.

Example reward strategy statements

What sort of reward statement or philosophy you decide to use will depend on the way you do things in your organization. I have given below three examples of the sort of documents that might form the basis of a model for you. They are all based on real statements developed within companies. I also give one real example that has been published online.

It is less the detail of the examples that I think is helpful, but the general structure and the sorts of things included. I would strongly advise against choosing any one of these as just right for you, but use them to give you some ideas of the sort of statement that would help. Using the style that would work in your organization, draw on these examples and what I have covered in the first part of this book to establish a reward statement or set of reward principles that will work for you that will give you the framework for your reward strategy.

Example 1: XYZ Limited

Reward and Recognition Strategy

Employee Reward is our single largest cost. It is therefore critical that we maximize the value of Reward to the company.

Reward has an important part to play in carrying strong messages, such as how someone's contribution and performance is seen or providing focus, but we recognize that reward is only one part of the range of drivers of people motivation.

▶

We need to be maximizing the effectiveness of reward whilst seeking to monitor efficiency savings.

Although reward can be made up of different parts – basic pay, variable pay, benefits and stock – we will manage this as total reward, emphasizing the same source of funding for all elements and the total value to people in the business.

Reward programmes should clearly support the goals and values of the business.

We compete for people in different markets and so recognize the competitive pressures in these markets. Specifically, we will monitor total reward data for the different markets in which we compete and look to position total reward competitively.

To support cross-divisional working and movement, we will have common reward programmes unless there is a strong market need to differentiate.

Example 2: ABC Group

Reward Policy statement

We recognize that our staff are a key resource and are the major factor that will differentiate ABC Group from the competition.

The reward policy will support and reinforce the strategic aims and objectives of the group. This will help to meet the needs of stakeholders – customers, staff and shareholders – to provide them with a return on their investment and a share in the success of the business.

The reward policy sets out the group's aims and objectives for the reward of our staff. The purpose of the policy is to ensure that the group attracts and retains sufficient appropriately skilled staff to fulfil strategic business objectives and to ensure that staff are fairly rewarded.

To achieve this the group will aim to ensure that:

- remuneration is externally competitive and internally equitable;

- base salaries are competitive when compared to an appropriate market sector;

- opportunities are given to staff to enhance total remuneration through performance-related bonuses, where appropriate;

- staff have as much choice in benefits as possible;

- the total remuneration package is communicated clearly to staff;

- pay, grading, bonuses and benefits will be applied consistently across the group unless there is a demonstrable reason for differentiation.

This policy lays out a framework for the construction and development of pay and benefits policies within the group; although detailed practice will vary, these will adhere to the overall group policy.

Group human resources is responsible for the development of pay and benefits policies and strategies. The responsibility for the implementation and management of these rests with line management and/or personnel operations.

Example 3: XCo

Reward and Recognition

1.1 Reward Philosophy

Reward will support the goals and values of the business – primarily the guiding principles. Working with the other elements of HR, it will help to attract and retain the best skills in the market.

1.2 Reward Policy

1.2.1 Overview

Although there are different elements within this reward strategy, they are not discrete, but there are important relationships between them. We will emphasize the total value proposition of working in XCo, of which current financial reward is part, rather than focusing on any one element. Total reward will be positioned above the market median. Unless there is a specific market reason for difference, a consistent approach will be taken.

Reward programmes will be simple, flexible and transparent. Where appropriate they will be linked to performance.

XCo's reward strategy will provide for non-bureaucratic and simple systems that will minimize administration; it will be flexible and adaptable.

The company recognizes that both itself and employees are obliged to pay taxes within the jurisdictions within which it operates. Although the company may help to minimize employee tax through effective structures, this will only be within the overall reward strategy.

1.2.2 Basic Pay

Market position

Basic pay will be set at around the median of the markets in which we compete. The markets may be function/discipline, geographic or a combination. This policy recognizes that the demand for particular skills is constantly moving and the market median for some specialized markets may readjust more frequently than others.

Drivers

Basic pay will normally be reviewed once per year. In cases of particularly high market inflation or demand for skills, a more frequent review may be warranted. XCo does not reward for skills per se, but the way in which skills are applied to add value to the business.

Recognizing the need to be competitive in the market, the overall pay budget will reflect the company's ability to pay. At an individual level a pay review will reflect both performance and potential.

Pay Structure

Underpinning basic pay will be a simple flexible structure; it will be non-bureaucratic and will support flexible management.

1.3 Variable Pay

Variable pay is cash award based on predetermined and defined outcomes. It is performance driven. Performance may be based on the individual, team, or group and is always in support of the business strategy. Variable pay will typically be based on performance over the financial year. Bonuses may be paid at the end of a project. They may be designed to run for a period of more than one financial year.

Variable pay when added to basic pay will provide an opportunity to move to around the 75th percentile for total reward. This reflects XCo's emphasis on performance.

The proportion of variable pay to basic pay will increase with the potential impact that an individual may have in the business.

1.4 Benefits

XCo provides benefits for different reasons:

- market need to offer certain benefits to attract or retain people;

- moral or social reasons as a responsible employer;

- financial reasons either because of some tax advantage or through the bulk purchasing power of the company.

Benefits are not designed to emphasize differentials between groups of people within the business. They should be as consistent as possible. Within the range of benefits offered, XCo will aim to provide as much choice as is practicable (including cash alternative), in line with employee needs.

1.5 Recognition and Value

We will strive to recognize and value the excellent work of our people using both financial and non-financial means. We will celebrate the success of teams and individuals in the business.

Tesco plc is a UK FTSE 30 company and one of the world's largest retailers with over 530,000 staff. It has a simple set of reward objectives and reward principles (shown below) that it applies to reward around the world.

Reward objectives

- **Attract** – Enable Tesco to recruit the right people.

- **Motivate** – Incentivize colleagues to deliver our business goals together.

- **Recognize** – Acknowledge individual contribution and performance.

- **Align** – Create shareholder value by focusing colleagues on making what matters better.

- **Retain** – Foster loyalty and pride in Tesco so that colleagues want to stay with us and strive to do their best.

◀

Reward principles

Fair

- policies are transparent, and applied consistently and equitably;
- reward decisions are trusted and properly governed;
- reward is legal and compliant.

Competitive

- we assess competitiveness on a total reward basis including financial and non-financial rewards;
- reward reflects an individual's role, experience, performance and contribution;
- reward is set with reference to external market practice and internal relativity.

Sustainable

- reward is aligned to the business strategy, reflects our performance, and is affordable;
- our reward framework is flexible to meet the changing needs of the business;
- we reward in a responsible way.

Simple

- reward is simple, clear, and easy to understand;
- we avoid unnecessary complexity;
- reward is delivered accurately.

(tescoplc.com, updated 9 May 2013)

Making changes over time

Change model

This book is not about change management; there are many books on that subject. But I just wanted to give you a couple of insights. First, a very simple model of one aspect of change (Figure 5.2) that I use all the time as a reward

FIGURE 5.2   Project model: developing options

consultant. I have found it invaluable to help think where we are in a reward change project.

The model illustrates the typical way in which a project works. There is an initial issue that is identified. You need to be clear exactly what the problem is and what you are trying to change. You need to open up a whole lot of ideas and thinking to consider a range of options before you can gradually close in on the final design. The model is particularly helpful to demonstrate that you should go into the potential change with an open mind and think widely round the subject rather than rush at a predetermined solution.

The second thing I wanted to share is an approach that Hoffmann *et al* (2012) developed for how to solve business problems, but which complements Figure 5.2. Whilst this was developed to solve wider business problems, I believe that this is a very helpful model that can be applied to changing reward.

1 *Understanding the central problem.* Too often, executives mistake the symptoms for the disease and act before they fully take stock of the problem.

2 *Applying a conceptual model.* A conceptual model lists the potential causes and solutions of the problem. When combined with business and operational constraints, it can be used to form a hypothesis about the cost and benefits of solutions.

3 *Using the conceptual model to focus data collection* and limit the temptation to boil the ocean. The conceptual model informs what data is critical and what is merely nice to have.

▶

4   *Analysing the data* to illuminate the causes and potential answers to the challenges the organization is facing, with a focus on defining solutions that stakeholders can reliably execute.

5   *Presenting the findings to stakeholders* to confirm the feasibility of the solution and develop a road map to successful action.

6   *Enabling the solution so the organization can take effective action.* This step almost always requires changes in processes, organization and people. Defining these changes and providing a road map to implement them are crucial to successfully realizing the full benefit of the analysis.

Strategic pragmatism

Nowadays, change is the constant. It comes from the internal and external factors discussed in Chapter 4. As opportunities present themselves from changes, for example, in legislation or taxation, or new products on the market or any of the changes within the organization, you need to consider the impact on reward.

You need to test out ideas against the organization's aims and values and reward philosophy. My view is that you also need to be pragmatic. Whilst you may have a great idea for changes to reward that you believe will help the organization meet its aims, its time may not have come. You can only operate within the reality of the organization. As Peter Drucker famously said, 'culture eats strategy for breakfast'. You can only make the sort of changes that the culture will allow.

In the discussion on reward strategy in Chapter 1 I emphasized the need for a sense of direction. You need to know what you are heading for. But you also need to think carefully about the pace of change. It may just not be possible to achieve all you want in the period you would like to. But the clarity of direction can ensure that you are always moving the right way even if at a slightly slower pace.

I call this approach '*strategic pragmatism*'. Having a clear sense of what is important to the organization and a sense of direction. You can frame changes against both of these, but it is pragmatism within this strategic framework that keeps moving reward on to help support the organization.

Unintended consequences

The world is a complex place and so too are organizations. Whilst an idea might seem excellent on paper, when it gets implemented there can be unintended consequences as other factors will come into play. It is most common in any contingent pay system – where salary, bonus or share allocation is contingent on a certain outcome. This can be difficult to spot in advance.

Sometimes you might think that the best thing that you can ask of your reward strategy is to do no harm. Being neutral can be much better than the potential unintended consequences. Let me give you a few examples of the sorts of things to look out for.

Targets

When you set a target or targets against which a payment may be made then, as I have already mentioned, if the individual values the payment for achieving the target they are likely to try to achieve it. This may mean reducing emphasis on other activities that are not targeted or finding ways to achieve the target that may cost the organization in other ways. For example, at an executive level, a target profit may be achieved by cutting costs as well as increasing revenue. But simply cutting costs may damage the business. You cannot keep cutting for success. At an administrator level, you can answer calls or letters quickly to meet a target but without giving customers the information they want.

Short term vs long term

A payment that is contingent on a short-term outcome may encourage short-term thinking and decisions that are not in the longer-term interests of the organization. So a payment of some kind may be made for achieving a particular financial result, but that may lead to not spending money this year on an investment that would give a longer-term result, because of the impact on the payment expected.

Assessments

Many performance-related pay systems link pay increases directly to a rating that is assessed based on performance of the individual, typically against meeting objectives. An organization may wish to emphasize the importance, as it sees it, of high pay for high performance and so weights pay increases heavily to those with the highest ratings. A potential consequence of such a system is that it may influence the behaviour of the assessor who may rate people based to some extent on their understanding of the weighting rather than on performance ie they work backwards.

Summary

Agreeing a written reward strategy with the leaders of your organization can be an excellent way to get them to think about what reward can and should be doing in the organization and its implications. Once agreed it should have a reasonable shelf life and you can refer back to it as you present proposed changes to reward over time.

As you design new reward programmes, in particular variable pay systems, try to look out for unintended consequences.

Questions

- What is there in the example reward philosophy statements that could fit with your organization?

- Can you do a first draft based on what you have read so far?

- How would it be best to consult with key stakeholders?

- How would you position it within your other policy statements?

- What process would you go through to get it out into the organization?

Communications 06

Effective communications is a critical element in bringing any reward strategy to life. In the world of reward management I see too many people fixated by the minutia of the design of a reward programme whilst they spend no time on communications. The only way you can get real value for the money the organization spends on reward is through effective communications.

Communications and reward

You must understand why you have the different elements of reward, how they fit together, what they are meant to be doing and how they relate to other HR programmes before you can communicate them.

If you want to give reward a chance of having an impact, people need to understand it. The most elegant reward structures will be valueless unless the stakeholders engage with them, value them and understand how they work. Without that you are wasting your time. I emphasized earlier that reward carries messages. Sometimes it is obvious, other times it may need some interpretation. But if reward carries messages, communications is fundamental. I give a simple model to illustrate the point shown as Figure 6.1

FIGURE 6.1   Technical and communications balance

Release the value – help employee engagement, communications
Technical changes, tax issues, programme design – not visible to employees

A lot of reward is about the technical issues – taxation, pay structures, compa ratios, spreadsheets. Much of this is undertaken at the desk with little visibility. It is important to design reward strategy and structures that will be the best fit for the organization. These are the core elements of reward that I show in Figure 6.1 as *below the line*. Consider them as below the surface that most people will not see.

However, to release the value of all of that work done *below the line* are the *above the line* activities. This is all about communicating and engaging with employees who will be affected by the changes being made.

Confidentiality

An individual's pay is normally kept confidential, although in the public sector and the most senior jobs in a quoted company it may be published. However, whilst this is a reasonable starting point, you cannot rely on employees keeping the information confidential. Gone are the days that an organization can control its external or employee brand. The internet put paid to that.

The Millennial generation, those born between 1980 and 1995, will make up 50 per cent of the workforce by 2020. PwC (2013) found that 43 per cent of millennials say they have discussed their pay with co-workers versus 24 per cent of non-millennials.

Data is much more accessible and is openly shared. What you pay and what it is like to work for your organization is no longer solely in your hands to communicate.

Communicating total reward

The CIPD Reward Risk survey (2012) found that the top risk identified by reward professionals in 2011 and 2012 was that 'Employees don't appreciate the value of total reward offering.' The report concludes that effective communication of the value of the total reward package remains a stand-out risk for organizations of all shapes and sizes. It seems that reward managers are more than ever focused on getting the most out of the existing reward offering.

Before you spend more money on more reward, you should first ensure that employees know what they already have and how it works. Benefits, pensions and share plans can cost a huge amount of money but it is rare that people understand them or appreciate their value. Therefore, you have to work very, very hard to get them to do so.

I ran an online survey in a financial services business as part of the research on flexible benefits. Over 50 per cent of people responded. 23 per cent of respondents did not know they had life assurance cover provided and 31 per cent of people did not know the company provided permanent health insurance. The cost of providing these benefits for the people who did not know they had them was close to £1,000,000! This information was material in supporting flex to improve understanding.

I once met with an executive of a business to help him go through his share plans. He thought that one set was share options and so, at the time, worth fairly little as the market price was low. In fact they were restricted stock, worth at the time more than £300,000.

Recognizing that most people do not understand the total value of their package has led to the growth or reward statements now used by many large organizations such as BP and Centrica.

Reward statements

Reward statements are not new; I received one from my first employer in 1978. Reward statements communicate the total value of all elements of reward (salary, bonus, benefits including pension and shares) to each employee. They will be in a common format but will show the details for each employee. They may be paper based or online. One of the advantages of paper-based statements is that they can easily be shared with family or a lender. But they would only be produced annually.

More commonly now reward statements are online. These are cheaper to produce, can be more dynamic and can be updated more easily for changes to the package. Figures 6.2 and 6.3 (courtesy of Strait Logics Limited) show pages from the sort of sophisticated online reward statements that are available.

In my experience, reward statements are very popular with employees as they help them see clearly the different parts of their reward package and what they are worth.

Reward statements help the employer get value from its spend on reward as they improve employees understanding of the value of the total package. This helps to ensure that employees do not simply think about basic pay, particularly where increases may be small. It is also important

FIGURE 6.2   Example online reward statement

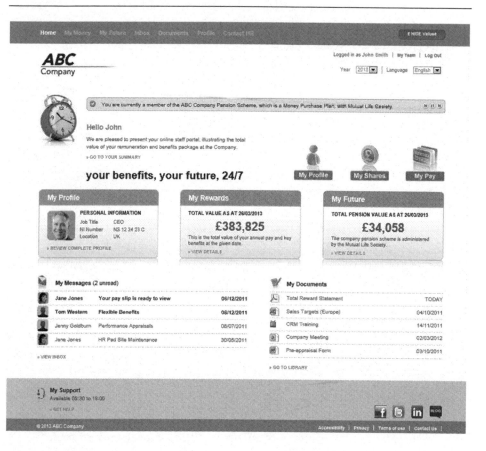

that employees value their total package, not just headline pay, if they are considering looking for a job outside the organization.

A point to consider in communicating total reward is the difference between the cost to the employer and the value to the employee. The normal approach is to show the total in terms of the cost to the employer. For cash elements such as salary, car allowance and bonus this is pretty well the same for both the employer and the employee at a gross level. Obviously tax and national insurance will impact the net, but this is rarely shown. But for benefits in particular there can be a significant difference.

The best examples would be insured benefits where the cost to the employer (and sometimes the tax cost to the employee) can be significantly lower than the cost to the employee if they were to buy a similar level of cover in the market. This is because the premiums will almost always be

FIGURE 6.3   Example online reward statement

lower for group cover than they would be for an individual. I will take private medical insurance (PMI) as the most extreme example.

- Firstly, group PMI will normally provide cover for all medical conditions regardless of whether they were present when the employee joined the scheme. This is not the case if you were to buy PMI as an individual where existing medical conditions would normally be excluded.

- Secondly, the cost to the employee would be the 'benefit-in-kind' cost of the benefit ie the tax payable on the benefit of the premium paid by the employer.

- Finally, premiums for group cover are normally considerably lower than for an individual.

If you put these three together the cost to the employee, for better cover, may be 20 per cent or 40 per cent of a much lower premium than they would have to pay. Therefore, taken together, the net cost to the employee can be less than 10 per cent of the cost had they bought cover themselves.

So in the case of PMI you have three potential 'prices' you can put on the benefit: the premium paid, the tax cost of the premium to the employee or the equivalent cost of buying cover for yourself. Typically, it is the premium paid that is shown. But I believe that it is also important to draw people's attention to the implicit value, which is much greater.

Flexible benefits (flex)

Unlike reward statements, flexible benefits (covered in Chapter 13) may not cover total reward. Flex is a great way to get people to understand, or at least to appreciate the benefits they have, but only some benefits may be 'flexed' within the plan. So whilst flex has the advantage over reward statements of requiring employees to be active in making choices, in itself it may only provide part of the picture.

Modern online systems can in effect combine total reward statements and flex through a reward portal. The reward statement element shows their details and allows them to drill down to the detail of the different plans. Then, once a year, through the same portal they can make changes to those things they may flex. For larger organizations this can be an excellent way to help maximize value – putting everything in one place so all elements of reward are covered.

Building communications into reward design

Whilst communicating reward may be seen as following the design there is an earlier element that needs to be thought through. That is, the level of involvement of employees during the design and development stages.

Other than for particularly sensitive changes, such as closing a defined benefit pension, my experience is that reward changes benefit from involving employees early on. This has a number of advantages:

- It is likely to give you a better final result ie the new arrangement or plan is more likely to be effective as employee groups often come up with some issues and ideas you had not considered.

- It may reinforce the desired culture of, for example, transparency, openness and involvement if these are important.

- It starts to build engagement with the change so that employees are involved in the design or change rather than it just being done to them.

- It starts the change and communications process; assuming you cannot involve every individual, then those people who are involved can start talking about the process with their colleagues.

You need to manage expectations so that employees are realistic about the likely outcomes. You can distinguish between reward 'levels' and reward 'design'. For example, I have worked with many employee groups in client organizations where we have explained at the start that the total spend is planned to remain unchanged but we want to review the design of reward to make it more appropriate.

Pay review process

In Chapter 9 I cover pay reviews and using market data. I have found that a surprisingly few organizations who use some rigour to determine market salary levels etc explain the process to their employees. Unless this is done it is no surprise that employees may think that decisions on budgets and market pay appear fairly random. Most people will not realize the research that goes into trying to be fair in relation to the external market.

If you have communicated a reward strategy or framework of principles, I hope you will have covered some reference to your position to the external pay market. This, then, is a helpful starting point to be able to explain a little more on how this is done. It does not need to be long and complex. Here is an example of the sort of explanation I am talking about.

> We strive to be fair in establishing pay levels across the business in comparison with the pay market in which we compete. To do this we participate in a number of salary surveys run by leading consultancies. We provide data on pay levels for particular jobs (we do not disclose any information about individuals) as do other organizations. The consultancy analyses the input and provides aggregated pay data for the different roles. We then compare our position against that of similar organizations and, within our pay policy, use this to help us determine competitive pay levels and pay increases.

I have been involved in a few organizations where there were complaints about pay levels. However, once the process was explained and people realized that there was some rigour and it was not just based on a 'finger in the air', the concerns diminished almost completely. So whatever your approach to pay levels I suggest you consider communicating something about how you do it.

Individual pay reviews

Much of this chapter is about the broad communication of reward to most or all employees, often due to a change in some part of the reward package. I just want to turn to communicating reward to individuals and what I see as frequently missed opportunities.

Almost all organizations will have an annual pay review. Some will use bonuses. The detail and the process will differ greatly. In some organizations there will be a standard pay increase for everyone or maybe a profit share. In these cases a standard communication for all employees is likely to be used. But particularly where there are differences in pay awards or bonuses between people, I think that there is an opportunity for a meaningful conversation.

It may be that a standard letter is produced by the HR department and sent directly to each employee. I think this should be avoided. Much better is for the line manager to have a conversation with the employee and hand over a letter. This is an opportunity for the line manager to help the individual interpret the message in the pay review (or bonus) and reinforce whatever they want to say about the last period and the next. Line managers may need some guidance on the way to manage the conversation, particularly where there may be a zero review.

The motivational value, if any, of a pay review does not last very long so we should do what we can to increase it. I believe that the organization can leverage more value out of the pay review event by encouraging these conversations.

Recruitment and selection

You need to ensure that those responsible for recruitment and selection are well briefed on the reward package so that they can explain enough about your reward programmes to potential recruits. You should ensure that the documentation given to those being recruited is effective in explaining the things people considering a job with your organization will want to know.

As part of their recruitment process, many organizations have developed an online system where potential recruits can log on and review the reward on offer in some detail. This can be interactive and allow the individual to do some simple modelling. This can be particularly helpful to explain flexible benefits.

A communications model

How you communicate a change will vary hugely based on its nature. A small change with little impact that may only affect a small number of people may be dealt with very simply. But a major change, good or bad, that is more complex and with greater impact for most people will need very careful planning.

You need to bear in mind that, quite reasonably, everyone will want the answer to the question, 'How will this change affect me?'

You should consider the relationship between the efficiency and effectiveness of different communications media. There is often a trade-off to be made as the most efficient is not likely to be the most effective. In practice, for a large reward change project a number of different media will be used as discussed below. But although some media will be more expensive than others, the marginal cost difference is usually fairly small compared with the total project and the downside risk of communicating poorly.

Here is a general approach to communicating significant reward changes. I will look specifically at delivering bad news in the following section.

Planning

- Plan – develop a communications plan including lead time to prepare materials, briefing of stakeholders, key dates to issue different communications etc.

- Establish key messages – what are the core messages about the change – background, what rationale etc? Do not worry about specifically how you will use them, but agree these core messages with the appropriate stakeholder. This is your initial communications collateral.

- Engaging stakeholders – you may already have a model for communicating change, but an important part is normally to brief the managers in advance of the broader communication to all employees. This can help give the managers of the organization the chance to help the communication and so keep them engaged and involved with the change.

- Ambassadors – you may have got to the point of communicating the change by involving many people through focus groups etc, in the initial design and development. These may be people who can be briefed in advance and can act as ambassadors for the change.

- Look and feel – you may have a design 'look' for the change – colours and name of reward change so that the themed look and feel can flow through all of the communications.

- Teaser – for a positive message you may wish to develop some simple announcements via desk drops or e-mail to act as teasers to generate interest. You may use them to build to a specified date for an announcement.

- Stories – the more you can make a concept concrete, the better will be the impact. Use stories and examples to illustrate what you mean. Think about some typical employees and see how you can show the change for people like them.

- External support – you may use external experts to help develop the communications plans. You may also be working with some technical providers, such as independent financial advisers or flexible benefits providers who can provide some direct support such as running roadshows to explain some details of the change, or resource a telephone helpline.

Communications channels

Think carefully about the messages and the most appropriate media for the audiences. One reason for using different communication channels is that some people will prefer one to another and so a range may be more effective. Determine what media you will use and when that will be built into the plan.

- Letter to home – this is relatively costly but can be personal and is easy to share with the family. There will be some inconsistency on timing as some people will be away; post may not be delivered on the same day for all; some will receive the letter before they go to work, others only when they get home.

- Booklet – where there is a lot of information, such as for a new flexible benefits scheme, you may wish to put together a simple booklet.

- E-mail – efficient and cheap and an accepted standard channel for most organizations but it is not good for long or complex messages.

E-mails can be missed with a lot of e-mail traffic although this can be reduced by announcing that an important message is coming.

- Technology – over 92 per cent of the UK adult population have a mobile phone of which more than 60 per cent are smart phones. More than 80 per cent also have broadband at home or through their mobile. So even though some employees may not have regular access to a computer at work, they are likely to have access at home.

- Texts – common (according to Ofcom in the UK, there are more than 200 texts sent per person per month) and cheap but only suitable for short messages, although there can be a link to more information.

- Intranet – you can link an e-mail or text to an intranet site with illustrations, models, question-and-answer section etc. For a change that is going to take place over some weeks or months, an intranet site can be updated regularly so you can point people to it for the latest position.

- Internal 'social media' – if you have an internal system such as Yammer you would normally use this as part of the communications mix to pick up issues and respond to points made and questions posted.

- Posters – where notice boards are used.

- Desk drop – this needs to be punchy and is likely to give summary information with where to go for more information.

- E-mail address – if you want to manage questions you may wish to set up a dedicated e-mail address to which people may post questions. You will, of course, need to ensure that you can handle the questions that come in.

- Telephone helpline – again to answer questions. This can be time consuming and expensive to manage, but can help to deal with concerns and issues very quickly.

- Questions and Answers – to complement initial communications you may develop a Q&A as a simple way to cover what you expect would be the main questions you will receive. An online Q&A can be kept up to date with questions that have come in via e-mail and telephone.

- Briefings – you may set up road shows, presentations, drop-in surgeries depending on the change, to help people get a more detailed understanding.

Communicating bad news

Sometimes you need to communicate bad news. For example, closing a defined benefit pension scheme to future accrual or paying no bonus because of poor trading results. Here are some points to consider in how to approach this:

- Ensure that your leadership are clear on the changes being made and are briefed so that the message given is consistent.

- You may wish to prepare a reactive press statement should the change be one that becomes of interest to the media. If the story does get into the media you have the statement ready.

- Where there is particular pressure on costs, there may be a number of negative changes being made. In such a case I suggest you think about getting all the bad news out at one time and take the inevitable negative reaction on the chin; deferring some decisions so that you have more bad news later on has the effect of 'death by 1,000 cuts' which can be much worse.

- Where possible plan for the change and give as much notice as possible. For example, if you are going to remove a benefit, say a fixed-value Christmas bonus, can you announce it a year in advance? A long lead time can make a negative message more acceptable as people have time to get used to it and, depending on the change, can make appropriate adjustments.

- Accept bad news as such and do not try to sugar-coat it with a false positive spin. You need to be honest and tell it how it is. Many people have to face much worse news in their personal lives and they get through it.

- Establish who will be best placed to give the news. Is it a letter from the CEO or HR director, or will it be cascaded down the organization through the management chain? The reward expert may need to be involved in explaining the detail after the main announcement.

- Depending on the nature of the change and timing and logistics you may have to announce the news in writing – by e-mail or letter. For example, this may be from the chief executive. However, face to face is much more effective to help people really understand and absorb the change. Face to face is particularly important if the change is very significant or is complex. So if possible, can everyone be briefed at the same time? If not, then would it be better to follow up the letter with roadshows or presentations? Some organizations have regular 'town hall' meetings. Others use videoconference and conference calls.

Here are two thoughts that might help frame your approach to delivering bad news:

- Employees may not like the message, but at least do they see that the company managed it as well as possible.

- The way you treat people now will be the way they treat the organization in a couple of year's time.

Summary

Effective communications is vital to release value from your reward strategy. Employees need to know what they've got and how it works.

To make the most impact it is not good enough to have well-designed reward programmes, they must be embedded so that everyone who is affected understands them.

You have to work hard to get communications right. It can take much more time and effort to get the communications piece right than the reward design itself.

Questions

- Do you know if the people in your organization understand what their total reward is, how much it is worth and how it works?

- Would some form of reward statements, or flex, help you get better value from what you spend on reward?

- Are you maximizing the existing opportunities to communicate key messages from reward, such as pay reviews?

- How can you involve people more in changes to reward?

CASE STUDY   Royal Horticultural Society

This case study illustrates the way in which effective communications and involvement can help ensure that significant changes can successfully be made in reward. Effective communications and involvement were at the heart of this significant change to the pay and associated structures of the RHS. A range of media were used and communications were built in from the start. The results show people have a good understanding of their pay and benefits and satisfaction with pay has steadily increased.

Background

The Royal Horticultural Society (RHS) is the UK's leading gardening charity dedicated to advancing horticulture and promoting good gardening. Its goal is to help people share a passion for plants, to encourage excellence in horticulture and inspire all those with an interest in gardening.

It has four gardens in North Yorkshire, Essex, Devon and Wisley in Surrey. The RHS is responsible for organizing flower shows around the country including the famous Chelsea Flower Show. The RHS publishes widely, both online and books and magazines. Its website (**www.rhs.org.uk**) attracts around 500,000 unique users a month and its book titles are amongst the bestsellers in gardening bookshops.

The RHS carries out wide-ranging scientific research into plants and its scientists are the recognized centre of excellence for independent horticultural science and advice.

The society provide a 'ladder of qualifications', from the RHS Level 1 Certificate (accessible to the amateur as well as the first step in vocational training for the professional horticulturist), through to the prestigious Master of Horticulture (RHS) qualification. The RHS is an Awarding Organization recognized by the Office of Qualifications and Examination Regulations (Ofqual), ensuring accessibility to RHS qualifications through colleges and other partners across the UK. It also offers practical training schemes through the School of Horticulture, public lectures, courses and workshops. In addition, the RHS promotes horticulture and gardening in schools and communities through its Campaign for School Gardening, Britain in Bloom and It's Your Neighbourhood schemes.

Issues

The RHS has a turnover of over £70m (2012) and employs about 750 staff in six locations around the country. Because of the breadth of its operations there are about 400 unique roles. In 2009, in the face of the economic downturn, the society restructured and for the first time made some roles redundant. This caused some disengagement amongst employees and the society needed to find ways to re-engage its people. Resources were very limited but pay was one of the issues that it needed to tackle according to feedback in the employee survey. It had no reward policy or strategies.

In the winter of 2009/10 the head of HR and the acting director general (the previous DG left in October 2009) visited all the RHS's six locations and met with many of its people in focus groups to understand more fully the range of issues that employees had both in terms of what they had gone through and their wishes for the future.

As a result of this they established an initial 'People plan' covering talent management, career development etc. An issue that came up frequently in the focus groups and elsewhere was pay levels.

Pay and benefits project

2010/11

It was felt that changes to reward would take two years to achieve. So to address the reward issues, in March 2010 RHS set up a Pay and Benefits Project Group to undertake a comprehensive review of pay and benefits and make recommendations for a clear reward strategy for 2011 onwards. The project group worked with an outside consultant and included the new director general who joined in summer 2010, senior managers, HR and the employee consultation group.

Initially the group looked at a sample of jobs across the organization and compared their pay and benefits with certain comparator organizations across the many markets in which they operated. Focus groups were also held to gather employees' views on the benefits provided.

The research showed that most roles were paid at a market rate, but some people in the lowest three bands (1–3) were behind the market. The existing salary bands were very long (partly to accommodate the wide range of roles) which led to unrealistic expectations that progress could be made to the top of the band. This was only one illustration of what was clearly a lack of understanding by employees of their pay and benefits. There were many different markets in which RHS competed and it was clear that one size fits all would not work.

They found that the RHS had a good range of benefits but there were considerable differences in eligibility. Also many people believed that benefits were at statutory minimum, which was not the case. Three reward changes were announced in March 2011:

- Some individuals in the lowest grades received a salary adjustment to bring them back to a reasonable market position.

- A new benefit programme was introduced. For example, death in service benefit was increased to four times salary for all; holiday entitlement was increased from 23 days to 25 days for the most junior roles, pension service requirements were also equalized for this group.

- There was a set of reward principles which would frame changes to reward as follows:

RHS Pay and benefit principles

Fair – through clear and transparent systems we will ensure a consistent approach to pay and benefits which builds trust and engagement.

Flexible – with our overall reward package we will aim to retain and attract high-calibre employees with the required skills and potential.

Encourage excellence and share success – we will recognize individual and team excellence in delivering high standards and working more effectively together across the society.

Build skills and expertise – we will build and develop our skills and talent to support RHS strategy and values.

Well communicated – we will ensure that all employees know how pay and benefits are structured across the society.

Affordable – we will ensure that our pay and benefit decisions appropriately reflect our charitable status.

A well-designed, comprehensive, four-sided pay and benefits newsletter was distributed to all staff explaining the background, the pay market comparison, the benefit changes and a schedule of all the benefits with a simple summary of each. There was also an explanation of what would be happening next.

Every Monday there is an e-mail round-up distributed to all staff across RHS. For those without access to e-mail, local communications co-ordinators print out the round-up and distribute on notice boards etc. This weekly communication is used by different parts of the RHS, including HR, to communicate current issues to everyone.

HR announced through the weekly round-up that it would be running open workshops at each site to help explain the reward changes and answer any questions. Local managers also encouraged people to attend. HR delivered two sessions at the smaller sites, as they are a seven-day, visitor service operation, and a number of sessions over a few days at the larger sites to ensure a high attendance. Over 90 per cent attended.

Prior to the announcement of the changes, HR briefed the 200 people managers by e-mail. This is their normal approach, although for some changes it may only be the 30 senior managers who are briefed in advance.

2011/12

The second phase of the pay and benefit project was to review the pay structures. The leadership team was asked for its views about what its members believed was required to support the RHS going forward. Results were also available from independent external pay benchmarking. Drawing on this and working with an external consultant, HR developed the idea of a simple five-level structure from the existing seven and a series of four job families as below, also showing the approximate number of staff in each:

- Horticulture (123)

- Retail (111)

- Visitor services (22)

- Catering (20)

For these groups there would be a structure with clear pay progression within a framework based on skills and competence. To achieve the optimum structure for the four job families each was developed working very closely with the line managers.

This was announced in April 2012. A well-designed 11-page, A4 colour booklet was distributed explaining the new reward policy and consolidating the changes announced a year earlier. As with the previous change, open workshops were held at every site. However, this time they were led by the local operations management rather than HR. This reinforced the role of the line management (as they had been very involved in the design, so had ownership) and made it clear it was an organization change, not an HR change.

Whilst the detail for each of the job families would be of most interest to those in the particular family, the sessions were open to all and all of the job families were discussed. The organization wanted to make it clear (in line with its principles) that this was all transparent; it had nothing to hide.

The way in which the salary system would work – starting salaries, progression, benchmarking to determine market rates etc – was clearly explained. But the RHS also said that where employees believe that their role has changed sufficiently, or the market has changed, they may make a business case for a pay review. They would need to provide evidence of comparable external salary rates if appropriate. In the first year (to April 2013) about 12 people (1.6 per cent of employees) had made a business case for their pay to be adjusted. This was a low take-up of the offer but it also generated goodwill as reflected in the June 2013 employee satisfaction survey showing 78 per cent of staff have a good understanding of their pay and benefits and satisfaction with pay has steadily increased.

Tax and National Insurance

07

This chapter covers the tax and payroll tax situation in the UK, but some of the underlying principles may apply in other jurisdictions. You should check the position with the local tax authorities or take appropriate local professional advice. Tax legislation is amended at least annually, so some details may have changed since this book was written.

The chapter is only able to skim the surface of tax issues as they relate to reward. It is designed to alert you to some key issues in how tax interrelates with reward. I hope that it will give you enough information to enable you to know when you need professional advice and have a better quality conversation with an adviser.

Information on UK taxation will apply to the majority of employees, but watch out for particular rules that apply for directors of companies and those earning less than £8,500. The limit was set originally to define higher paid employees. However, as you can see it has eroded somewhat with inflation, having been frozen in 1979. Had it been increased with average earnings the limit would now be over £50,000.

General principles

Driving reward strategy

As discussed in Chapter 4, taxation will be one of the influences on reward strategy. For example, in the 1980s company cars were relatively lightly taxed and so were a common feature of a management benefit package. But in the 2000s cars have been taxed progressively more and so this has been a strong influence on providing a taxable car allowance rather than a car.

A fundamental principle in considering the impact of taxation is that you should not let the tax opportunities drive your reward strategy. Certainly take tax changes into account and you may be able to arrange things to maximize tax breaks from time to time. But you need to get your reward strategy agreed to meet your agenda and then find the efficient way of delivering value, not simply have a reward programme because it is tax efficient. For example, long-service awards. There are some tax concessions for awards made, within limits, at 20 years and thereafter. But if long service awards do not fit your culture you should not use them just because of the tax break.

Having said that, you need to keep up to date with tax changes that may impact reward, and in particular advantageous reward programmes that become available. Monitor what is changing in tax and national insurance, especially with finance bills as they relate to reward, and consider if you can take advantage of the opportunities provided.

Employer and employee responsibilities

The employer has certain obligations to report to Her Majesty's Revenue & Customs (HMRC) and collect and remit tax and National Insurance Contributions (NIC) within set time limits, operate PAYE and issue relevant tax documents – P60s, P45s, P11Ds etc.

For the majority of employees being paid through the PAYE system, there is little for them to do. They may or may not be required to complete an annual tax return, depending on their circumstances. Generally, only higher-paid employees or those with other earnings or more complex benefits such as share options need to complete an annual return. But whilst the employer may be accountable to collect tax and NIC to remit to HMRC, the personal tax liability remains with the employee.

Whilst you may be able to arrange some elements of reward to minimize tax for employees, ultimately personal taxation is the responsibility and liability of the individual, not the employer. A business can only operate within the tax rules that apply at any one time and they change pretty frequently – at least once a year.

An organization needs to consider how much it will explain and communicate tax issues that are the responsibility of the employee although arising out of a company reward. It is not appropriate for an employer to give financial or tax *advice*. It may wish to give information or point employees to sources of advice or information, or it may wish just to alert employees to a tax issue. On the other hand, the provision of financial or tax advice to employees (by a qualified outside provider) could be one benefit as part of an overall reward package.

For example, in recent years the tax position of company pensions has changed a number of times. This includes increases and reductions in the Lifetime Allowance (LTA) and annual allowance. Based on individual circumstances an employee may be best advised to take one of the forms of 'protection' allowed by the government. However, whilst the employer may choose to alert employees to the potential issue, it is for the employee to take responsibility for their own affairs and take appropriate advice and action, not the employer.

Taxation of various reward programmes

What is taxable

A good starting point is to assume that anything of value provided to an employee is taxable. Whilst it is, of course, much more complex, this should encourage you to always ask the question, 'What are the tax and national insurance implications of what we are proposing?'

Whilst most people will recognize that salary is taxable, as you move further away from pay, it becomes less clear and employees and employers can make inappropriate assumptions.

- **Cash** – be it salary, bonus, allowance or any other cash payment it is almost always taxable. Any cash payments should be made through payroll to ensure that any tax and national insurance liability is settled. If, unusually, a payment itself is made in hard cash, then it should still be processed through payroll with an appropriate adjustment.

- **Vouchers** – there are particular HMRC rules on vouchers which, because of their close equivalence to cash, are almost always taxable as cash. However, there are specific concessions, such as childcare vouchers, which are free of tax within certain limits.

- **Benefits** – this is complex as some benefits are taxable and other not, some are subject to NIC and others not. I give a list of some of the most common benefits and their current tax position later in this chapter.

- **Shares** – again the tax position on shares is complex and depends on the particular arrangement. Some plans that are approved by HMRC carry tax benefits if operated within certain limits, for example free of tax or subject to Capital Gains Tax (CGT) rather than income tax.

Tax concessions

There are many tax concessions and tax-efficient opportunities approved by HMRC that you should consider and see where there may be a way to use them for delivering extra value or help deliver a strategic aim. They are all available on the HMRC website, but here are a few examples, with others mentioned elsewhere in this chapter:

- A loan to an employee (not director) up to £10,000 interest-free with no benefit-in-kind tax charge for the individual. This limit increased from £5,000 from 6 April 2014. An interesting application could be to help retention – say, provide an interest-free loan to a new graduate joining which is written off after three years, but repayable if they resign. Or a similar arrangement where the amount is written off based on some performance criteria, but otherwise repayable. There would be no tax liability during the term of the interest-free loan, but writing off the loan will be liable to tax and NIC as if it was a cash payment.

- Annual functions provided by the employer which are open to all employees (or at least all employees at a particular location) and where the average cost per head does not exceed £150 (including VAT) in the tax year does not give rise to a tax charge. This concession typically covers the Christmas party.

- Employer paid, or reimbursed, removal costs to move to a new location or take up a new job up to a maximum of £8,000 are free of tax.

- Employer-provided accommodation where: required to do the job eg school caretaker; it allows you to perform your job better and it is customary in that employment eg clergyman or police officer; there are special security risks so accommodation is provided for your safety eg members of the armed forces.

Bonuses

A bonus will be taxable once paid to the employee and should always be paid through payroll. But just a word of caution on bonus design. It is very important that an employee does not acquire an absolute right to a bonus payment much earlier than the date it is paid. If they did, there could be a tax and NIC liability created at the point that the right is acquired well before the bonus is actually paid. Whilst this unintentional design error is rare I have come across it. So if in doubt get a professional opinion. Bonuses are covered in Chapter 10.

Share plans

Share plans (covered in Chapter 12) are taxed in different ways. The tax position of the main UK plans is summarized here.

Save as you earn (SAYE)

Employees save a fixed monthly amount of between £5 and £250 for a fixed period, normally three or five years. Based on the amount being saved employees are granted options to buy shares, with a maximum 20 per cent discount to market value. After the end of the fixed period the proceeds, including any bonus, can be used to exercise the option. As an HMRC-approved plan, there is no tax or NIC liability when the option is exercised. If they do not wish to exercise the option, the proceeds are repaid in cash, tax free.

Share Incentive Plans (SIP)

The tax situation for shares within an HMRC-approved SIP varies according to the type of shares. Companies can give up to £3,000 worth of 'free' shares a year to each employee. Employees can purchase up to £1,500 worth of 'partnership' shares a year. This can be rewarded by the company giving up to two 'matching' shares for each share an employee buys. Employees can also invest up to £1,500 out of dividends from the plan shares in 'dividend' shares. There may be no tax or NIC liability so long as the shares are held for long enough.

Company Share Ownership Plans (CSOP)

There is no tax charge when options are granted under an HMRC-approved CSOP. The maximum value of share options at grant is £30,000 in total. Options may not to be granted at less than market value and may not be exercisable within three years. Gains are then chargeable to CGT not income tax.

Unapproved share option

A share option granted outside a CSOP will be taxable for income tax and NIC on any gains. However, an unapproved share option can be much more flexible as it does not need to conform to the CSOP rules. For executive share options, the relatively low limit of £30,000 for CSOP means that most options are unapproved. However, where this is the case it is also common to have a CSOP that shelters the first £30,000 of options.

Restricted stock

A restricted stock grant should not be taxable on grant whilst there are restrictions that mean it may or may not acquire a value. At the point that the grant vests and the restrictions are lifted, so that shares are transferred to the employee, income tax and NIC are due.

Benefits

One driver of your benefit policy, as discussed in Chapter 13, is the tax status of benefits. If you can deliver higher value to employees at no or little cost to the organization then you should certainly consider it. But of course the tax rates and limits will change so that a benefit that was tax efficient may no longer be so. It is helpful, therefore, to be as flexible as possible.

Whilst the tax position of any particular benefit is normally fairly straightforward, overall it is complex simply because of the range of different tax and NIC treatment and associated limits. I have given below a number of fairly common benefits with their current tax status.

Benefits not subject to income tax or national insurance:

- life assurance;
- long-term disability insurance;
- discounted or free company restaurant meals as long as they are provided for all employees;
- employee assistance programmes;
- pension contributions below the annual allowance;
- childcare vouchers below annual limits;
- travel season ticket loan (<£10,000 after 5 April 2014);
- a mobile phone (including smart phone) and rental and calls if paid by the employer;
- annual medical checks;
- additional holiday;
- car-parking spaces at or near work;
- sporting or recreational facilities for employees and their families eg a company gym.

Benefits subject to tax but not employee's national insurance:

- private medical insurance;
- dental insurance;
- critical illness insurance;
- personal accident insurance;
- travel insurance;
- hospital cash plan;
- company car;
- free fuel (for company car).

Benefits subject to tax and national insurance:

- retail vouchers;
- car allowance.

Tax on company cars and fuel benefit have changed considerably over the last few years and currently the taxable amount is based on a percentage of a sum dependent on a range of factors. In the face of increased taxation, more employers provide a cash allowance than provide a car or fuel.

Salary sacrifice or salary exchange

Salary sacrifice (or salary exchange as it is becoming more commonly known) is a way of packaging employees' benefits and salaries whereby an employee reduces their contractual salary; the employer then provides some benefit(s) in place of the salary given up. The result is that it reduces the amount of NIC paid by both.

Salary sacrifice can be used for a range of benefits and is a fundamental part of making a flexible benefits system work (covered in Chapter 13). Benefits that are currently often part of salary sacrifice are: pension, 'buying' additional holiday, childcare vouchers, cycles, providing employees with car-parking space, most insured benefits and even cars, and mobile devices and phones. I will use pension contributions as an example to explain how it works.

An employee has a contractual salary of £40,000 and pays 10 per cent pa (£4,000) into their company pension. The employer also pays 10 per cent of salary into the individual's pension, so a total of £8,000 pa is being contributed. The employee pays income tax, plus national insurance of 12 per cent on most of their earnings. The employee receives tax relief on the contribution (of £4,000) to pension but will also have paid national insurance on their salary out of which the £4,000 is paid.

The employer pays national insurance at a rate of 13.8 per cent on the salaries it pays.

The employee then reduces their contractual salary down to £36,000 and no longer contributes to their pension. But the employer now agrees to pay a total of £8,000 pa into the pension, so the amount being saved into the pension has not changed.

There is no difference to the employee's tax position, but they have saved 12 per cent NIC (£480) on the £4,000 of salary sacrificed. The employer is now paying a lower salary and so pays £552 less NIC (£4,000 × 13.8 per cent).

The net result is that the same is being contributed into the pension but both the employee and the employer make a saving. The employer may enhance the contribution it makes to the pension, using some or all of this saving, as can the employee.

For salary sacrifice, employees normally opt to change their contractual salary for no less than 12 months. If a salary sacrifice arrangement allows an employee to swap between cash earnings and a non-cash benefit whenever they like, then they have not really sacrificed their entitlement to the cash earnings, as is required. In those circumstances, any expected tax and NIC advantages under the salary sacrifice arrangement will not apply. However, if an employee's financial or personal circumstances change unexpectedly, eg marriage or divorce, HMRC accepts that it may be necessary to change the terms of a salary sacrifice arrangement under a 'lifestyle change'.

You need to ensure that a new contractual salary does not go below the national minimum wage. There may also be some issues relating to state benefits for some people if they reduce their salary.

Non-cash awards

General situation

Just because it is not cash you should still assume that a gift or award is taxable. If you are using a non-cash recognition award or incentive, it is normal practice for the employer to settle any employee tax and NIC that arises. It is therefore important to discuss this with your tax department or tax advisers early on if you are considering such a plan. A potential risk of local informal arrangements to provide employees with non-cash awards is that any tax or NIC liability is not correctly accounted for. You will need to ensure that you set up a system to capture information on non-cash awards given to ensure any tax obligations are met. This is one benefit of using an external provider to facilitate such gifts. The third-party organization will be able to provide management information to capture the required data to help you remain compliant.

Whatever cost estimates or budget you set will need to take the tax cost into account. It is better to provide a lower value gift and pay the tax than a higher value one where the employee finds themself paying tax they did not expect. The enthusiasm and goodwill generated from a non-cash award is immediately damaged, even destroyed, if the employee suddenly finds themself taxed on the benefit. Some organizations have found people refuse to accept a gift on which they may have to pay tax. In these situations the message is generally that 'the tax I am going to have to pay is more valuable to me than the gift, that I can do without – so don't bother!' (Rose, 2001).

Trivial awards

A gift may not be taxable if it is considered 'trivial' by HMRC. Although HMRC uses the term 'trivial' it does not define it. There are no set rules for determining the type of benefit and monetary limit below which benefits are deemed to be trivial. HMRC expects employers to apply common sense and judgement both to the type and the amount of benefits that they consider to be trivial. However, HMRC does give some guidance. It notes that trivial benefits are often, but not always, perishable and/or consumable. HMRC does consider two categories, small gifts and seasonal gifts:

- Small gifts – such as an arrangement of flowers made in recognition of a particular event (eg an employee's marriage or birth of a child), and – importantly – that do not form part of any reward for the employee's services.

- Seasonal gifts – such as a turkey, an ordinary bottle of wine or a box of chocolates at Christmas.

It may be possible, therefore, to consider a gift of a bottle wine or a bunch of flowers or similar as part of a non-cash scheme to be trivial and so not taxable. But if you move to a case of wine or a Christmas hamper then it is almost certainly going to be subject to tax. You should discuss with your local Inspector of Taxes to agree a sensible way to handle your circumstances for trivial awards. For example, HSBC (see the case study in Chapter 11) agreed a limit of £10, below which any award is trivial. Cash benefits, benefits with a money's worth and vouchers, however small in amount, should not be regarded as trivial.

The most common way for organizations to settle any tax due on items which are not accepted by HMRC as trivial is through a PAYE Settlement Agreement (PSA).

PAYE Settlement Agreements (PSA)

A PSA is a flexible voluntary arrangement that an employer can use to settle any PAYE tax and NIC due to HMRC on items that are minor, irregular or impractical to apply PAYE/NIC to, or apportion the value of a particular benefit. The tax due on the expenses and benefits covered by the PSA would normally be payable by employees and the tax the company pays must be 'grossed up' taking account of the tax rates payable by the employees covered by the PSA.

For practical purposes it may be that small cash and money's worth benefits can be included in a PSA. This can be a convenient way for employers to deal with the position on small (if not trivial) awards without involving the individual employee. That said, it is important to tell the employee this is your intention so that they are clear that they do not need to worry about the tax themselves.

Suggestion schemes

HMRC allows some awards as part of a suggestion scheme to be exempt from tax and NIC. For an award to qualify for this exemption:

- the suggestion scheme must be open to all your employees – or to an entire group of employees, such as everyone based in a particular office;
- the suggestion leading to the award must relate to your business;

- the employee receiving the award couldn't reasonably be expected to have made the suggestion in the course of their normal duties of employment;
- the suggestion can't have been made at a meeting held for the purposes of proposing suggestions;
- the award must be either an 'encouragement award' or a 'financial benefit' award.

An encouragement award is one made to an employee for a suggestion that has merit or that shows special effort on the employee's part. Encouragement awards are exempt from tax and NIC up to a small limit of (currently) £25.

A financial benefit award is one made to an employee for a suggestion that meets the following three conditions:

- it relates to an improvement in efficiency or effectiveness;
- you must have decided to adopt the suggestion;
- you must reasonably expect the suggestion's implementation to lead to a financial benefit.

Financial benefit awards are exempt from tax and NIC up to the greater of the following limits, subject to an overall limit of (currently) £5,000 ($7,500):

- 50 per cent of the financial benefit you reasonably expect the suggestion to lead to in the first year following its adoption; or
- 10 per cent of the financial benefit you reasonably expect in the first five years following adoption.

If you make an encouragement award or financial benefit award up to the limits, then you have no reporting requirements and no tax or NIC to pay. If you make an award above the limits set any excess counts as earnings and must be put through PAYE.

Long-service awards

There are currently tax exemptions for long-service awards provided they fall within certain limits. The awards should be:

- in the form of a tangible article or shares in an employing company (or another company in a group of companies);
- for a minimum recognition period of service of 20 years;

- up to a maximum spend of £50 per year of service; and
- with a minimum 10-year break between awards.

So long as these four criteria are met the service award is free of tax and does not need to be reported. If a higher value is used than the £50 per year of service then any excess over the limit is taxable.

Expenses

Expenses are not part of reward as they should be incurred as part of the job and so whilst reimbursed should leave the employee broadly neutral. There are detailed HMRC rules about expenses. But there are some elements of expenses that interact with reward policy. For example:

- HMRC allows expenses to be claimed below certain car mileage rates per mile (based on a number of situations) tax free.
- Taxi fares to take someone home after working late will be tax free within certain guidelines.
- There are daily allowances that may be paid tax free when working away from the normal place of work.

So whilst these sorts of payments may be claimed through the expenses system, operated by the finance function, the policy of what the company will reimburse is something that HR should be involved with as part of the terms and conditions and reward.

Summary

Whilst taxation will always be a significant influence it should not drive reward policy. Rather, monitor what is changing in tax and national insurance as it relates to reward and consider if you can take advantage of the opportunities provided.

This chapter on tax and NIC is a general guide only on the position in the UK and should not be relied upon as the legislation changes regularly. You are therefore strongly advised to take professional advice at the time. You may also find that the HMRC website will give you useful information. It is certainly a good first step.

Questions

- Have you reviewed the benefits you provide to ensure that the correct tax and NIC is being applied?

- Are there some HMRC-approved plans or benefits with low or no tax that could fit your reward strategy and increase value?

- Could you use salary sacrifice to give better value for some benefits to employees?

- Have you established a position on the relative responsibilities of the employer and employee for tax, in particular when taxation changes?

- Are you sure that no tax *advice* is being given to employees inappropriately?

REWARD IN PRACTICE

Grades and pay structures

08

In this first chapter of Part II, I deal with grades and pay structures which are often thought of as the foundations of reward. Whilst for most organizations a pay structure will be tied to a grade structure, they are not synonymous. Let me clarify the difference.

A **grade structure** is a way of grouping broadly similar jobs in an organization into a hierarchy that provides some degree of internal relativity. There may be as few as three grades or more than 20. A grade structure allows people to see where there may be similar sized jobs in other parts of the organization, so it can help career development. Where benefits are based on seniority, different benefits may be tied to the different grades. For example, car allowance may become payable at a given grade. However, an organization can have a grade structure but have individual salaries and so no pay structure or salary scales.

A **pay structure** is a hierarchy of pay or salary levels showing the rates of pay for employees performing a particular job or function at each level of the organization. It therefore seeks to help address internal pay relativities and is normally based on a grade structure. A pay structure normally has some form of range of pay for each level (grade) and typically has a minimum and maximum pay rate, and a series of mid-range opportunities for pay increases. There may be a mid-point which is normally defined as the rate for the fully competent job holder. The salary range also normally reflects the external market, being determined by market pay rates, established through market pay surveys.

I will explain each in turn and how they can come together. Inevitably, there is some overlap between the two sections of this chapter.

Grade structures

To repeat what I said in the introduction, a grade structure is a way of grouping similar jobs in an organization into a hierarchy which provides some degree of internal relativity. There may be as few as three grades or more than 20.

Why use a grade structure?

I suggest that there are four main reasons to use grades:

- To help establish pay scales – pay scales are linked by the grades into ranges, as discussed below.

- To help ensure appropriate internal pay relativity – by their nature the hierarchical grade structure and associated pay structure should help ensure pay levels are differentiated appropriately.

- To link to benefits in a hierarchical structure – unless benefits are single status, ie the same for everyone, a grade structure is used to peg benefits for different levels. I give an example in the box on page 101.

- To help everyone see where there are similar sized jobs – this helps internal recruitment and career development, so people can see where there are opportunities in different parts of the organization.

The first two points are the most common. However, although the main reason that organizations use grade structures is as the basis for a pay structure it does not automatically follow. See the Which? case study at the end of this chapter.

If one or more of these four is an issue in your organization you may wish to introduce a grade structure.

Job size

A fundamental concept underpinning a grade structure is 'job size'. This reflects the relative significance of one role against another. It is not based on pay. So you do not compare jobs and assume that one that is paid more is a bigger job, as that may have much more to do with the salary market for different disciplines. It is also not about the individual job holder but the job itself. Having said that, particularly for more senior jobs, the job holder may influence the size of the job to the extent to which they take on more or broaden or deepen their accountabilities.

You may have jobs that are quite different in their dimensions, as illustrated in Figure 8.1, but are considered the same size. In this example, the way in which each will make an impact will be quite different. The pay markets will also be very different.

Job size is normally determined by some form of job evaluation which is discussed below. If you are introducing a grade structure you will need to think about what sort of job evaluation you will use.

FIGURE 8.1 Job size

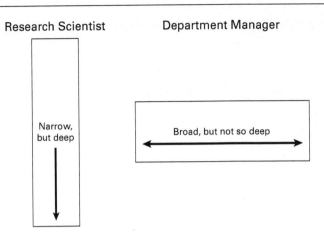

Job evaluation

Job evaluation (je) can be analytical or non-analytical, although in practice some approaches use a combination. But in either case you will need to draft some level of job description for every job to be evaluated.

Analytical

Analytical je analyses each job based on a set of defined factors, such as: decision making, skills, impact and accountability. There are usually different levels within each factor with some points associated with each. The total of the points give a job size that may be compared with others.

Probably the most well-known analytical je system is the Hay Guide Chart Method (Hay Group). This uses three main factors that are subdivided into eight separate dimensions as follows:

- Know-how – is the sum total of every capability or skill, however acquired, needed for fully competent job performance. Know-how has three dimensions:
  - Practical/technical knowledge
  - Planning, organizing and integrating (managerial) knowledge
  - Communicating and influencing skills

▶

◀

- Problem solving – refers to the use of know-how to identify, delineate, and resolve problems. Problem solving has two dimensions:
  - Thinking environment
  - Thinking challenge
- Accountability – the type and level of value a job can add. It has three dimensions:
  - Freedom to act
  - Scope
  - Impact

Analytical je can be done using an online system that normally requires answering a series of questions. The questions will have been validated and will be designed to bring out the separate factors that have been established to determine job size.

Pros and cons

An analytical je scheme is more robust and will enable you to see the relative difference in job size. It can provide a defence against a claim of equal pay for work of equal value, but only if you can demonstrate that the scheme is free of sex bias. The Equality and Human Rights Commission provide helpful checklists on their website (**www.equalityhumanrights.com**) dealing with this. It may be more likely to help identify structural issues in organizational design than a non-analytical approach. An analytical job evaluation scheme can be used to provide a robust grade structure into which jobs may be 'slotted' as illustrated in the case study below.

It can be very time consuming to set up a grade structure in the first place and maintain it. For example, some organizations have a fairly lengthy process to re-evaluate a new or changed job using an analytical system as its basis. However, this tends to go along with a traditional grade structure with 20-plus grades, which is one reason why broad-banding (discussed later) has become more common.

Non-analytical

Unlike the analytical method that breaks down jobs into their component parts, a non-analytical method ranks the whole job. Typically, jobs are matched against a series of profile job descriptions each of which is likely to be associated with a grade. This is called 'job classification'.

An alternative method is 'job ranking', where jobs are ranked against each other based on perceived value to establish a hierarchy. Paired comparison may be used that compares every job with every other job in pairs. By establishing which job is perceived as the larger in each pairing, a hierarchy of job size is established.

Pros and cons

Non-analytical je is fairly simple to operate and so is quicker to implement than an analytical system. However, it is not so robust and does not help understand the relative difference in job size, only the hierarchy.

The Equality and Human Rights Commission states that non-analytical schemes are prone to sex discrimination because comparative judgements about jobs made by the evaluators will have little objective basis, other than the traditional value of the job. Whether the jobholders are predominantly male or predominantly female may influence the placing of that job within the overall rank order. Non-analytical job evaluation can therefore perpetuate a situation in which the jobs most frequently performed by women are regarded as being of less value than the jobs mostly performed by men. A non-analytical job evaluation scheme does not provide you with a defence against a claim of equal pay for work of equal value.

Harmonizing benefits and people development

I introduced a grade structure into a UK business where the main driver was not pay. This organization had three operating divisions with different approaches to pay, bonus and benefits. But the business strategy was to get them to work more closely with each other – to cross-sell to customers, share resources and develop employees across the business as a whole. One of the barriers that had been identified was the significant difference in the benefits. This really got in the way of people working together and easily moving between the divisions. In one division they had a formal grade structure with nine grades and associated salary bands, in another they had eight grades with loose associated salary bands and in the third there were no grades or salary bands.

To harmonize benefits we first needed a single grade structure as the foundation on which to 'hang' the benefits. A single grade structure would also help determine differences in job size across the whole business and lead to better opportunities to be able to develop and promote people. The

▶

three divisions were in different markets with a different approach to pay and they were all concerned to a greater or lesser extent that a new grade structure would lead to a single associated pay structure imposed from the centre.

We emphasized that the grade structure was to harmonize benefits, which had been agreed and to help people development; each division could decide how it wanted to operate pay and, importantly, job titles.

Initially, benchmark jobs were identified and were evaluated using the Hay job evaluation system. This enabled a nine-grade structure to be established, based on the clusters of jobs, with a number of benchmark jobs fixed for each grade. Other jobs were then slotted into the structure based on a template shown as Figure 8.2 and were tested against the benchmarks. From time to time Hay was asked to evaluate jobs.

The result was a single grade structure across the whole business, covering all the UK employees from the CEO down, harmonized benefits aligned with the grades, more clarity on job size and more movement between the divisions. Each division retained an approach to pay and job titles that worked best for their market. The grade structure developed for the UK was then taken up by the US parent and rolled out across the rest of the world.

Broad-banding

What is broad-banding?

Broad-banding uses a small number of grades, typically around five although in the range of three to 10, and is designed to allow for much greater flexibility than traditional graded structures. In essence, broad-banding is a de-layered structure. The trend has been to move from a larger number of narrow bands to a smaller number of broad bands, as illustrated in Figure 8.3.

The rationale for broad-banding

The rigidity of traditional grade structures, of maybe 20+ grades, does not reflect the sort of flexible working processes required in the fast-changing environment of modern organizations where organizational change has developed flatter, more team-oriented cultures. A less hierarchical organizational structure and culture has meant that the traditional grades have

FIGURE 8.2 Grade-level descriptions

Grade	Capsule description
1	Scans the external environment and is strategically focused across a long-term horizon setting business plans and policies. • Most senior roles in business, including board and leader of the largest business units. • Strategic intent: set corporate direction and strategy.
2	Translates and reshapes policies for application in a major organizational unit, looking well beyond the year ahead. May also hold a small number of critical business relationships which generate significant levels of revenue. • Typically Heads of major businesses within the business; responsible for the management and utilization of significant resources in a discrete part of the business, both direct revenue generation and support. Accountable for overall performance of the business unit. • Strategic development: determine discipline specific policy and provide senior level input on company-wide plans and policies of strategic importance • A leading expert practitioner in their discipline.
3	High revenue generation, either directly, through projects or management of a specific organizational unit. Develop operating plans and translate policy for area. Main focus is on the year ahead but with input to longer-term plans. • Typically Heads of Functions – cross-functional co-ordination roles. Also large revenue/sales generator roles, or large project/programme management roles. May head smaller businesses. • Set broad objectives within their area. • Expertise and business development roles; objectives setting, people and budget management.
4	The role concentrates on the next 12 months. Emphasis on supporting policy development and developing local plans. May head function with focus on their own area or may play an important role in the management of a medium-size business. • May run a sizable team or department, typically providing services or support to one part of the business. Also may be a middle to large revenue generator. • Senior professional or technical roles providing support across the business or with specific expertise to one part of the business.

FIGURE 8.2 *Continued*

Grade	Capsule description
5	Includes a range of managerial and professional roles responsible for revenue generation or managing projects. Focused on the year ahead in application of policy and delivery within plan; emphasis on interpretation and incremental improvement. • Roles will include direct revenue generator roles, heads of a team/area, technical experts with significant experience and project managers. • Will have a deep understanding of their business area and very solid expertise in their field. • Operational improvement: organize and equip team so best able to deliver plans. • Manage the development and delivery of services.
6	Focused on the provision of (specialist) professional/technical information, analysis and advice which contributes to and supports the achievement of organization unit objectives and revenue generation. • As first level management, may involve managing a small team of technical/junior professionals. • Typically project or team based work with solid technical/conceptual input often contributing to revenue generation. • Provides advice, support guidance and training to colleagues. • Maintains standards and develops new systems/procedures which impact on own work area. • Day-to-day work of managing conflicting demands and goals.
7	Operating within well defined boundaries: overall direction given but there will be some scope for initiative and more independent working within guidelines. • Involved in parts of projects, building expertise. • In specialized/technical administrative functions an understanding of the whole process and context in which work is taking place is required. • Could supervise or provide support, guidance and training to process orientated work. • Prioritization and organizing of work.
8	Direction and guidance provided on a regular basis but much of the day-to-day work is undertaken without detailed instruction. • Systematic roles requiring simple technical input. • May include providing support and guidance to less experienced colleagues. • Core branch/department secretarial roles
9	Supervised, either directly or through routine/process restrictions. Work tends to follow an established sequence and is typically reactive, there will be some scope for prioritizing within the day. • Routine roles requiring basic administration skills, including word processing. • Most basic roles in the organization, often task-based.

FIGURE 8.3   Narrow band to broad band

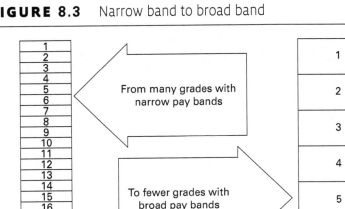

become counter-cultural. Flatter structures have led to a reduction in traditional promotional opportunities, so that career development now includes lateral as well as vertical moves.

Traditional grade structures can lead to people defining their status solely in terms of the grade. This often results in 'grade drift' where individuals tend to rise up the many grades over time, so that the 'average grade' gradually increases. The question becomes, 'What do I have to do to get to the next higher grade?' rather than the question a modern organization would want asked, 'How can I develop?'

The main reasons for introducing broad-banding are:

- reduce fixation on grade progression;
- improve organizational flexibility;
- de-emphasize hierarchy and minimize grade drift;
- support a new culture;
- emphasize career development;
- encourage skill development.

If some of these issues are relevant to your organization you may wish to consider broad-banding. Broad-banding has been getting gradually more popular. It is now a common approach in the private sector. The 2013 CIPD Reward Management survey reported that 27 per cent of participating organizations use broad-banding.

Implementing broad-banding

Broad-banding can be implemented in a number of ways. Some organizations do no more than simply reduce the number of grades. They may just convert the existing grades into the new boarder structure. Whilst this is simple, it will carry forwards into the new structure the various anomalies that have almost always been created over time. For example, roles that have been over-graded or are no longer needed. Therefore, I would not recommend this approach.

More common, and ultimately more valuable, is to introduce broad-banding as part of a wider change in the organization such as team-working where broad-banding can help. Rather than simply converting from old grades to fewer new ones, a more holistic review is undertaken to examine the nature of the roles that exist. This way involves some job evaluation. Like any fundamental change to the grade structure, moving to broad-banding can act as a catalyst to reviewing the structure of the organization and the relevance of some roles.

One way to consider the number of broad bands is the natural levels that there seem to be in the organization. Some organizations define levels in very broad terms such as:

1 strategy and leadership;

2 implementing strategy and management;

3 technical leadership;

4 operational management;

5 operations and support.

The main steps to implement broad-banding are:

- Establish the rationale and get support from the key stakeholders.
- Identify a group of benchmark jobs. These should reflect the range of jobs in the organization in terms of seniority and across different functions. Choose jobs where there are many job holders and some unique jobs. Aim for around 10 per cent of jobs.
- Draft job descriptions for the benchmark jobs.
- Decide on the method of job evaluation.
- Evaluate the jobs using the je method agreed.
- Review the total evaluated benchmark jobs and see to what extent they cluster into levels. This may reflect your understanding of the natural levels that occur in your organizational structure.

- Group the benchmark jobs into the grades (levels) you have established.
- Test out the number of job grades with stakeholders and the benchmark jobs allocated to each and adjust the number of grades if needed.
- Evaluate/slot the remaining jobs into the established grades.

Job families

Job families can be used with any form of grade structure (broad band, narrow band etc.) This is not separate from grades but rather establishes a series of families of jobs (IT, HR, Sales etc) which are overlaid on the grade structure, as illustrated in Figure 8.4. Here, five job families are shown in a five-grade structure. Normally all of the roles are shown by grade and by job family.

As you can see in this illustration, not all grades are used for every job family; it purely depends on where the job sits in the hierarchy of internal relativity.

Job families allow the organization to group together jobs in the same family regardless of which part of the organization they may sit within. It

FIGURE 8.4 Example job families

| Grade | Job families | | | | |
	Sales	IT	HR	Finance	Operations
1	Regional sales manager	Head of IT operations Head of development	Head of HR	Head of finance	Head of operations
2	Senior sales executive	Senior programmer Online development specialist		Divisional accountant	
3	Sales executive	Programmer Business analyst	HR Business partner		Team leader
4		IT Helpdesk adviser			Customer adviser
5	Sales support assistant		HR Assistant	Accounts assistant	

also allows pay structures to be established by job family reflecting the different level of market rates between families. Whilst using a job family approach does not shut off career opportunities outside the job family, it more realistically reflects the way in which many people progress their careers. This has a significant benefit for larger organizations. By bringing all of the roles together in a single job family for any one discipline wherever they sit in the organization, individuals can see where their career could develop in the same family. For lateral moves it also shows jobs in other families at a similar level.

Implementing job families

Job families may be implemented at the same time as a new grading structure or may be introduced as a way of grouping jobs within an existing grade structure.

Where a grade structure exists that is not being changed here is a simple approach to implementing jobs into families:

1 Identify the job families that exist – where similar type work is undertaken at different levels. Common groupings to look for are: finance, IT, marketing, sales, facilities, HR, administration, operations. Some groupings will be specific to your sort of organization depending on its sector, such as: actuaries, architects, scientists, designers etc.

2 Identify what jobs exist in each family and list them by family – most will fit fairly easily into one of the families you have identified. Some you will be less clear about. For these you may need to either:
   – place them into one of the families, based on typical career paths, or
   – create a new family if there are sufficient job holders, or
   – leave outside the job family model (see RHS case study in Chapter 6).

3 If appropriate, establish pay ranges for each job family (see the following section).

4 Communicate as works best in your organization.

The Which? case study at the end of this chapter illustrates the way in which job families can be established.

Pay structures

A pay structure is a hierarchy of pay or salary levels showing the rates of pay for employees performing a particular job or function at each level of an organization. It therefore seeks to address appropriate internal pay relativities and is normally based on a grade structure. A pay structure normally has some form of range of pay for each level (grade) and typically has a minimum and maximum pay rate, and a series of mid-range opportunities for pay increases. The salary range also normally reflects the external market, being determined by market pay rates, established through market pay surveys.

The benefits of a pay structure

As I discussed in Part I of this book, perceived inequity in pay between individuals can be a major cause of disengagement. More so than external comparison. Pay structures – normally using some form of pay scale – are therefore important in helping an organization ensure that pay level differences can be justified and are equitable based on some fair rationale. Most organizations will make the pay scales available to employees and explain how they are determined and how individuals can make progress.

The pay structure will often be used to help set increases on promotion to a new job. For example, this may be based on the position of the individual's existing salary in the salary range for the new role to which they have been promoted.

Whilst internal equity is very important, pay structures are also used to key into the external pay market. So rates for jobs based on external market data can be established within a pay structure. Organizations need to explain this process to their employees so that they can see that the pay levels used within the structure are based on data and not just plucked out of the air.

Pay structures can help an organization manage the total pay bill by providing a clear framework within which an individual's pay can be changed; for example, if there is a pay scale with a maximum level of pay, individuals are not normally paid above that maximum.

Pay structures can also help the process of managing pay levels. For example, with a single structure you can manage market data and internal relativities more easily than with only individual salaries. Which? found that the HR team were spending a disproportionate amount of time on externally benchmarking pay levels before they introduced a single grade structure and associated pay levels.

However, a pay structure using salary scales can build expectations that someone in a particular salary scale will be able to increase their salary to the top of the scale.

Types of pay structure

Table 8.1 below shows the range of usage of base pay structures from the 2013 CIPD Reward Management survey.

TABLE 8.1 Usage of pay structures

	%
Individual rates/ranges/spot salaries	49
Narrow-graded	37
Pay spines/service-related	32
Job family	30
Broad-banded	29

I discuss each of these approaches to pay in the following sections.

Individual rates of pay

Particularly in smaller organizations, although in some larger organizations as well, there may be no formal pay structure. Rather, spot salaries or individual pay rates are used. This is where individuals are on a salary unrelated to a particular structure. More so for smaller organizations, this can be a reasonable and pragmatic approach, but there needs to be care that it does not lead to internal pay inequality.

Larger organizations are more likely to use individual rates where there are many unique jobs that can be keyed into good external market data. In some cases there is a combination so that even though a formal pay structure exists, some roles are outside it. This may be for jobs with considerable market movement or where there are unique features about the job or the job holder.

Some organizations have taken the view that the more formal structures, even broad-banded, are rather artificial and do not reflect the reality of their organization. They therefore decide to use spot salaries and do away with any more formal structure.

Narrow-graded pay structure

This is the traditional pay structure based on a relatively large number of grades as illustrated in Figure 8.5.

FIGURE 8.5 Example narrow band structure

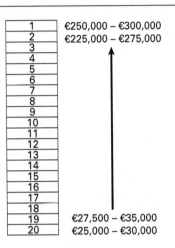

1	€250,000 – €300,000
2	€225,000 – €275,000

19	€27,500 – €35,000
20	€25,000 – €30,000

Jobs of approximately the same size are placed in each grade, often using job evaluation. But there is a range of salary for each grade to give flexibility to reflect the different performance, experience etc of different job holders. The range may also help to deal with slight differences in salary markets. For significant differences however, it is more common to use a different set of salary ranges.

For example, there may be one salary scale that covers the majority of jobs in the organization, but one or two higher salary scales to deal with those higher-paying salary markets which cannot be accommodated in the standard ranges. This may be because of location or discipline. So, for example, there could be one salary scale for London and one for the rest of the country, or there could be an additional set of salary ranges for specialist highly paid roles. An alternative approach is to use the single salary scale, but have additional allowances for 'cost of living' or specialism.

You should consider if additional salary scales are really needed as the more you have the higher the cost of maintenance. So you should carefully consider what the nature of any differences are, how many jobs are affected and how material is the difference. It may be best to see if you can manage with only one or two scales before developing any more.

There is normally a stated minimum, mid-point and maximum for each pay range for each grade. The mid-point is normally considered to be the salary for a fully competent job holder. The range is normally expressed in one of two ways:

As a percentage of the mid-point. The minimum and maximum are expressed as a percentage of the mid-point. For example, a range might be expressed as 80 per cent to 120 per cent where the mid-point is 100 per cent. So a range could be:

TABLE 8.2   Example pay range

Minimum	Mid-point	Maximum
£30,000	£37,500	£45,000
80%	100%	120%

As a percentage of the minimum. This is simply the maximum expressed as a percentage of the minimum. The percentage is normally in the range 25 per cent to 50 per cent. For example, a 40 per cent range with a minimum salary of £30,000 would have a maximum salary of £42,000.

The pay ranges for each grade also normally overlap with the next one. This is to reflect that the most highly performing people in one salary band may be contributing more than a relatively inexperienced individual in the next band. The overlap can be as high as 50 per cent and in general the degree of overlap in pay ranges has increased over the years to provide more flexibility.

Pay spines

Pay spines are mostly used in the public sector and also not-for-profit; they are rare in commercial companies. They are a single 'spine' of incremental pay points from the starting salary of the most junior role to the largest salary that is payable to the most senior. In practice, the spine is normally divided into sections to create spines for groups of jobs rather than for the whole organization which would be unwieldy as there could be over 100 points in a single organizational pay spine.

The difference between one salary point and the next is an increment. The size of increments is normally in the range 1.5 per cent to 5 per cent. An individual will normally move up the spine points, by receiving an increment to their salary each year until they are at the top of the scale. This pay structure almost always goes along side service based pay progression, hence its prevalence in the public sector where this is much more common than the private sector. The Shropshire Council case study at the end of this chapter refers to the use of increments.

Pay spines are rarely introduced now as most organizations are looking for a more flexible approach to pay structures typically based on contribution rather than time served.

Job family pay structure

As discussed earlier in this chapter, job families are typically an overlay to a grade structure. Depending on the pay markets for the different job families, you may establish different salary ranges by job family, but using the single grade structure. This is a good illustration of the point I made at the start of this chapter that grade structures and pay structures are not synonymous.

As market pay is typically based on type of role, using job families allows a more coherent approach to pay across the organization. The alternative is that pockets of different pay practice can develop in different parts of the organization for jobs in the same discipline.

It does not follow that with job families there will be different salary ranges for each family, it is just that job families give more flexibility to do so if needed and justified by differences in the pay market. So job families can be very effective in providing a clear set of career opportunities throughout the organization and the flexibility to meet different salary markets, whilst still providing a common framework for the organization. Job families are commonly used with a broad-banded structure (as in the Which? case study) discussed below.

An issue to watch out for with a job family structure is that it can result in unequal pay for work of equal value between job families. This can arise if jobs of the same size are paid differently when pay levels vary between families to cater for market rate pressures. Such variations may be difficult to justify objectively.

Broad-banded pay structure

I discussed broad-banding in the first section of this chapter as a grading structure. Now I will develop that as a pay structure. A broad-band pay

FIGURE 8.6   Narrow band to broad band

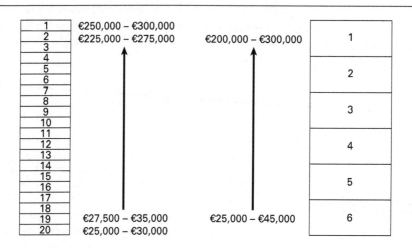

structure will cover the same total range of salaries as a traditional structure, but in broader bands, as illustrated in Figure 8.6.

Fewer bands give much more flexibility, which is one of the main reasons
for introducing it. However, you need to be careful to manage expectations
of individuals within a band. Controlling pay decisions can also be a problem in broad-banded graded systems. So it is common to use some form of
pay zones within the broad bands to help clarify the realistic expected salary

FIGURE 8.7   Pay zones

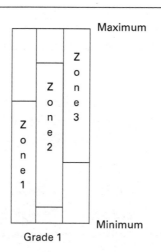

range for different roles that sit in the same band. These may be ranges of pay for jobs or job families. The size of a pay zones will be sufficient to allow for pay progression for a job. Pay zones may also help counter some concerns over equal pay issues.

There would typically be two or three pay zones identified within a broad band but it will depend on the market based salary ranges that are needed to accommodate the roles within a particular band. Figure 8.7 illustrates how three pay zones may fit within a single grade within a broad-band structure.

How you develop pay structures

Unless you are starting with a clean sheet in a new organization there will be an approach to pay that has been established. What a new pay structure should look like will depend on many factors relating to the organization:

- Organization structure – a flatter structure with little emphasis on hierarchy would suggest a broad-banded approach; a more hierarchical structure would suggest a narrow band approach.

- Organizational size – the smaller organization will almost certainly want informal simple systems, so spot salaries or a simple broad-banded salary structure.

- Homogeneity of jobs – if the organization operates in one main field so that jobs are broadly from the same or similar salary market, a narrow band structure would work; with many different types of roles, job families and/or spot salaries should be considered.

- Culture – team working, informal with decisions made at the lowest level and an emphasis on contribution rather than seniority would suggest a broad-banded structure.

This is summarized in Table 8.3.

So to determine the most appropriate type of pay structure for your organization, you need to go back to some of the strategic issues I presented in Part I. You first need to understand the culture of the organization. You also need to review the type of roles you have in the organization and how they relate to the external pay market. Of course the pay structure will be closely tied in with your approach to grades.

You may want to think about the degree of fit between the pay and grading structure you have at the moment and the organization's aims and culture against Table 8.3.

TABLE 8.3 Factors influencing pay structures

	Organization size		Organization structure		Homogeneity of jobs		Organization culture	
	Small	Large	Flat	Hierarchical	Broad	Similar	Team, informal, decisions made low down	Seniority, decisions go up
Narrow-banded		✓		✓		✓		✓
Broad-banded	✓		✓		✓		✓	
Job families		✓			✓			
Spot salaries	✓		✓		✓		✓	

Summary

Grade structures and pay structures are different and it is helpful to be clear about what each is for. Whilst there are very many different types of structures (with a particular difference between the public and private sectors), the trend seems to be moving to broader bands and, where appropriate, job families.

Employers are looking for their grade structures and pay structures to give them the sort of flexibility that reflects modern organizations but with sufficient consistency to ensure fairness and equity.

Questions

- If you have a grade structure, what is it for and is it helping?

- If you do not have a grade structure, could it help?

- Broad bands and job families are a growing trend; is this a model that would help your reward strategy?

- Would a single pay structure or a number of pay structures be most appropriate for your organization?

Case studies

I have included two different case studies for this chapter. The first is Which? and the second is Shropshire Council. Each illustrates a different approach to changes to grade structures.

Shropshire Council had 1,000 technical, professional and managerial staff in 22 highly overlapping grades. They implemented a new simpler grade and salary structure to more clearly differentiate between roles. The case study shows how the organization used a combination of a points-based analytical job-evaluation system and panel approach to implement the new system very effectively.

Which? had 450 staff but over 100 different manager roles, 300 salary bands and job descriptions and a large number of job titles. They were able to rationalize this complex range of practices and implement a single grade structure with a series of overlaying job families and pay structures. This provided a single corporate structure but also reflected the relevant differences between jobs.

CASE STUDY   Which?

Which? is the commercial and campaigning brand of the Consumers' Association, an independent registered charity and not-for-profit social business. Having started in 1957, Which? is now the largest consumer body in the UK. It has total subscriptions to its publications of over 1.3m with over 635,000 members subscribing to *Which?* magazine and over 298,000 online subscribers. Other magazines include *Which? Money*, *Which? Computing*, *Which? Travel* and *Which? Gardening*.

As an independent organization Which? provides unbiased advice to consumers through a range of free and paid for services and products including Which? Consumer Rights, Which? Legal Services, Which? Travel and Which? Mortgage Advice. In addition to publishing magazines and websites, Which? undertakes research and campaigns with consumers to get them a better deal. The group turnover is over £80m. There are over 500 employees across four sites in London, Hertford, Bristol and Edinburgh.

Issues

In 2009 the newly appointed HR director ran an engagement survey to enable her and the leadership of Which? to understand the levels of engagement and views from staff about working there. The results came through at the end of 2009 and showed three areas in particular that needed attention:

- **Reward** – how reward worked and how it linked to performance; a lack of understanding of the value of benefits.

- **Career development** – how to develop one's career; a lack of career development opportunities across Which?

- **Performance** – performance management was not seen as effective.

It was decided that they would seek to address reward and career development first in 2010 and look at performance following that.

Reward and career development project

Analysis

Initially Which? undertook desk research to look in detail at the existing reward structures. It drilled down to the job titles, job descriptions, where people were on salary scales, the entry levels etc. It found that:

- There were three main reward structures plus a range of other structures for different support roles. There was a particular divide between campaigning, where reward was primarily driven by service, and marketing which was more about performance and bonuses.

- With around 450 staff at the time, there were over 100 different manager roles.

- There were 300 salary bands and job descriptions.

- There were a large number of different job titles. In some parts of the organization they had proliferated to provide some career steps but for jobs which were almost identical. In one fairly small function there were seven job levels between entry and the manager of the function.

- There were many people at the top or above the top of salary bands and people often joined Which? close to the top of a salary band.

Which? had a corporate aim to change some of the culture and practices in the organization. It wanted to bring more of a commercial focus without losing the service and campaigning role and to bring more of the organization together – reducing silos. It was clear that the difference between the pay structures was working against this.

The pay, grading and career structure was extremely disjointed and complex, for an organization with fewer than 500 employees, therefore administratively expensive. For example, with no grading structure HR had to spend considerable time benchmarking individual roles. The structures had grown over time in different parts of the organization and emphasized their differences. It became clear that some people in Which? moved up within their division and then left the organization whilst there were opportunities in other parts of the organization. Clearly this was misaligned with the corporate aims of bringing the organization together and reducing unnecessary differences.

The HR team had to achieve the buy-in of the leadership team to the project. It explained the criticality of making changes based on the employee research and the positive impact a better system would make. It engaged an external reward consultant to help with the project to introduce a single flexible structure to replace the myriad of differences.

Level structure

The initial thinking was that a simple grade structure with job families would provide the sort of framework to meet the organization's aims. The team therefore worked on developing a single level (grading) structure for the whole of Which? plus a set of job families.

It reviewed all the 300 jobs using the existing job descriptions to see what natural levels fell out. It 'sized' the jobs using four factors:

1 primary focus of the role;

2 accountability and impact;

3 skills and complexity;

4 level of problem solving and decision making.

The team grouped the jobs into what seemed to be natural clusters based on the size of the jobs. To help test out the thinking on the number of levels, Which? sent out questionnaires to about 25 per cent of employees. It also held focus groups with around 35 employees and the leadership team to gain more qualitative information. Finally, based on the analysis and discussions, they established that seven job levels would fit the organization best.

Job families

Based on the 300 job descriptions they also developed an initial set of job families. Working with the heads of departments and other managers, the project team refined this initial set and eventually came to seven job families:

- professional;

- marketing;

- operations support;

- IT/Technology;

- research;

- communications;

- publishing.

Which? explain a job family as: '...a collection of roles that do similar types of work or where knowledge, skill and competence requirements are similar. A job family can help to identify how you might develop your career up and/or across Which?'.

Single integrated framework

This was brought together in the 'One Which? One Reward framework' shown below as Table 8.4.

Each role was placed at one of the seven levels in the job family. A two-page job level profile was produced for each role showing:

- the job level (1–7);

- descriptor (eg leadership/management);

- job family;

- the primary focus (a few word summarizing the focus of the role);

- an explanation of the role under four headings used to 'size' the role: Accountability/Impact, Skills/Complexity, Problem Solving/Decision Making and Performance Measures;

- the generic description of the behaviours for this level role for each of the six values: Ambition, Bravery, Today Not Tomorrow, Personal Responsibility, Collaboration and Flexibility.

Salary ranges

A salary range was established for each of the 54 roles shown in Table 8.3 plus the CMG. The roles were benchmarked using external data and a mid-point salary was established for each. A minimum and maximum was also set based on the market data upper quartile and lower quartile. This produced salary ranges of different widths. The narrowest was where the maximum salary was 15 per cent higher than the minimum and the widest was where the maximum was 55 per cent higher than the minimum.

Whilst 60 salary bands may seem rather a lot, they ensured that roles were well aligned to a relevant market median and tied in with the level and job family structure. It was also a significant reduction from the original 300 salary bands.

Implementation

The single seven-level seven job family structure was implemented across the organization in the second half of 2010. There was a very considerable amount of communications including posters, leaflets and manager briefings. Each employee was given the role level, job title and job family for their role as well as the generic information.

When people were moved to the new structure, the majority were within the new salary bands. Approximately 9 per cent were above the band maximum and

TABLE 8.4   One Which? One Reward framework

Job family >	Professional	Marketing	Ops Support	IT/Tech	Research	Comms	Publishing
1	Corporate Management Group (CMG)						
2	□	○		○	○	○	○
3	○	○	○	○	○	○	○
4	○	○	○	○	○	○ □	○ □
5	□ ◆	□	○ ◆	○	○ □	□	□
6	□ ◆	□ ◆	◆	□ ◆	□ ◆	□ ◆	□
7			◆		◆	◆	

Job level >

CMG – The primary focus of these roles is strategic business direction and leadership.

○ – Leadership/management. At the most senior levels, the primary focus of these roles is strategic development, delivery and leadership for the area of responsibility. It will also include roles where contribution to strategy, delivery and management is, or may be, required.

□ – Specialist. The primary focus of these roles is to drive and/or support key activities through specialist knowledge. At the most senior levels, the primary focus of these roles is strategic development, delivery and leadership through areas of expertise. It will also include roles where contribution to strategy, technical support, implementation and advice is or may be, required.

◆ – Support. The primary focus of these roles is front line support for internal and/or external customers.

were 'red circled' and only receive an unconsolidated payment until their salary moves back into the band as the band is adjusted. Fewer than 10 per cent were at the bottom of a band and received a salary adjustment.

Which? had a set of values that it had established some years before. It therefore wanted to link the values to the new structure. Workshops were held with managers and employees to establish the different behaviours expected at each level for each value. The types of behaviour are consistent for each level regardless of job family.

In 2012 the One Which? One Reward framework, shown as Table 8.4, was developed into an interactive tool on the intranet. Employees could look at any of the roles and see other roles in other parts of the organization at similar levels. They could see the competences needed to develop up their job family and what development opportunities are available.

Results

Whilst there was an appeals process, no employee appealed against their position in the new structure when it was implemented in 2010.

There has been a considerable increase in the number of people moving to another part of the organization through rotation and secondment, with promotions up three-fold following implementation.

The average compa ratio is 102 per cent, which shows that people are close to the mid-point of the salary scales. Which? is able to recruit people within the new salary structures with over 85 per cent brought in around the mid-point rather than at the top of the old scales.

In 2013 Which? benchmarked the whole framework against the external pay market and found that other than a few small adjustments it was working well.

CASE STUDY   Shropshire Council

Background

Shropshire Council is a unitary authority which was created on 1 April 2009. It replaced the former two-tier local government structure in the non-metropolitan county of Shropshire. Shropshire is part of the Central Region which borders the West Midlands to the East and Wales to the West.

Shropshire Council covers a predominantly rural area of some 1,235 square miles (320,000 hectares). The county has a population of just over 300,000. Shrewsbury is the county town and the largest in Shropshire with a population of around 95,000. The second largest town is Oswestry with a population of just 18,000.

The council employs around 6,500 staff, of which around 900 are based at its main site in Shrewsbury. The employees of the council are structured within services, which are themselves structured as part of directorates. Beneath director level there are a number of group managers, who oversee the council's individual service managers. The service managers then oversee much of the council's day-to-day administrative functions and, with the help of their officers, provide its frontline services.

Grade structure – issues

The majority of technical, professional and managerial employees are classed as principal officers. This population of about 1,000 individuals in 450 roles were positioned in 22 highly overlapping salary bands (PO1–PO22). More junior jobs were in grades 1–10 and PO1 started immediately above grade 10. There were four increment points for each grade and they overlapped by three points with the next band. By 2012 this structure had been in existence for more than 20 years.

It was extremely difficult to differentiate between the different grades as they were so tightly packed, which posed difficulties in determining the grading of posts.

In 2012 the council wanted to improve the position for these PO grades, to simplify the system and make the difference between levels of POs much clearer. As the council wanted to make sure the process was as streamlined as possible, various approaches were reviewed before the approach outlined below was agreed.

Changes made

100 benchmark jobs were selected spanning all departments and across all of the 22 PO grades; these included both single and multiple occupancy posts. The PwC, Monks Six Factor job-evaluation methodology was developed and applied. The factors used in the system are:

- people skills;
- external impact;
- decision making;
- specialist skills;
- knowledge;
- innovation/creative thinking.

The council examined the way the benchmark jobs were distributed based on the evaluations and felt that they naturally fell into four levels. In place of the 22 PO grades, the council introduced four new grades, 11–14, above the unchanged grades 1–10. Each of the four grades had five increments and there was no overlap between the increment points. This now clearly distinguished pay and grade between the levels within the PO population.

A generic role profile was drafted for each of the four grades. Each of the job descriptions for the remaining 350 roles was to be matched against the role profiles to determine into which grade the job would fit. This was carried out by a joint panel made up of one management and one trade union representative. A moderation panel consisting of different management and trade union representative then reviewed and validated or challenged the outcome.

As part of the process various issues were thrown up. One significant issue was how to implement the revised grading structure at a time when other significant changes were taking place such as terms and conditions changes, and the fact that the new grading was very different. It was decided to approach this by implementing the revised grading over time as sections were restructured. This allowed for structures to be designed taking account of the revised grades. However, it was agreed that where any PO graded jobs were not already assimilated on to the new grades by 2014 they would be moved on to them even if there was no restructuring.

Other issues included the situation where a manager and their reports might be in the same grade, which questioned if the role was necessary or more should be required of it. So the restructure did not simply fit all roles into the new structure, but challenged some of the apparent anomalies in roles and structure that the project found.

Whilst the matching process was undertaken with rigour, an individual could request their job to be fully evaluated using the points factor system. They would need to take into account that it could go up or down as a consequence.

When individuals were placed into one of the new grades and salary bands, some had salaries within the band, which were unchanged. Where a salary was above the new maximum, their salary was held for 12 months but then reduced to the top increment for the band. Where people were below the lowest increment, their salary was increased to that point.

In the first 12 months there had been only one appeal to the grade to which a role was allocated.

09

Managing pay data and pay reviews

Pay data

One way or another you need information on the reward market within which you are competing. In smaller organizations it may be very informal and unstructured – simply paying what you need to recruit people. But as an organization gets bigger it is likely to have to take a more structured approach and more formally use market data to be able to compare its pay levels in the external market.

Types of data

There are broadly two types of data:

- changes in pay rates: percentage pay increases in the market; and
- current pay levels: what particular jobs are paid.

Most of this section relates to the latter, but a few words about changes in pay rates first. Many organizations look for data showing the rates of pay increases to help establish overall budgets and overall pay pots for salary reviews. Sources of market pay movement include published data in journals such as *IDS* and *IRS* based on pay settlements. The Office for National Statistics publishes regular data online such as the Annual Survey of Hours and Earnings. You can also look at the rate of inflation – such as RPI or CPI if that is relevant for you. Salary survey providers will also typically show the rates of increase as well as salary levels for particular jobs.

You do need to take care though that the overall changes in pay in the market are relevant to you based on your pay position. For example, if the salaries in your organization are already high in the market, you may feel that it is appropriate to set a pay increase percentage budget below the market movement.

Purposes of pay data

Market reward data can be used for a number of reasons:

- establish salaries for new jobs;
- determine salary levels for recruitment;
- inform annual pay review budgets;
- inform annual pay review decisions;
- inform pay decisions throughout the year for individual cases;
- establish salary ranges for salary scales;
- change salary structures;
- identify pay trends.

Market

We often talk about market pay data and so a key starting point is to consider what we mean by market. This is a fairly fluid concept as there is never a single pay market. Other than the smallest, all organizations are likely to be competing in a number of pay markets. There are five main factors that can define a pay market:

- **Function or discipline** – the particular skill or profession, such as accountant, sales, secretary, actuary.
- **Level or seniority** – reflecting the seniority of the particular role. This may differentiate between roles within a discipline, such as finance director and cost accountant.
- **Sector** – this could be broad sectors such as private sector, public sector, not-for-profit or charity and particular industrial sectors such as manufacturing, retail, oil and gas, or financial services.
- **Organizational size** – typically this will be measured by turnover or number of employees.
- **Location** – where the job is located, for example, Edinburgh, Leeds, the South East, Central London.

These five factors will overlap when you are looking at the market for some jobs. Some of the factors are more important depending on the seniority of the job. For example, location is generally a more significant factor for the more junior jobs than it is for the most senior.

One global business I met found that they had to explain a particular factor of pay markets for their operations across Europe in the eurozone. Germany, the Netherlands and Ireland had higher total cash than France or Italy. But it is not a single eurozone pay market; there may be a single currency but there are different salary markets by country etc.

One way to help think about the pay markets is to analyse where your employees move to and where new employees come from. This will help in particular for thinking about location, sector and organizational size.

It is important to understand the nature of the market so that you can try to obtain data that is most relevant for the jobs you are reviewing.

Exercise

Which factor or factors are most important in considering what the market for the following roles is?

1   Call centre customer adviser

2   Nurse

3   IT director

4   Machine operator

5   Internal legal adviser

I would suggest the following:

1 Call centre customer adviser – location.

2 Nurse – discipline, location and sector.

3 IT director – organization size and sector, possibly location.

4 Machine operator – location.

5 Internal legal adviser – discipline, seniority, sector.

Sources of pay data

There are many potential sources of pay data. But I would divide them into three broad categories:

- the worthless;
- the cautious;
- the reliable.

Worthless

Wine bar source – the individual who tells you that he was chatting with some people in the wine bar (also read pub, club or pretty well anywhere else) who told him about the salaries at Big Co or the package that Mr X just went for. It might alert you to the need to improve the communication in your organization on how you determine market value, but otherwise I suggest that you ignore this.

Generic surveys – typically, published on the internet and in some newspapers and magazines. This sort of survey will tell you things like the average salary for an HR manager in the UK is £36,000 or that the average package for a finance director is £61,000. This sort of generic information does not take into account any of the factors that I said define a market and gives some very broad figures that cannot help determine any salary for a particular role. The methodology is normally also going to be very suspect. So again, ignore this.

Treat with caution

The following four sources can all help provide some qualitative, and sometimes quantitative, information about the current salary market. But they are not as rigorous as the most reliable sources.

Industrial/occupational surveys are often conducted by employer or trade associations on jobs in a particular industry eg chemical engineers. Therefore, they can be helpful in specialist areas. But job matching may still not be that precise and the data may be collected directly from the individual employees (members). Therefore, there may be bias in that the sample is self-selecting and, for example, might tend to the higher paid. The best of these, however, can be a good source, but be cautious and review the methodology.

Recruitment consultants and agencies should have an idea of the salaries being offered for roles they work on and so help give a sense of the current market. But some may also have a vested interest to try to inflate salaries as their fees may be a percentage of salary.

Job adverts may also give a sense of the current market. But the role may not be described well enough to give a clear understanding of what is required for it, compared with those you may be dealing with. Also, whilst the advert may show a salary, you do not know how much the organization will end up having to pay.

Exit interviews with those leaving your organization and interviews with joiners may give some helpful data. I have found that well-structured exit interviews can be very valuable to help understand issues in the organization, but you need to take care in using them to gauge the salary market. Many people leaving the organization may be prepared to tell you what their new package will be, but you would need to know how different the job is. For example, the individual may be moving to a larger job, so the move is a promotion. You should ask about this to help you take a view on the relative salary size. Also, one example is not a reliable sample, so you would need a number of examples to start to determine a pattern.

Reliable

Whilst their quality can vary considerably I believe that salary surveys are the most reliable and valid sources of data. I deal with salary surveys in the following section.

Salary surveys

A salary survey would be run by an independent organization that would collect pay and associated data from participating employers for individuals doing specified jobs. The job would normally be described using a job capsule or some sizing mechanism. The data would be analysed and aggregated data would be provided in a report or online for employers to use to help them make pay related decisions.

Validity of salary surveys

Whilst you may be able to buy some survey data without providing data from your own organization, many surveys are only available to organizations who participate by providing their pay data. Salary surveys vary in quality and so you need to consider a number of factors before relying on the data from a survey. I have listed below the main factors you should consider:

Survey provider – check on the record and professionalism of the survey provider. There are many survey providers who are rigorous and professional in their approach. Here are a few examples:

- Global: Aon Hewitt, Hay, Mercer, Towers Watson.
- Sector specialist: Radford for IT and McLagan for investment banking (both part of Aon Hewitt).
- Smaller local: Alan Jones and Compensation Research.

It is important to consider organizations whose main business is survey data or, like some of the major accountancy firms, have survey specialists as they are more likely to be reliable. Some organizations run surveys as a marketing opportunity to get press coverage; these are best avoided even though they may be free.

Methodology – look out for when the data was collected. It is likely to be some months before a survey is published. Although many survey providers have an online data base that you can access at any time. Most surveys will collect data from each participating employer who will input their data for the relevant populations. But be wary of a survey that asks individuals to input their own data, as I mentioned earlier.

Job matching – this is really part of methodology but is worth a point on its own as it can be a major source of inaccuracy in the data collected. A critical element of any survey is that the data provided is based on similar jobs. That is, all of the participant organizations only input data for jobs of the same size and discipline etc. The survey provider will use some form of job-matching methodology. It may be based on a job-evaluation system, such as Hay or a similar job-level approach such as Towers Watson. Alternatively, it may be based on a capsule job description, or series of capsules to help determine the right level. Whilst no system can be flawless, any of these approaches is likely to give a reasonable basis for effective job matching. Surveys that use just a job title to match the job should be avoided.

Sample size – whilst the overall sample size may be large, matches for any one job may be quite small. In general, the smaller the sample size the less reliable will be the data. It becomes dangerous to rely on data from a very small sample. Reputable survey providers will give a detailed breakdown of the participating organizations, number of job holders etc. They will also only present analysis where the sample size is large enough. So for some roles they may only show a median salary, but for others, with a larger sample, they may also show the quartile ranges, discussed below.

Club surveys

In the UK and many other developed countries there are very many reliable salary surveys available across sectors and geographies. However, there may be a particular niche salary market for which there is no salary survey available. This is likely to be based on geography or a specialised sector. In this sort of situation you may consider developing a club survey. This is where a group of employers club together and appoint a survey provider to run a survey for the group. Normally, each employer will pay, although sometimes one or two may sponsor the survey. The survey company collect the data and it remains confidential to them. They analyse the data and provide ano-nymized median and quartile data etc for the participant organizations.

Key terms

Survey data is normally analysed and presented using particular statistical terms which you need to know.

Salary surveys mostly use median salary as the most typical salary from a set of salaries, rather than arithmetic mean. The mean (or simple average) is the total of all the salaries in the group divided by the number of salaries in the group. Where, for example, the mean is much greater than the median you will usually see a relatively small number of very high salaries that skew the data.

The median is the middle salary from a group of salaries, with an equal number higher and lower. This is simple with an odd number in a group. Where a group has an even number of salaries you take the mean of the two in the middle.

So the median of: £34,000, £39,000 and £41,000 is £39,000 – the middle salary. The mean is £38,000 (£34,000 + £39,000 + £41,000)/3.

Exercise

What is the median and mean of the following group of salaries?

| £44,000 | £43,500 | £69,000 | £43,000 | £45,000 |
| £63,500 | £42,000 | £47,000 | £44,000 |

The median of the group is the middle salary, £44,000

£69,000

£63,500

£47,000

£45,000

£44,000

£44,000

£43,500

£43,000

£42,000

The mean of the group is the total of all the salaries divided by nine, so £49,000, £5,000 more than the median. As you can see from this exercise, there are two salaries, £69,000 and £63,500, which pull the mean up considerably. If these two salaries were excluded the mean drops to a little over £44,000. If you scan your eye down the list £44,000 looks more representative of the salary for this role than £49,000.

In addition to median, the other term that is used considerably is 'quartile'. The quartiles divide the data set into four equal groups, each group comprising a quarter of the data as illustrated in Figure 9.1.

FIGURE 9.1   Median and quartiles

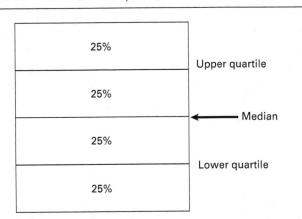

Whilst a quartile can be defined as the 25 per cent range, it is more common to use median, upper and lower quartile.

- Upper quartile is where 25 per cent are above the point and 75 per cent below. So 'above' or 'in' the upper quartile are salaries in a group of the top 25 per cent.

- Lower quartile is where 75 per cent are above and 25 per cent below. So 'below' or 'in' the lower quartile are salaries in the group of the bottom 25 per cent.

Using survey data

Whether you participate in one or more survey or buy those that are available, you are likely to use the data to inform pay decisions, typically for the annual pay review. But maybe also for individual pay decisions during the year. Here are a few pointers to using data from surveys:

Aging – the data may have been collected some months ago and so you may need to age the data to bring it up to date to take account of pay movement in the intervening period. With very low inflation and low pay increases this may be of little importance, but you should consider if this needs to be done. If so, you should increase the survey data by a factor taking into account pay increases. For example, the salary data you have was collected six months ago; you have data that shows salary increases are running at approximately 3 per cent, so increase the data by 1.5 per cent. Some organizations would 'age' data not to the pay review date, but to the mid-year ie halfway between one pay review and the next.

Presenting numbers – the median and quartile data will be shown in the survey down to the last £1. So a median salary may be shown as, for example, £74,873. If you are just using this data for yourself for analysis and comparison, fine. But if you are to share survey data with other stakeholders then I would always round the numbers. My concern is that an unrounded number conveys a degree of spurious accuracy and tends to focus people inappropriately on what may appear to be a very precise looking number. So in the example, I would show a median of £74,873 as £75,000.

Exercise

How would you round the following:

£125,329   £67,217

£36,549   £24,217

£17,423   £51,729

I would probably round as follows:

£125,000   £67,000

£36,500   £24,200

£17,400   £52,000

Median – a median, or any other number from a survey needs to be used with care. Just because a survey shows a median salary of, say £74,873, it does not mean that anyone paid a bit over or under that is over- or underpaid. The median is simply a statistical outcome of a set of data and is a reasonable approximation for the rate for the job. But individual salaries will vary considerably for very many reasons. The rate for the individual and the median (rate for the job) will be different. I think it is healthy in most cases, to consider a range above and below median as the area where a salary is 'around median'. It depends on the job and spread of salaries, but something like plus or minus 5 per cent – 10 per cent of median is likely to be considered as around median.

Base and total cash – survey data normally shows basic salary and total cash. Check the definition of total cash for the survey you are using, but it is usually basic salary plus bonus and other variable pay. Whilst basic pay can be compared fairly based on the data, total cash is rather more complex. The main problem is that bonuses may be driven to a large extent by the performance of the organization. So if your company has had a particularly good year whilst the economy has not been doing well, your total cash position might go up against the market. The opposite may also be true. So if you are significantly ahead or behind the market for basic salary that may be of concern. However, you need to be more cautious in drawing conclusions on your total cash position without thinking through the context.

Practice, policy and market – you may wish to use the survey data to give an overall position of your pay against the market. One way to do this is to present your organization salary data graphically showing salary on the left-hand axis and grade or job on the bottom axis. You can show the overall salary position against the market and your salary scales if you have them. So the practice line is your current position, the market line is the market data and your policy line is you salary mid-points. This is illustrated in Figure 9.2.

FIGURE 9.2 Graph of pay practice, policy and market

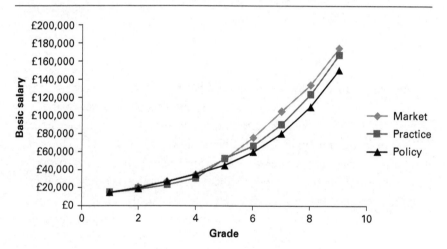

Historic – whilst the data may be valid, it is by definition based on the pay of existing employees in organizations. Pay levels at recruitment on the other hand are about the reality of the pay market at the time. So do not discount the experience in recruiting people, as it may be that pay for people in the market now is higher or lower than shown in the survey data.

Pay reviews

As discussed above, one of the uses of market pay data is to inform annual pay reviews. In countries with high inflation, pay reviews may be more frequent but in most locations an annual review of some kind is common.

Pay review budget

An organization will normally budget for the annual pay review at the start of the financial year, although it may be difficult to forecast the pay budget that is going to be required, maybe nine months later. The population will have changed, as will the external market. Ideally you should work with finance colleagues to take into account pay increase trends to help establish the budget. There needs to be some flexibility as the circumstances will change, otherwise, as I have observed in some organizations, the budget set by finance becomes fixed regardless of changed circumstances.

The other point to note on budgeting, relates to the date of the pay review in relation to the financial year. The impact of a general pay increase implemented part-way through a financial year will only increase salaries for part of the year. It will only have a full impact the following year, but subject to turnover etc, which is discussed below.

Table 9.1 shows the main factors that employers said determined the size of the pay review from the 2013 CIPD Reward Management survey.

TABLE 9.1 Factors influencing pay reviews

	%
Ability to pay	78.8
Going rate	45.9
Movement in market rates	44.9
Inflation	42.4
Recruitment/retention issues	40.0
Government funding	34.4

It is no surprise that the most common factor is the organization's ability to pay. Without the money, other factors become secondary. Often there will be a rebudget later in the year as you get closer to the pay review. This may be a further opportunity to work with finance colleagues to refine the budget based on the latest data you have. Where annual increments are used (almost exclusively in the public sector) this will have been budgeted for separately to what is probably a flat rate increase.

Cost of salary increases

The budgeted cost will normally be expressed as a percentage increase in salaries on a day one basis – that is the annualized cost of the salary increase on implementation. It will not be the cost over the year as there are many other factors that will have an influence. It is notoriously difficult to forecast the true cost of an annual salary increase because of the dynamic nature of an organization. Employees join and leave and also get promoted during the year.

Organizations often use very tight controls on the annual review budget but do not try to impose similar controls during the year. Some organizations have sought to control 'in-year' increases by having a second review date, normally six months after the main review. It is only at this second date that salary increases due to particular market pressures etc and promotions during the year may be implemented. This is then monitored and controlled.

Typically, employees who are more experienced leave and get replaced by someone who is less experienced and hence is paid less. Obviously, this will vary from case to case depending on the market conditions. But it has the effect of balancing out other increases during the year. In terms of aggregate salaries, there is always some recruitment lag. This is the gap between someone leaving and a replacement starting. During the intervening period there is no salary being paid for that role.

In aggregate the number of employees will have a significant impact. If the organization is growing or contracting the total salary costs will obviously move.

Pay policy

In Part I of this book I discussed a number of factors that would help you create a reward policy and strategy. Within that you may have a statement on your position on pay that will frame any pay review. Here are two examples of the sort of statements that set the scene for pay reviews:

Intel, the largest semiconductor chip maker's stated practice on pay is:

'Deliver base and variable cash compensation that is above market in total, and ensure top performers receive the top rates of pay.'

The Royal borough of Kingston Pay policy statement 2013/14

General Principles

In setting pay, remuneration for council staff at all levels needs to be adequate to secure and retain high-quality employees dedicated to the service of the public, while not being unnecessarily generous or otherwise excessive or perceived as such. At the same time there must be sufficient flexibility to cope with a variety of circumstances (foreseeable or not), such as local or occupation-specific labour market conditions.

The pay review system you use should be based on your reward principles or policy that I covered in Part 1 of this book.

Individual pay changes

Table 9.2 shows the criteria organizations used to change individual pay, from the 2013 CIPD Reward Management survey.

I cover some of the different approaches to pay reviews in the following sections.

Service-based

An incremental pay structure (as covered in Chapter 8), most commonly used in the public sector, allows the individual employee's salary to increase by one incremental point (typically 1.5–5 per cent) every year until they hit the top of the salary scale. The aim is to reflect acquired skills and knowledge in theory converted into effectiveness over time. In addition, there will normally be an annual cost of living adjustment to reflect inflation.

Whilst most incremental systems operate as described, with one increment increase per year, there are also variations where for particular performance or demonstrable increases in competence etc there may be two or possibly even three increments awarded.

TABLE 9.2 Criteria used in reviewing individual pay

	%
Individual performance	71.5
Competencies	64.7
Market rates	64.2
Skills	57.6
Employee potential/value/retention	51.3
Length of service	31.1
Union/staff pressures	27.1
Living wage pressures	24.0
Shareholder views	19.8
National minimum wage	18.8

Common to any approach that has a fixed pay range, there is a question of what to do once someone is at the top of their salary band as they may receive no more increments. In most cases they would just continue to receive any cost of living increase. But in some organizations there may be a non-consolidated lump sum payment especially to reflect excellent performance.

Cost-of-living/market movement

As I mentioned above, in an incremental system recipients may receive an annual cost of living increase as well as an increment. This is one reason why pay levels in the public sector in the UK have outstripped those in the private sector over recent years.

Some organizations may aim just to use a standard increase for everyone. This is obviously very simple. Where salary increases are very low, as they have been for many years, many organizations have felt that the administrative cost is disproportionately high to try to differentiate between individuals where there is little to play with. The two case studies at the end of this chapter reflect this to some extent.

Individual performance

Individual performance remains the most common factor, although a significant part of the mix is competencies. This reflects the shift in the approach to performance management over some years to take into account both the 'what' of performance – the outputs, usually framed as objectives – and the 'how' – the way in which the job is done, that is the competencies used.

A common approach to capture individual performance for determining a pay review is to use some form of annual appraisal with a rating – typically one of around five. This may aim to reflect both the what and the how and is a part of the annual performance management cycle.

Performance management should be about helping improve the performance of individuals and teams to help improve the performance of the whole organization. The core of performance management for individuals is the answers to the two questions:

- What is expected of me?
- How am I doing?

However, performance management can become, in the eyes of most employees, simply the process that is used to determine pay reviews. This is a classic issue of potentially contaminating effective performance management – goals, feedback, support, development – with a pay focus.

In pursuit of fairness and objectivity organizations often look for objectives to be set that are SMART (specific, measurable, achievable, realistic and time bound). But part of the problem can be that objectives are set that are easy to measure, rather than those that add value. Objectives may also be too narrow. In the worst cases people achieve results in a changing environment in spite of the fixed objectives rather because of them. International think tank ODI dropped 'SMART' and instead encouraged people to agree objectives that were meaningful and were clear about what success looked like. In the following employee survey the response to the statement 'my last performance appraisal was fair and objective' went from 61 per cent positive to 86 per cent.

The annual rating system can be criticized as being too simplistic, demeaning and insensitive to the complexity of changes in organizations today. They can also be the focus of the contamination of what otherwise could be a sensible conversation as part of a whole approach to true performance management. Whilst I believe that an annual review should be part of a whole approach to performance management, I am very cautious about using ratings. My experience is that they are primarily used for the annual pay review and little else. This really should be challenged. Many high-performing organizations such as Arup, Specsavers and the National Theatre do not use ratings.

Pay matrix

Where an organization uses annual ratings they are often used in some sort of pay matrix such as shown as Table 9.3. This will typically give the rating on one side and the position in the salary scale, if there is one, on the other axis. The range of salary increases that may be used is shown for each intersection. The manager uses this matrix to propose salary changes for their team members within an overall budget available.

As I mentioned earlier, with low inflation and relatively low salary increases, it is questionable if there is much value in spending a significant amount of time on what might be extremely small differences in salary. Some organizations who may have used such a matrix in the past have moved away from this to a much more informal approach with broad guidelines and an overall budget.

TABLE 9.3　Example pay matrix

Performance rating	Position in salary range		
	High	Mid-point +/–	Low
5	3–4.5%	4–5.5%	5–7%
4	2–3%	2.5–3.5%	3–4.5%
3	1–2%	1.5–2.5%	2–3%
2	0%	0%	1–2%
1	0%	0%	0%

Online pay review systems

There are many online pay administration systems available which help manage pay reviews. They will normally interface with the main HR database and finance system.

The system will have the relevant details for each employee, salary etc. There may be some form of matrix in the background limiting the salary increases available. The reviewing manager may be presented with a suggested salary for each individual that the manager may change within the guidelines.

Online pay systems can speed up the whole process considerably. There will be workflow built in so that the data can move up the organization for approvals. This can be particularly valuable in a global business where a manager may have people reporting who work in different countries. Using such a system can mean that the elapse time for running a pay review can be shortened, although it still depends on the various stakeholders meeting a timetable.

Pay review and pay progression

An annual pay review with, perhaps, an element of market pay movement and performance may be fine for most people in work. But there may be some employees, particularly when they are fairly early in their career, who would be expected to make more significant pay progress. In some systems they may be promoted into a higher grade. But with wider pay ranges and broad-banded systems much of the pay progression to reflect experience and value in the market needs to be managed by pay progress within a pay range rather than by being formally promoted into a higher grade.

An annual pay review will not cope with this sort of progression unless it is planned for. Many organizations that have trainees, for example on graduate programmes or other technical or professional trainees, will have specified pay reviews that operate in addition to the annual pay round. This is to ensure that those who may be developing strongly in their careers have their pay reviewed more frequently to ensure that it reflects their market position and helps protect the talent pipeline.

The message

Where there is discretion as to the size of a pay increase (other than pure incremental systems), there is an opportunity to give a message with the award. Informing an individual of a pay review (or bonus) is an ideal opportunity to ensure that the individual gets the message that the review is meant to convey. Too often this is wasted with a standard letter produced by HR rather than a meaningful conversation about the rationale for the pay decision. I discuss this further in Chapter 6 on communications.

Summary

This chapter has just highlighted a number of issues that I think are important in using salary surveys and managing pay reviews. You need to understand the market(s) in which you compete and take care in the sources you use for pay data and how you use them. However, it is only a summary. If you are going to use salary survey data professionally, I suggest that you look for some training to help you. Some of the major survey providers run courses as do the CIPD.

Questions

- Should you look for a training course to give you more detail on salary surveys and pay reviews?

- Are you clear on the pay markets in which you compete?

- What are your current sources of pay data; are they fit for purpose?

- Do you have a clear statement to explain simply how pay reviews work in your organization?

- Should you reassess the pay review process?

Case studies

I have included two different case studies for this chapter. The first is Specsavers and the second is the National Theatre.

The National Theatre is one of the leading theatres in the world. The case study illustrates how a hugely successful organization can manage very effectively with a very simple and non-bureaucratic pay review process.

The pay review process at Specsavers reflects its values and fits well in the context of its approach to reward and its pay mix. The case study shows how the organization brings together a number of reward components as part of an annual review so that the pay review is positioned as only one of three elements emphasizing total reward, not just basic salary.

CASE STUDY Specsavers

Specsavers remains a family-owned company having been founded in 1984 with one store in Bristol. Specsavers is now a well-known high street brand and the world's largest private optical group with over 1,650 stores in 10 countries. Each store is part-owned and managed by its own directors, who are shareholders of their own businesses but who are supported by key specialists in support offices who provide a range of services, such as marketing, accounting, IT and wholesaling.

There are more than 2,500 partners and over 30,000 employees. Specsavers is the largest employer of registered optometrists and dispensing opticians (around 3,500) in the UK. In 2012, global revenue was £1.8bn. The financial year runs from 1 March to the end of February.

Specsavers directly employs about 450 people in its headquarters in Guernsey and in support offices across the UK. It is a strongly values-based business encapsulated in the following:

- Treat people as we would like to be treated ourselves

- Passionate about:
  - Our customers: the lifeblood of our business
  - Our people: supporting our staff to be the best they can be
  - Partnership: at the heart of everything we do
  - Communities: giving back to and working with our local communities
  - Results: keep it simple, get it done, deliver on our promises

Reward

The approach to reward overall reflects the core values, in particular to keep things simple. To the extent to which pay varies for individuals is to a large extent based upon the way in which people behave within the values as well as the outcomes.

Specsavers has five simple bands or levels with benefits tied to each. All employees are eligible for a quarterly bonus and an annual profit-share award. The final quarterly bonus and the profit share are payable in June along with the annual pay review. Given the low levels of market pay changes this means that the pay award becomes, what might be, only a relatively small (or lower key) part of the total announced at the time. Particularly with low market pay increases,

Specsavers takes the view that it wants to 'get pay right' so that it can effectively take concerns about salary off the table – in order to talk about other more meaningful things to their people – the things that really do make a difference.

Performance management

Specsavers encourages regular meaningful conversations between managers and their teams. These are centred around the four simple questions:

- What went well?

- What didn't go so well?

- What can you do better?

- How can I help?

There is an annual review which is documented but they do not use performance ratings. The annual discussion is also based on the four questions for the whole year and covers behaviours against the values as well as outcomes; what people do and how they do it. The regular discussions seek to ensure that the managers can make good judgements about elements of individual reward that may be based on behaviours and outcomes.

Approach to pay reviews

Each year Specsavers reviews a range of market data to understand the levels of pay increases in the market. This includes data from its main data provider, other published and subscription services and general business contacts. Based on this data, the head of reward makes a proposal to the board for a pay review budget in February, for the annual pay review effective from 1 June covering the head office staff in each of the 10 countries in which Specsavers operates.

Using the approved pay budget, in May each line manager is e-mailed a pay review schedule listing their staff with basic details including current salary and bonus history. It is also pre-populated with the standard pay increase. There is an 'exceptions' column that they may complete.

Specsavers believes that the salary for most people is pretty well positioned. With market pay increases being generally suppressed and pay pots generally being relatively small, the starting view is that there will be a standard increase for everyone unless there are exceptional circumstances. The line managers may propose a higher or lower review than the standard which they enter on the sheet with their justification. The exceptions are reviewed by the relevant senior managers as a group to review the consistency of approach. The exceptions are then approved by the relevant board director. Finally, there is a board level review of all the exceptions to make sure any adjustments are approached in a consistent way.

It controls the overall budget for pay increases at the board level but does not try to impose a fixed budget at the level of each line manager. In practice, Specsavers' experience is that there are around 10 per cent of exceptions approved; approximately half higher and half lower than the standard increase.

After the final approval, the results are communicated to the line managers and local HR business partners in June. Managers are encouraged to talk to each of their reports to explain the pay review increase they have been awarded as well as the final quarter's bonus and why they are receiving what they are.

On the last Friday before 24 June (pay day) each individual receives a personalized reward update showing their new salary, bonus and the amount of annual profit share they will receive. This is an important date in the calendar and there is a degree of celebration surrounding it, in particular the profit share.

In addition to the annual pay review there are some areas of the business, for example call centres, where employees can make progress up a salary scale based on acquiring additional skills.

Specsavers believes that its simple, relatively low-key approach to pay reviews reflects the values of the business and works well particularly in the context of having a bonus and profit-share arrangement.

It is interesting to note that engagement levels in Specsavers are up around the level you would expect for a high-performing organization – and the reward related scores are higher than average in both UK and global terms.

CASE STUDY   The National Theatre

Background

The National Theatre is a company limited by guarantee and a registered charity, established in 1963. It is the leading theatre in the UK and has a worldwide reputation for its productions. It has extended the opportunity for people to see its productions through the innovative NT Live, where productions are streamed into cinemas around the world. The National Theatre has also successfully transferred productions to the West End and to the USA. Worldwide audiences are around

2.3 million. In its three theatres on the South Bank in London, it presents an eclectic mix of new plays and classics from the world repertoire with seven or eight productions in repertory at any one time.

The South Bank theatres have averaged over 90 per cent capacity in the last few years. With, currently, four productions in the West End, the National Theatre's audiences are likely to represent over 40 per cent of London's total play-goers with over 1,750 performances.

In 2011/12 the NT income was £80m, more than doubled in 10 years. The breakdown of income is approximately:

Box office including transfers	56%
Public subsidy from Arts Council England	23%
Trading and other activities	13%
Fundraising	8%

The objectives of the NT are:

- The artistic programme and artistic development. The NT presents a balanced artistic programme, staging around 20 productions a year from the whole of world drama, with a specific responsibility for the creation of new work and representing the widest range of voices.

- Audiences. The NT is tireless in trying to reach more people, broaden our audiences and give them an unparalleled experience.

- Learning and engagement. The NT aims to be an inspirational, internationally recognized resource for lifelong learning about and through theatre.

- Leadership. As a national theatre, the NT takes responsibility for fostering the health of the wider British theatre.

- Sustainability. The NT operates in a financially and environmentally responsible manner, whilst striving to increase self-generated income.

- Innovation. The NT actively considers the way in which it operates, and strives to innovate in all areas of its activity.

The NT employs around 1,100 people (just over 1,000 full-time equivalent in 2012) and will employ over 500 actors and musicians over a year for particular productions.

The 1,100 splits to around 700 technical and front of house staff where pay levels are negotiated with the union and 400 where there are individual pay reviews.

Pay review process

Initially, a nominal standard percentage rise is built into the budget in December. This is primarily based on a reasonable approximation of how the forthcoming year's budget will be balanced in the light of funding increases or cuts. Whilst used for budgeting, the final agreement of the actual pay rise budget will be made in the following March prior to the annual review date for the non-unionized staff of 1 April.

In January the head of HR writes to the 15 senior managers (heads of departments) asking them to review if any individuals should receive more than the standard increase. At this point the same managers are asked to discuss their team development plans and diversity objectives for the forthcoming year.

The main rationale for any proposals above the standard is based on any material changes to responsibilities. In February the head of HR then meets with each of the 15 senior managers to discuss their proposals. Based on the overall requests the total is reviewed against the initial budget and adjustments are made. This produces a final list of requests outside the standard.

In mid-March the head of HR then meets with the three members of the executive to review all of the individuals on the list and finalize the budget. They review the nominal budget figure and test it in the light of the February RPI figures and any additional sense of financial expectations across the last three months of the financial year (to the end of March). For example, if a production has been a hit and might therefore generate additional surplus via transfer in the next year, or looking at whether a greater increase should be granted to the lower paid. In practice the margin of difference is in the region of 0.5 – 1 per cent.

The executive members take an overall view of the changes requested to seek to ensure that there is an unbiased and fair distribution. Typically, fewer than 10 per cent will receive an increase above the standard. It is unusual for someone to receive less than the standard, but it is possible where, for example, there has been a material reduction in responsibility. The executive then approves a final list.

The head of HR then notifies the departmental heads of the outcome in March and writes to each individual directly with their pay review.

10 Bonus plans

Introduction

Prevalence of bonuses

Bonuses come in all sorts of shapes and sizes, from a weekly low-level prize to annual (and longer) executive plans paying potentially a multiple of annual salary. Table 10.1 shows the range and prevalence of bonuses reported in the 2013 CIPD Reward Management survey.

Types of bonus

Using the data in Table 10.1 as a starter, in Table 10.2 below I note some of the main types of bonus and where they might be used, before discussing how best to approach bonuses.

I do not propose going through each type of bonus. Rather, I will suggest an overall approach. But whatever type of bonus plan you might be considering, there are some vital things you need to take into account. I have been in meetings where people came armed with proposed details of a bonus plan before we had even agreed what its purpose was. Designing the bonus plan is the last stage, not the first. Like decorating a room, it is all about the preparation. You need to understand a whole lot of other things first. Once you really know those, the design (if a bonus is relevant at all) will become clear.

Whilst I mention some issues relating to sales bonuses and commissions, I do not deal with them in detail. Detailed design issues such as caps and thresholds and different bonus periods can all have a significant effect on sales. For example, a cap can encourage successful sales people to push a sale into the follow period. Sales plans are a particular type of plan that needs specific expertise to design successfully.

TABLE 10.1 Percentage of respondent organizations

	Individual-performance related					Group-performance related			
	Individual bonuses	Combination schemes*	Sales commission	Other individual cash-based incentives	Ad hoc/project based schemes	Profit sharing	Goal sharing	Non-monetary incentives	Gain sharing
All	59.8	49.4	36.5	17.4	19.5	39.7	50.3	21.2	11.9
By sector									
Manufacturing and production	51.8	66.1	35.7	10.7	25.0	47.6	52.4	16.7	11.9
Private sector services	69.7	51.6	53.3	23.8	18.9	44.7	55.3	16.5	15.3
Public sector	48.8	32.6	4.7	14.0	14.0	11.8	35.3	47.1	0.0
Voluntary, community and not-for-profit	45.0	25.0	30.0	5.0	20.0	0.0	14.3	42.9	0.0
By occupation group									
Management/professional	58.8	47.5	29.8	13.0	17.2	39.0	48.2	19.1	12.1
Other employees	46.0	40.0	25.6	15.3	14.0	38.0	42.6	21.7	5.4

* combination schemes depend on a mix of individual, group and/or organizational performance.

TABLE 10.2   Main types of bonus

Bonus type	Main features	Typical time frame	Usage
Individual bonus	Payable to individuals based on their achievements, often linked to annual objectives	Annual	As part of performance management to encourage and reflect individual achievement
Combination schemes	Individual bonus typically based on two or three factors in combination, such as individual, division and organization performance	Annual	To encourage individuals to balance out their actions to meet their individual goals as well as support others to achieve broader goals
Sales commission	Individual bonus paying on sales or sales revenue	Monthly or quarterly	To incentivize a sales person to maximize sales
Project bonus	Team or individual bonus for successfully delivering a project	End of project	To encourage the team to work together to achieve the project on time and to cost
Total Reward	A discretionary bonus awarded as part of the annual pay review process in lieu of (some) salary increase	Annual	In place of part of a pay review for a high performer who is already on a high salary
Profit sharing	Group-wide bonus that pays a cash amount or a percentage of salary depending on the profit that is made	Annual	To encourage people in the business to focus on the success of the whole business rather than just their part

TABLE 10.2 *Continued*

Bonus type	Main features	Typical time frame	Usage
Goal sharing	Group bonus based on achieving broad, typically company or division wide goals	Annual	To get people behind one or more key corporate goals
Team bonus	Bonus paid to a team for their collective achievement	Quarterly or annual	To encourage team behaviours to achieve a positive result
Gain sharing	Group-wide bonus based on a formula that relates bonus to improvements in productivity and performance which are under the control of employees	Quarterly or annual	To bring people in the business together to share the value of improvements; part of cultural change
Pool base	Create a bonus pool and allocate a % share to participants; pool size varies according to some KPIs	Annual	To bring a management group to work together to achieve the KPIs
Spot bonus	Immediate low-level bonus to recognize particular success	Daily	To recognize a positive behaviour or output immediately
Deferred bonus	Executive bonus where part or all of the bonus is deferred for, typically, three years before it is paid; the deferred element may be in company shares	Annual with three-year deferral	To help retain executives and tie them into the longer-term results of the business

Bonus design framework

Here is a fairly simple framework of six steps that you can follow to design a bonus plan. Of course they overlap and you may find you need to go back to an earlier stage, but they are a helpful guide.

FIGURE 10.1　Six step bonus design framework

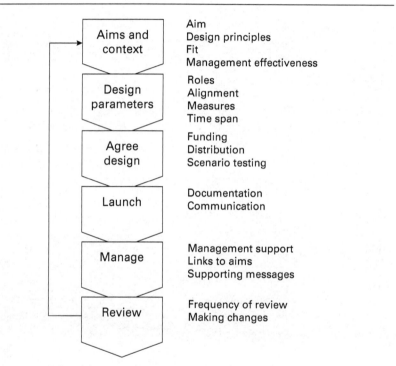

In the following sections I will take you through each of these steps, giving a practical approach of how to review and design bonuses.

Aims and context

Aim

The absolutely critical question you must answer to start with is, 'What is the bonus for?' This can be quite a difficult question to answer, particularly if you have had bonuses operating for some time. They have always been there rather than they are there for a particular purpose. You should agree a written answer with whoever are the main stakeholders. 'The purpose of the XYZ bonus plan is to...'. I am afraid that '... to help recruit, retain and motivate...' is just not good enough as we discussed in Chapter 1 on reward strategy. Maybe these questions will help:

- What is the problem that the bonus is trying to help solve?
- What will be different if the bonus is successful?
- How will people behave differently, or achieve different results?
- Is the bonus to encourage exceptional performance or will it be part of business as usual; what is the message the bonus is meant to carry?

You also need to consider the relationship between bonus and basic pay. So you should be able to answer the question, 'What is basic pay for and what is bonus for?' Sometimes there is confusion and double counting as they are both driven from the same outcomes. So I hope as part of your reward strategy you will have considered this relationship and their strategic fit and can articulate the difference.

I would strongly advise that you spend some time on this vital stage. You need to be careful to look for the ultimate aim, not the means. If you can really distil the essence of what you are trying to achieve, you may decide that a bonus is not actually the right answer. So I would try to keep a fairly open mind. You need to be thinking if it is actually possible for a bonus to deliver the aim you agree, particularly in the context of the organization.

Fit

A bonus will not manage for you. It can only help you focus attention on ends and behaviours but it must be part of the culture and management style of the organization. Like all other parts of reward (and other HR programmes) simply grafting on a bonus is unlikely to be successful without thinking about how it will fit. For example, an all-employee profit share can be very successful in the right context or little short of a waste of money having no impact if the fit is wrong.

The John Lewis partnership is one of the most successful retailers in the UK. It is unique in that it is owned by the 85,000 partners (employees) who share the profits. It has a very strong culture and values. In 2013 partners received a profit share bonus of 17 per cent of salary. The bonus announcement is a highlight of the year. It is strongly communicated and aligned closely with the business success. Whilst the profit share is only a part of the culture it is central.

▶

Moog Inc is a very successful US hi-tech engineering business with over 11,000 employees in 27 countries. Moog operate no individual bonuses or sales commission. They have only a single global profit share which emphasizes their core values to team work and shared responsibility.

On the other hand a profit share can just become institutionalized and expected in the wrong culture.

I worked in a private sector organization which had an annual tax efficient profit share (under the legislation at the time). It had been paying out the maximum of 10 per cent of salary for a few years but it was not tied into total reward. So tough annual pay negotiations were around basic pay increases of 2.5 per cent or 3.0 per cent, but they were overshadowed by the 10 per cent profit share that was ignored.

The nature of the bonus itself would need to fit the organization. For some organizations cash may be inappropriate, so maybe small non-cash awards would be better, as discussed in Chapter 11. Some research has shown that in some circumstances a bonus, coined as a pro-social bonus that may only be used by the recipient for others or to give to charity can be more motivating than a regular cash bonus for them to spend on themselves (Anik *et al*, 2013).

Some annual bonus plans are launched at the start of the year and a pay-out made after the end of the year, but nothing is said about them during the year. They never touch the sides. But to get an annual plan to have impact it needs to be aligned with the key messages – how the business is doing, and what else can we do individually and collectively to help keep it on track? So it's all about context and fit.

In 2011 Intel, the world's largest semiconductor chip maker, found an error in the design of one of its products. This meant that it had to scrap 14,000,000 units and manufacture 28,000,000 new units in factories in the US, Israel and Ireland in 14 weeks; half the time this would normally be planned to take.

Communication was key. In Ireland, the leadership explained the issue to everyone at the factory. It was going to be a huge challenge. But they worked through what had to be done and how they were going to achieve it. To focus everyone on the local target, they set up electronic displays in the factory entrance showing the target and how they were tracking to it. These displays were updated on the basis of daily output achieved, along with other communications to ensure everyone at the factory knew what progress was being made.

Intel also wanted to provide some financial incentive reflecting the gain if they collectively achieved the goal. They wanted a simple system that emphasized that everyone in each of the three factories could help achieve this challenging target. They introduced a gainsharing bonus so that each of the people in the factories, including the team leaders and managers, would receive $1,000 so long as the goal was reached – at least 28,000,000 units manufactured by the end of 14 weeks.

They actually managed to beat the target: the three factories produced 32,000,000 units within the revised time frame.

Incentives or rewards

A significant problem with bonus plans is that they often do not encourage people to do what you would like them to do; so they have little effect. A much worse problem can be when they do exactly what they are designed for and have a very significant effect. This may sound like the sort of problem you would like to have – a reward programme impacting behaviour and outcomes as you would like it to.

The problem is that if you design a bonus plan to incentivize behaviour you may well get what you are incentivizing and nothing else. The theory that helps to explain this is Expectancy Theory (Vroom, 1964). In essence, Vroom found that the strength of motivation will vary according to the individual's

- desire for a particular outcome;
- expectancy that an action will lead to that outcome; and
- view that the action (goal) can be achieved.

In other words, in the context of incentive bonuses, if the participant values a potential bonus and can see that they can achieve a certain outcome which will give them that bonus, they are likely to seek to achieve the outcome to get the bonus. Whilst at one level this might seem obvious, it is helpful as we think about constructing bonus plans, in particular those that are designed to incentivize.

It is actually fraught with danger, because you have to be absolutely clear what the outcome is that you want the bonused individual to achieve. So, as discussed earlier, a key factor to consider is, 'What does success look like?' What is the outcome you are seeking? Be very careful to distinguish between any short-term achievements and the ultimate goal.

The recent past is littered with mis-selling scandals. Very many of these were caused by organizations that set their goals in generating revenue in the short term without thinking through the longer-term consequences. As mentioned in Part One, whilst they may have talked about valuing the customer, the bonus plans paid out on sales. It should come as no surprise then that those targeted and bonused to achieve sales did exactly that. However, huge fines and compensation had to be paid and significant reputational damage was done. One financial services business I talked to said that the total cost of putting right a particular mis-selling issue was very considerably more than the value of all the sales made.

There are some illustrative examples shown in FSA (2013) final guidance. Whilst the report is focused on financial services, the examples of poor practice show very clearly how a poorly designed bonus plan can undermine an organization, regardless of the sector.

There are some things where it is counterproductive to try to incentivize, as discussed in Chapter 3. For example, research has shown that creativity and innovation are reduced where you introduce a financial incentive.

FIGURE 10.2   Control and clarity of goal matrix

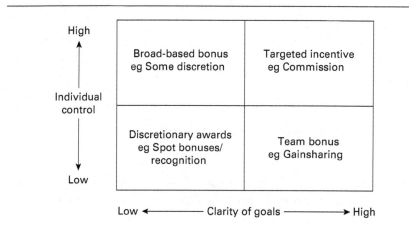

One way to consider this issue is in relation to the clarity of goals and the degree of control the individual has over the outcome. This is illustrated in Figure 10.2. Where the outcomes are very clear and specific and the individual has high control, with little support or dependency on others, targeted incentives may be considered. But as you can see, in other situations depending on the relationship between goals and control, alternative bonus mechanisms are likely to be more appropriate.

A reward rather than an incentive is likely to focus on broad outcomes and may reinforce what people are already doing. This point is expanded in Chapter 11 on non-cash reward. But, as discussed in Chapter 3, the belief system in the organization will influence thinking about what a bonus should be doing. So here are two truths:

- if you want to see what an organization values, look at what it pays for, not what it says;
- if the bonus is attractive, people will do what the bonus targets, so it must be what you want.

Management effectiveness and training

You need to understand how effective your management is at communicating messages. How will they be able to operate the bonus plan you are thinking about? Managers don't need bonus plans to help them manage. But if you are going to introduce bonus plans then look at how people do manage in the organization and what further training they may require to help embed the bonus to make it as effective as possible. As I have said before, bonuses do not manage for you. If a manager believes that they can abdicate responsibility for managing performance because the bonus will drive the right outcomes, you are in trouble.

The bonus may include a degree of management discretion – judgement – so your managers need to be clear about the nature of the discretion they have and need to be briefed on using the discretion fairly.

Design principles

As part of the process of taking a strategic approach to bonuses, having established the main contextual issues, I recommend you start to develop a set of design principles that you can agree with the key stakeholders. This is likely to help frame the design of a particular bonus although it could be to set the scene for all bonuses – although this would be more of a bonus strategy.

The design principles are not the bonus plan, but the main agreed principles to which the design should adhere. Some may be in conflict. I would not shy away from this, but you need to recognize that there may be some trade-off between one principle and another. The benefit of agreeing design principles is that you can get stakeholders to focus on the things that are important to help achieve the aims but not get fixated by the detail of design.

Here is an example of a set of bonus design principles that was used to help design an annual bonus. Like other examples in this book, I am not suggesting that you should follow this model precisely. But I hope it helps illustrate what I mean by design principles and allows you to develop what is appropriate in your circumstances.

XYZ Co Annual bonus design principles

1   As both basic salary and bonus make up the 'total cash', the market position for an individual should be taken into account in considering bonus levels.

2   At the start of the financial year a participant should have a reasonable understanding of the range of potential bonus they may earn and what has to be achieved for the bonus to pay out.

3   Bonus should not focus on individual performance at the potential cost of the larger unit to which they contributes.

4   The bonus plan should be as simple as possible.

5   Bonus will be expressed as a percentage of salary.

6   Potential bonus will be expressed as both target and maximum. The minimum bonus will be zero.

7   The bonus plan will be fully documented including provision for changes in circumstances (such as leavers etc). Every participant will have a copy of the documentation.

8   Effective feedback systems will be available to show people on a regular basis how they and the parts of the business on which their bonus depends are doing.

Design parameters

Roles

Firstly, you should be clear about the target population of employees who you expect to participate in the plan. You need to be quite specific, put it in writing and agree it with key stakeholders to ensure there are no misunderstandings.

As I mentioned earlier, part of Expectancy Theory is that the individual should be able to see the connection between what they do and the outcome. So in bonus terms this is saying that if you are going to use individual bonuses, based on individual results, the individual should be able to control the outcome. But we need to question very carefully the nature of any roles for which we are considering introducing a bonus.

In a modern organization, how many people have that degree of control? I would say very few indeed. Almost always to achieve a result we work directly or indirectly with others. Even when you look at sales roles you often find that individuals will support each other. So a vital question to ask is, 'How do people work together to achieve a result?' You need to probe to really get to the answer, but whilst the starting assumption might be a bonus based on individual results, that is unlikely to reflect reality and may destroy value rather than improve it. For example, if your bonus plan is based on the individual and their results, it is likely to encourage individual behaviours – not supporting others, keeping things to yourself and protecting your own results regardless of the corporate consequences.

Almost no one can achieve results on their own, so consider carefully if it should be an individual or team plan or at least with outcomes to which the individual contributes rather than for which they are directly accountable. You may want to use two or three measures in combination (such as individual and division) to reflect these elements. So key questions to ask are:

- What do you really want people to do?
- To what extent do people work on their own or with others to achieve success?

Time span

The key question here to ask is, 'Over what time period does the individual (or team) make an impact?' I have come across many cases where there is complete misalignment between the span of time of impact and the bonus period. For example, people doing a job with an immediate impact but getting an annual bonus. Ideally, the time span of impact and the bonus period should be aligned with any pay-out following very soon after the event. So this might get you to think about more than one bonus plan.

In general, the more senior the person, the longer the time scale over which they make an impact. For example, the directors of a company should be setting the goals and strategy looking ahead well past the current year. You might argue that even an annual bonus is inappropriate for the leaders of an organization as they should be planning and delivering over a longer period. That is as least one reason why some element of deferral of bonus has become more common for executives.

Whilst no one would put in place a bonus for executive using weekly results, there are plenty of organizations who have annual bonuses (that they believe incentivize) for relatively junior people for whom a year is normally much too long. For example, a call-centre adviser is likely to make an impact day-to-day, or maybe week-to-week. So in this sort of situation, consider spot bonuses, immediate prizes and recognition as a better fit than an annual bonus. They can make a particularly big impact for short-term incentives. This is discussed in Chapter 11.

You might decide that a form of annual profit share would help the organization explain some of the key financial measures and may get people to look at what they are doing over the year. This would apply for everyone and may try to encourage joint working and focus on a common goal as discussed earlier. It can be most effective in a relatively small organization. But to make an impact with this sort of annual programme you need to embed it and ensure that leaders and managers use it to help communicate things that are relevant to each team and individual.

Horizontal and vertical alignment

It is common to have different bonus plans at different levels and sometimes for different functions in the organization. This makes sense given the points I have just made about time span. So the executive bonus plan may look very different to the plan for people in more junior roles in the organization. But you should consider the vertical alignment. That is, check that the bonus plan at one level is not driving people in a different direction to the plan above or below them.

For example, if front-line employees have a bonus that reflects excellence in customer service but customer service does not feature in the bonus of the people above them, there is likely to be conflict in the ways in which the two groups see success.

There is also horizontal alignment. This is checking that bonus plans of people at similar levels who may need to work together, or depend on outputs from others to do their job are not in conflict. For example, you may have some people whose bonus reflects only their individual outputs. But others are looking to those people for support. It is inevitable that there will be little sharing with others if the bonus drives individual results.

So look at the vertical and horizontal alignment between bonus plans. They can be different plans with a different emphasis but they must be aligned and not in conflict. Look at what success is all about and adapt bonus plans to reflect the reality of the way people need to work together.

Measures

If measures are being used as part of the bonus they are likely to fall out of the corporate or individual objective-setting system. It is common that people find things that are measurable and use them as objectives, but often a measure does not help you determine outcomes or value. Counting the number of words in a poem or weighing a statue will not help you appreciate their value.

There is a tendency to look for 'objective' measures to underpin a bonus. However, searching for something 'measurable' rather than 'value adding' can lead to a situation coined the Macnamara Fallacy (Handy, 1994):

'The first step is to measure whatever can be easily measured. This is OK as far as it goes.

The second step is to disregard that which can't be easily measured or to give it an arbitrary quantitative value. This is artificial and misleading.

The third step is to presume that what can't be measured easily really isn't important. This is blindness.

The fourth step is to say that what can't be easily measured really doesn't exist. This is suicide.'

Bonus plans are often designed to avoid what is seen as subjectivity underpinning them. But another way to consider this is that we require people to use assessment or judgement every day, often based on incomplete data. The test is going back to what ultimately you are trying to achieve rather than strive for perceived objectivity through measures at all costs.

It may be that a mix of measures is needed to carry a balanced message (eg individual, team and company performance measures). I would advise against more than three as otherwise it becomes too complex and unfocused.

Of course the sort of measures used, if any, should be based on the aim of the bonus plan. But the management information needs to be available for the measures. There is no point in deciding that a particular measure should be used where there is no management information available.

Where a quoted company uses a bonus based on business-wide financial measures, such as a profit share, there will be limited opportunities to communicate how you are doing as the information may be price sensitive and therefore controlled by disclosure rules. You are likely to be restricted to the annual results and quarterly updates.

Agree design

Funding

Funding is not about what you pay to an individual, team or department; that is distribution. Funding is establishing where the money is to come from. Whilst this might have been discussed earlier in the process, it will need firming up now.

One of the advantages for an organization of paying bonus rather than salary is the lower long-term cost and flexibility. Whilst an increase in salary will increase the costs of other benefits which are based on salary such as pension and life assurance, bonus is normally not counted as the basis for such benefits. Most bonuses are structured to be non-contractual and so there is flexibility for the company to pay higher or lower bonuses dependent on profitability.

If times are tough for the business, it is easier to reduce a non-contractual bonus than it is to reduce pay. The alternative may be redundancies. So bonuses may be funded directly from the profit of the business. This does assume that this flexibility is clear in the bonus plan rules and you explain to people the finances of the organization so as to manage expectations.

You will need to work with your finance colleagues normally to agree the funding. The finance function of the company will normally approve the basis of funding for a bonus plan. They will want to budget for the bonus funding as part of the annual budget cycle. Whilst sometimes this will be a fixed budget to fund, typically, small bonuses, it is more likely to vary with profitability or another financial measure. The funding may be a simple percentage of this year's profit or may also reflect improvement over last year.

You need to recognize where funding for any one bonus plan could pay out a substantial bonus whilst the business overall makes little or no profit. This may be a conscious decision as without the bonus the overall finances could be worse. But it needs to be agreed.

In some bonus plans there is even a bonus-funding table shown so it is clear to everyone how the initial funding will be calculated. An example is shown as Table 10.3.

TABLE 10.3   Example bonus funding table

% of target earnings before interest, taxes, depreciation and amortization (EBITDA) achieved	Bonus funding (%)
125+	140
120	130
115	120
110	112
105	105
103	103
102	102
101	100
100 (target)	**100**
99	99
98	98
97	97
96	95
95	92
94	89
93	85
92	80
91	75
90	69
85	35
Below 85	Nil

Sales bonus funding, and in fact the basis of distribution to individuals or teams, may be based on revenue rather than profitability. This is fraught with danger as I have seen many such plans paying bonus or commission on sales, but the company making little or no profit. As was coined in the retail business, 'Revenue is vanity but profit is sanity.' Whilst the individual sales person may primarily affect the revenue, it is important to take into account the costs of sales at least to some extent, as there is almost always the opportunity to affect costs as well. A particular concern is where the sales person can agree discounts which may have little effect on their revenue-driven commission, but could significantly affect profitability.

Where a bonus is payable over a longer period, for example it has a deferral period, the amount due will be accrued (spread) over the period, so that the cost of the bonus is charged against the profits of different years. This can be fairly complex and is clearly something for your finance colleagues to deal with. But it is important to note that the funding may get spread over more than one year.

Distribution

You will need to establish what participants would get from the bonus plan and how it would be calculated against outcomes. There are almost endless permutations of ways to deal with this, but here are some pointers covering a range of issues:

- Bonus set as a percentage of salary – assumes that individual's impact is related to their seniority and the actual cash amount is valued similarly by participants as in proportion to their salary.

- Flat payment to all – carries the message of equal contribution of a team – mostly used for short-term bonuses, such as a bonus at the end of a project.

- Minimum bonus – generally the minimum bonus is zero assuming that bonus payout relates to outcomes. Otherwise it becomes a guaranteed bonus. I would advise that this should be considered for the first year of employment only. Long-term minima or guarantees are a bad idea.

- Maximum bonus – there may be a maximum (or cap) to ensure that windfall outcomes are not over-rewarded and also to keep a reference point with the external pay market.

- Target bonus – this may be stated as the bonus payable for a set of outcomes, but will lead to expectations.

- Threshold – the minimum performance point that triggers funding or a bonus payment. This might be set a few points below target.

- Accelerator – an increasing rate of bonus or funding typically for over-achievement.

- Decelerator – a reducing rate of bonus or funding, typically for performance below target.

- Multiplier – combining two (or possibly more) factors together by multiplying them together. For example, the initial pot is established by taking a percentage of an outcome which is then multiplied by a factor of between 0 and 2 depending on a second measure. Typically used where both measures are important and a minimum level must be achieved in each.

- Adder – combining two or more factors by adding them together. Typically used when achievement in either or both is acceptable.

Scenario testing

One influence on bonus plan design will be the range of likely outcomes and the degree of direct or indirect impact the participants of the bonus may have. This is particularly important for annual and longer bonuses, but you need to think about them for most types of bonus other than immediate or very short-term plans.

For example, could there be a very high impact due to changes in the market rather than what the participants actually do?

The unexpected does happen – quite often actually – so it is very important to think about the potential range of outcomes as illustrated in Figure 10.3.

FIGURE 10.3   Range of possible outcomes to consider

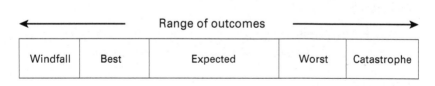

Whilst there is likely to be some discretion in the operation of the plan, it is far better to consider the range of outcomes and build them into the design. If you present some outcomes where the decision makers would make a payment using discretion, then try to document that in the plan.

Launch

Documentation

If you are implementing a short-term bonus, or competition over a few days or weeks with low value payments you will need to ensure that everyone understands it, but the documentation can be pretty light. However, as the term of a plan and the potential value increases it is very important to ensure that the plan is well documented. Certainly any bonus plan that covers a year or more must be documented in some form of plan rules.

The document you use needs to be in the corporate style and its prime use is to explain the details of the plan. But it needs to be sufficiently robust that it covers the range of circumstances that may take place and ensure it is clear when a payment will and will not be made. You would be strongly advised to use an expert to draft a set of bonus plan rules.

You may want a lawyer to review the drafting, but be careful to ensure that you do not turn a well-written and clear document into something that is overly legal.

Whilst I would not advise someone without the skills and experience to write a set of bonus plan rules I give below an outline of sections that might be used and some ideas on what each section would cover.

Introduction

- Short background to set the scene, overall summary, discretion.

Objective

- At least one sentence starting with something like, 'The objective of this bonus plan is to...'

Participants

- Who will participate in the plan and how you will deal with new starters and existing employees transferring in or out of the function.

Plan outline

- Explanation of how it works.

Payment

- When it will be paid, through payroll, subject to tax and national insurance.

▶

◀

Example

- One or more worked examples illustrating how it works and showing any important variables – for example when a maximum cuts in.

Changes in circumstance

- Cover the changes that might happen and how you would deal with it: dismissal, resignation, death, sickness absence, maternity and paternity leave etc.

Definition of terms

The documentation can form part of the communications plan covered in Chapter 6.

Manage

As raised earlier, to be effective a bonus plan needs to be owned by the management. So for an annual plan in particular, you may need to look to what extent it is being used to help communicate messages about the corporate, department or individual success. For example, if there are quarterly corporate announcements on results is there any reference to the bonus, where relevant?

Bonus plans depend upon line management to make them effective and they will only work if line management is committed to them and use them appropriately in their management role. At the core of this is effective communications. There should be an active programme of briefings for managers when a bonus plan is launched or when there are major changes. You should provide support in the form of guidance and training, and perhaps briefing documentation.

When it comes to a payment, ideally, the manager needs to be engaged and should ensure that the individual gets the right message about what the particular bonus payout means.

Review

I suggest that all bonus plans should be reviewed annually. If you are introducing an annual plan I suggest that you communicate it only as a one-year plan, so it is shown as the, say, 2014 bonus plan. This gives you the opportunity of reviewing it before the start of the next year and making any adjustments necessary.

You may wish to take views from any of the stakeholders – HR, line managers etc to gauge how the plan has done both in terms of direct impact on results and also behaviours. You may wish to do a short survey of participants or run a couple of focus groups to see what those affected think about the plan.

It may be that you wish to make no changes, so simply re-label the previous one. But I have seen many examples of bonus plans that have not been reviewed for many years even though there have been substantial changes in the business.

Bonus design checklist

The following checklist summarizes much of what this section covers and introduces some additional points to look out for.

Bonus design checklist

1. Who is the target group?

- Directors/senior managers/managers/staff – do you need different plans for each?

- At what organizational level will it apply – group, division, unit, individual?

- Will it be for individuals or teams?

- What is the relationship with other parts of organization?

- How do the individuals work together and depend on others?

2. Objectives of the plan

- Will the plan reflect business objectives?

- What do target group(s) need to do to help achieve business objectives?

- Will the plan encourage target group(s) to focus on priorities?

- Will the plan make target group(s) more aware of the factors that govern company performance?

- Will the plan enable target group(s) to share the company's success?

▶

- Will the plan reward personal commitment and success?

- How will it link with salary reviews?

- How will it link with recognition plans?

3. Types of plan

Incentive or reward?

Reward – would be a payment for work done where the targets were not set at the start of the period but, typically, a good level of achievement was reached eg profit share plan.

Incentive – targets or objectives are set at the start as are the basis for and amounts of payments. It is clear to individuals what behaviour is required of them to achieve a particular level of payment ie there is a clear relationship between the achievement of a target and a given payment

The choice of the type of plan will depend on the:

- culture and values of the organization;

- degree to which functions are inter-related or free-standing;

- extent to which the company is planning-based;

- extent to which year to year performance is predictable;

- degree of complexity in the mix of measures to be used.

4. Choice of performance measures

The choice of performance measures is critical. Key considerations include business priorities; the extent to which individual/group can influence results; the existence of reliable measures and the ability to track performance. There is the danger of choosing a measure because it exists rather than because it is right. In general the performance measures used in a bonus plan should relate closely to the measures used in running the business. The broad choices will be:

- financial vs non-financial;

- quantifiable vs non-quantifiable;

- short term vs long term.

5. Key issues in plan design

- *Competitive base rates and benefits* – basic pay and benefits should be competitive. Fluctuations in total earnings should not threaten basic living standards.

- *Significant payments* – very small payments have little motivational value.

- *Simple and clear* – complex systems do not motivate.

- *Appropriate to business needs* – any plan must reflect business priorities. There should be a balance between the needs of shareholders (and other stakeholders) and employees.

- *Felt fair* – the plan must be acceptable/equitable in its underlying principles, how it compares with other plans in the company and to some extent its comparisons with plans in the market.

- *Communications* – ensure that key stakeholders, managers and participants are briefed effectively including bonus documentation. A bonus that is not understood is useless.

- *The target mix* – can have a mix of performance targets ie financial and non-financial; individual, team and company performance measures; short term and long term.

- *Discretionary element* – many plans which have a mix of targets have a discretionary element. This can avoid the pitfalls of rigid/mechanistic measures.

- *Link with performance appraisal* – discussions on setting and achievement of targets should take place as part of performance appraisal procedure. Be very wary of a mechanistic link to an appraisal score.

- *Level of payments* – setting of target level (as per cent of salary). Is it meaningful? Is it self-financing? – upper limit – there may be a need to 'cap' payment.

- *Treatment of exceptional circumstances* – it may be necessary to make provisions for dealing with exceptional circumstances outside the control of the target group(s) to curb excessive gains/hardships.

- *Frequency of payment* – annually (after annual results), quarterly, monthly?

- *Thresholds and ceilings on payments* – will payment start below, at or above target performance; similarly will the maximum be capped?

- *Accelerator/decelerator* – the extent to which the marginal gain increases or decreases.

- *Plan duration and reviews* – all plans need to be reviewed regularly; ideally annually.

- *Administration* – who will approve the plan? Rules and procedures should be written: formula for calculating payments; eligibility to join plan; timing of payments; treatment of leavers, new joiners, internal transfers, death etc.

6. Scenario planning

Model the payments from the plan in a variety of scenarios, in particular reflecting the extremes of performance and outcomes. What would the organization do in each?

Summary

Bonuses can have a place, but they will do nothing on their own. They can provide flexibility as part of total reward without being a fixed cost. They can carry strong messages about what is important. But if they provide a large enough carrot, participants are likely to seek to achieve exactly what they target, and nothing else. This can be a significant problem and is something of a paradox.

Whilst organizations often want a bonus to act as an incentive, when it does it may end up producing a different result than the organization was after, particularly in the long term – the danger of unintended consequences. On the other hand if bonus is very small and is not going to act as an incentive, what exactly is it doing?

The fundamental question is, do you believe that people need the extrinsic motivation that a bonus is meant to provide? Or should a bonus be positioned to reflect overall success and try to support the intrinsic motivation of the engaged employee? This is developed in the next chapter on recognition and non-cash reward.

Maybe the best way to think about bonuses is as a small part of the whole. They should help managers to reinforce key messages about performance at different levels and they should make people feel good when they get them.

Questions

- Are you clear what you are asking your bonus plans to do; is it realistic?

- Are your bonuses documented sufficiently so that it explains how the plan works and the main changes to circumstances are covered?

- Are you making best use of your bonus plans in helping manage rather than leaving them drifting unattached to the rest of the organization?

- When did you last your review plans? If not in the last 18 months, I suggest that you do so.

CASE STUDY McDonald's

McDonald's has three bonus plans that appropriately balance incentive and reward, use bonus periods that are relevant to the populations covered, align key measures, give focus to the balance of outcomes and emphasize team success.

Background

McDonald's is the world's largest restaurant chain with more than 34,000 restaurants in 118 countries and employing 1.8 million people.

McDonald's opened its first restaurant in the UK in 1974. There are now over 1,200 restaurants in the UK of which around 825 are owned and operated through franchisees who collectively employ around 55,000 people. McDonald's directly owns around 400 restaurants where it employs around 35,000 people – approximately 29,500 crew members and 5,000 shift leaders and managers. There are another 550 people in its head office and regional management. This case study focuses on the bonus plans for the company-owned restaurants and the head office and regional management staff.

McDonald's global philosophy is to decentralize as much as possible so as to ensure that discretion is used to meet the needs of the local markets. This is contained in a global framework document that states what must be dealt with at the corporate centre in Chicago, what can be varied within a region (eg Europe) and what can be varied in each market (country). In terms of reward, stock is dealt with at the centre and there is one common bonus framework for non-restaurant staff. Hourly-paid employees are paid fortnightly and salaried employees are paid twice monthly. The financial year is the calendar year.

Bonus plans

McDonald's has three bonus plans that are designed to incentivize achieving goals and behaviours and reward success. They are each aligned with some key measures and each has a bonus period that fits the population. Each is covered below.

Restaurants

In the restaurants there are two bonus plans; one for the restaurant management team (salaried managers and hourly-paid shift leaders) and one for all other employees, collectively referred to below as 'crew'. Restaurants typically run four shifts a day. Each restaurant is run as a profit centre.

Crew

Crew members are in a monthly bonus plan based only on customer satisfaction. This is measured through two monthly mystery shopper visits per restaurant. McDonald's have established that there are five key factors that are important to customers and these are scored along with other measures by the mystery shoppers. Also the speed of service is noted against standard service times. To qualify for a crew bonus the restaurant must score 100 per cent for the five customer satisfaction factors for the month and achieve a high overall visit score. The restaurants are then ranked by speed of service as a tie breaker, if required. The crew employees in the top 10 per cent of the qualifying restaurants are eligible for a bonus.

Each month the results are published of the top 10 per cent of restaurants. There is a certain level of competition between restaurants wanting to be seen to achieve this standard. The bonus is in the form of hourly pay enhanced by 50p for the fortnightly pay period starting the following month. These periods are set at the start of the year.

With four shifts a day, over a month it could be any of a large number of crew members who were involved in the two mystery shopper visits. But the point is that it is all about the team effort. Also, as a monthly bonus there are 12 opportunities a year for a restaurant to achieve the bonus. The bonus is very short term to meet the nature of the role. The message carried by the bonus is clear – deliver all the vital ingredients of customer service to provide customers with a great experience. This focuses on exactly what crew members can do and how they can make an impact.

Restaurant Management Team

Restaurant managers and shift team leaders are all in a quarterly bonus plan based on three factors. There is also an annual element, payable with the final quarterly bonus based on two other factors.

In December each year a bonus plan document is distributed to the participants showing the plan for the forthcoming year and highlighting any changes from the previous year's plan. There is a schedule showing the payment dates for bonuses, which is six–eight weeks after the end of each quarter. Targets are set for each quarter throughout the year, rather than for the year as a whole. This enables more realistic stretching, but achievable targets to be set. So with the December communication are the targets only for the first quarter.

The three factors on which bonus is payable each quarter are:

- Customer satisfaction – based on the mystery shopper results, which are the same as those for the crew.

- Comparable sales – the change in sales revenue for the quarter compared to the same period in the prior year.

- Profit – operating profit.

For each of the three factors there is a qualifying standard below which no bonus is payable for that element. Where a restaurant does qualify there is a pre-announced £ value bonus payable for the quarter depending on the seniority of the role. The qualifying restaurants are ranked and those in the top 10 per cent receive a double bonus.

At the same time as the last quarter bonus is payable there is also the annual element that is payable. This is based on two people measures for the restaurant:

- the turnover of hourly-paid employees for the year, and

- employee satisfaction as measured in the annual employee attitude survey, 'Your Viewpoint'.

An example of the summary given to participants is shown as Figure 10.4 below. The actual amount of bonus is not shown as this is confidential.

Each quarter when the results are announced the revenue and profit targets for the next quarter are also given. The customer and employee measures are set for the year.

The management team bonus is based on an interrelated balance of factors that can be directly influenced by the management team at the restaurant. The

FIGURE 10.4 Bonus payment table

	POSITION	SRFM	2nd Assistant	1st Assistant	Unit Manager	Business Manager
Quarterly Bonus Measures	**Mystery Shopper:**	⇩	⇩	⇩	⇩	⇩
	Top 10% of Qualifying Restaurants Nationally Enhanced bonus	£xxx	£xxx	£xxx	£xxx	£xxx
	Remaining Qualifying Restaurants Nationally Standard bonus	£xxx	£xxx	£xxx	£xxx	£xxx
	Comparable Sales:					
	Top 10% of Qualifying Restaurants Nationally Enhanced bonus	£xxx	£xxx	£xxx	£xxx	£xxx
	Remaining Qualifying Restaurants Nationally Standard bonus	£xxx	£xxx	£xxx	£xxx	£xxx
	Profit – Carry Down:					
	Top 10% of Qualifying Restaurants Nationally Enhanced bonus	£xxx	£xxx	£xxx	£xxx	£xxx
	Remaining Qualifying Restaurants Nationally Standard bonus	£xxx	£xxx	£xxx	£xxx	£xxx
	Maximum Enhanced bonus per quarter	**£xxx**	**£xxx**	**£xxx**	**£xxx**	**£xxx**
	Maximum Standard bonus per quarter	**£xxx**	**£xxx**	**£xxx**	**£xxx**	**£xxx**
Annual Bonus Measures	**Annual People Measures:**					
	Hourly-Paid Turnover National Target of xx%	£xxx	£xxx	£xxx	£xxx	£xxx
	'Your Viewpoint' – Overall Commitment score National target of xx%	£xxx	£xxx	£xxx	£xxx	£xxx
	Maximum Annual Bonus	**£xxx**	**£xxx**	**£xxx**	**£xxx**	**£xxx**

management team has accountability for growing sales and delivering profit, which are two of the factors. But this is balanced out with the customer satisfaction and people measures. There is alignment with the crew bonus through the customer satisfaction measure which the whole team can influence.

The message is clear through the bonus that the managers need to keep an eye on all of the key factors to run a successful restaurant – customer satisfaction, employee satisfaction, revenue and profit. To ensure a balanced approach is adopted, each of the three quarterly measures are equally weighted to discourage behaviours targeted at achieving one of the measures at the expense of the others.

This is a genuine quarterly bonus where each quarter there are new financial targets to aim for. If no bonus or a partial bonus is achieved for one quarter there is the next quarter to aim for. Even if the restaurant qualifies for a bonus for each factor, there is then the opportunity to push harder to get to the top 10 per cent and double bonus. So there is both an absolute element and a competitive element based on relative performance. McDonald's see the balance between absolute and relative performance as important in the way in which they manage performance. The bonus is simply set as a cash value, so everyone can see what their potential bonus is.

Head office and regional staff

All head office and regional staff are on the same bonus framework but with different annual target bonuses as a percentage of salary. The bonus plan is known as the Target Incentive Plan (TIP).

The actual annual bonus paid is the target bonus multiplied by a factor relating to achievement of company-wide operating income and other targets for the UK (team performance factor) and a factor reflecting individual employee performance (individual performance factor).

- **Target bonus** is between 5 per cent and 20 per cent of salary depending on seniority.

- **Team performance factor** is between nil (below threshold operating income) and 175 per cent (maximum operating income). It has an additional modifier that can increase or decrease by a further 25 per cent, making the maximum 200 per cent. The modifier is based on three or four factors that are changed from time to time, but have included, mystery shopper score, external brand perception scores and customer volumes.

- **Individual performance factor** is between nil and 150 per cent depending on the annual performance rating. This uses four ratings as shown in Table 10.4.

TABLE 10.4 Performance ratings

Annual rating	Factor
Exceptional performance	115–150%
Significant performance	75–110%
Some improvement required	0–50%
Unacceptable performance	0%

Bonuses are paid in February, after the year end. Should the operating income be below the target threshold then there would be no bonus payable under the plan. At an individual level poor performance could lead to no bonus. As you can see from the table above, there is flexibility in the individual bonus factor. This allows managers to adjust bonus for individuals within each rating. Salary increases are effective 31 December and are paid from February backdated. The flexibility in the individual bonus factors also allows some adjustments between salary increases and bonus as they are announced at the same time.

Whilst in theory, the maximum bonus would be 3 times target (target × 200% × 150%), a corporate maximum of 250 per cent of target is applied to help overall budgeting.

McDonald's makes the bonus live throughout the year as part of the communications on how the business is doing. A monthly meeting is held for all UK head office and regional staff at the head office in London. There is a live link to the meeting so people unable to attend in person may watch the meeting online. During the business summary a 'TIP slide' is shown giving the year to date operating income – the main component of the bonus. This clearly relates the state of the business with potential bonus.

The UK also use a bonus calculator that sits on the intranet. Any employee can use it at any time to see what their potential bonus could be depending on the business performance. This aims to engage the TIP participants and helps explain and embed how the plan works. This is illustrated as Figure 10.5.

FIGURE 10.5   Bonus plan calculator

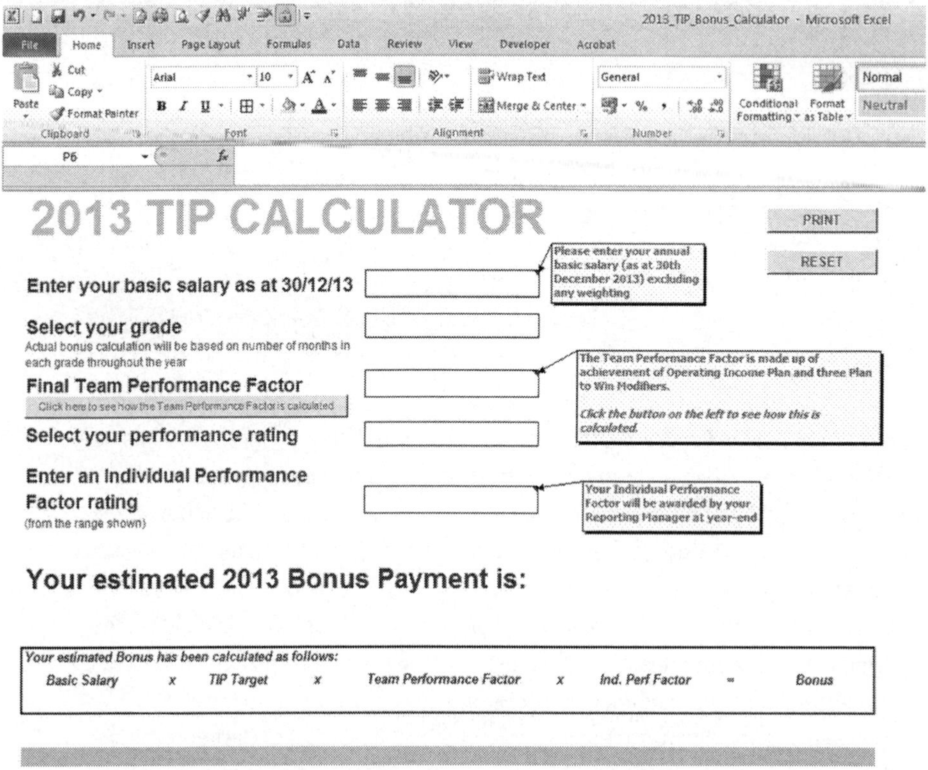

Summary

The three bonus plans are summarized in Table 10.5 below

Impact

Whilst the bonus cannot be taken in isolation in having a causal impact, it is part of a whole approach to managing performance and sharing success. Certainly, McDonald's in the UK has had impressive financial performance over the last few years.

The compensation and benefits team will have occasional focus group discussions with managers to check their views on the plans and comments are taken into account in future adjustments to the plans. The overall views that they get are that the plans are effective.

TABLE 10.5   Summary of bonus plans

	Restaurant crew	Restaurant management team	Head office and regional staff
Participants	29,500	5,000	550
Bonus period	Monthly	Quarterly and annual	Annual
Key factors	Customer satisfaction	Quarterly: customer satisfaction sales Profit Annual: Crew turnover and Employee satisfaction	UK Operating income Other key Company measures Personal performance
Measures	Absolute and relative	Absolute and relative	Absolute
Bonus type	Increase in hourly rate for fortnight following	Fixed cash by level of manager	Percentage of salary

The 2012 annual employee attitude survey shows an increase in scores from 2004:

- I am proud to work for McDonald's   +24 points

- I am motivated at work   +16 points

- I am paid fairly   +16 points

Also since 2004 the crew turnover rate has halved.

11 Recognition and non-cash reward

Introduction

In Chapter 10 I discussed the things to look out for when reviewing and designing bonus plans. I raised some issues that suggested that using recognition and/or non-cash can work more effectively than bonus:

- Where the time span of impact is short – do not use annual bonus plans but immediate or very short-term non-cash awards.
- Where a direct financial incentive is unlikely to work – use recognition.
- Complement bonus plans with non-cash.

Whilst I believe that more effective use of recognition will deliver more value than bonuses, it is not a nil sum game. For reasons I will discuss here, I believe that recognition is important for everyone. The 2013 CIPD Reward Management survey shows that around 35 per cent of organizations currently use individual or group-recognition awards.

Reward and recognition are often linked together, sometimes within a job title. But whilst reward is about the components I have discussed in this book, recognition is something different. Recognition is more about behavioural change than reward. The underlying principles of recognition are also different to those that many attribute to reward. In Figure 2.2 I positioned recognition between reward and learning and development. Although this book is about reward, I believe that recognition has an important complementary role and non-cash reward can enhance reward practices. So in simple terms, I believe that a reward practitioner needs a good understanding of recognition.

In writing this chapter I have drawn on my last book, *A Guide to Non-cash Reward* (2011), which covers the subject in detail.

Recognition

Definition

I define recognition as, 'A process of acknowledging or giving special attention to a high level of accomplishment or performance, such as customer care or support to colleagues, which is not dependent on achievement against a given target or objective. It can be day-to-day, informal, or formal' (Rose, 2011). The core of this definition, is that recognition is not based on targets.

A much simpler way of thinking about recognition is '...catch them doing something right' (Blanchard and Johnson, 1993). We seem to be hardwired to look for the negative in people and situations, encapsulated in the view of an engineering director who said, 'My people know when they are doing a good job, 'cause I'll tell them when they're not.' Recognition is all about trying to counter that attitude.

Recognition versus incentives

Recognition programmes are not incentive plans. Incentives seek to change behaviour by using the incentive of a carrot. An incentive plan (and some performance-related pay plans) carries the message, 'You do that and I will give you this.' A recognition programme, on the other hand, seeks to reinforce the great things people are already doing, so the message is, 'What you just did was great, thanks very much.'

Going back to Chapter 3 on motivation, incentives are an extrinsic motivator, whereas recognition is acknowledging the intrinsic motivation of the individual.

Recognition programmes typically seek to recognize behaviours (and maybe achievements) that fulfil overall values, such as excellent customer service, but are difficult to record in terms of objectives even if it was desirable to do so. It may be difficult to define precisely the behaviour that will be recognized, for example in the area of customer service, in particular given the emphasis on empowerment, but it might be captured in the phrase, 'I'll know it when I see it.' This is not to say that a recognition programme should be unfocused, simply that it is not an incentive scheme.

British Airways simply, but effectively, differentiates as follows:

- Reward – is about pay or compensation
- Incentives – are about meeting targets
- Recognition – is about saying 'thank you'

Juran (2003) says:

- Rewards are salary increases, bonuses, and promotions keyed to job performance and usually conferred in private, primarily focusing on conduct of operations using performance appraisal or merit ratings.

- Recognition is typically non-financial and consists of 'ceremonial' actions taken to publicize meritorious performance.

I have summarized the three key differences between recognition and incentives in Table 11.1.

TABLE 11.1   Recognition continuum

	Recognition	**Incentives**
Motivation Theory	Reinforcement	Expectancy
Impact	The message	The prize
Cost (€)	Low	High

The motivation theories, which are covered in the Appendix, are quite different. Of most importance is to distinguish between where the impact is placed. With an incentive, the outcome (prize or money) must be valued by the participants, so typically will be large. But it is quite the opposite with recognition. A prize may complement the recognition but that is not core – it is the message that makes the impact with recognition, not the prize. This is where many recognition plans come unstuck. Using a 'reward focus' puts emphasis in the wrong place. Recognition is about reinforcing the great things people already do, not incentivizing them to do something.

Of course, with the emphasis on the message rather than the prize, the cost of recognition is very low compared with a financial incentive. Recognition can make a huge impact for its cost compared with expensive incentive plans. I would suggest that most organizations would do well to carve out a very small amount from their bonus budget (or an even smaller amount from their pay budget) and spend it on recognition instead.

Impact of recognition

Hertzberg found that lack of recognition for work done was a very significant factor for negative feelings about the job. It was also most often the only factor present in the situation, compared with others that more commonly appeared in combination. The research found that whereas achievement on its own can be a source of good feelings about the job, recognition is rarely independent of achievement. 'A feeling that you have achieved and a feeling that you have been recognized are the two most frequent feelings that are associated with an increase in job satisfaction.' (Hertzberg *et al*, 1959) Hertzberg also said that the act of recognition, which is not related to a specific sense of achievement, becomes a fairly trivial factor. (Hertzberg, 1968).

Maslow (1970) believed that people need both self-respect or self-esteem and the esteem of others (recognition). The Appendix provides more on Hertzberg and Maslow.

Recognition and engagement

There is now considerable evidence to show that there is a correlation between engaged employees and organizational performance. Improving engagement also correlates with improving performance. Much of the evidence is summarized very effectively in the MacLeod and Clark (2009) report.

Gallup has done some substantial work on examining engagement within organizations. It has surveyed over 4 million employees worldwide. Analysis it did of more than 10,000 business units and over 30 industries found that individuals who receive regular recognition and praise:

- increase their productivity;
- increase their engagement amongst colleagues;
- are more likely to stay with their organization;
- receive higher loyalty and satisfaction scores from their customers;
- have better safety records and fewer accidents on the job (Rath and Clifton, 2004).

There are very many pieces of research across organizations that have found recognition to be a very significant factor, such as:

- A survey of 1,500 US employees found that the number one workplace motivator was recognition. Specifically, the top motivator was personal congratulations from the manager for a job well done, which should be immediate and specific (Caudron, 1995).

- A survey of companies across eight countries found that praise was ranked as the top motivator of front-line employees, just ahead of money and time off (The Ascent Group, 2009).
- The US Department of Labor report that the number one reason why people leave their job is because they 'do not feel appreciated' (Rath and Clifton, 2004).
- The Roffey Park Management Institute (2007) found that the fourth biggest motivator of managers was recognition by others. The third biggest demotivator of managers was a lack of recognition.

A lack of effective recognition when people have really put themselves out can cost an organization in many different ways as the following quote illustrates:

> 'Recently we were very busy and a few of us worked a lot of hours to help out, but we didn't get any thanks for it. We're just not appreciated at work. If someone were looking for a job, I wouldn't tell them to get one where I work.'
>
> *Susan, 43, Customer Service Representative* (CIPD, 2006)

When someone feels like Susan does, they will lose pride in their organization. Instead of being an ambassador for their company they can be turned into a detractor. And all for the sake of a few words of thanks and genuine appreciation. It doesn't take much. With poor recognition, employees may not only discourage others from joining the organization, but they may also be more likely to leave.

Recognition plans

It is helpful to consider recognition as a continuum as shown in Figure 11.1.

FIGURE 11.1   Contrast between incentive and recognition

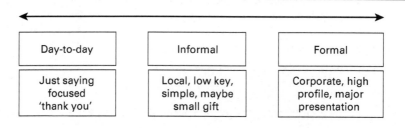

In my experience, organizations tend to look to 'solve recognition' by implementing formal plans shown on the right, but I suggest that the place to start is on the left. Encourage local informal recognition.

How to do it

Key factors

Recognition can be oral and face to face, and ideally with something to remember, or it may be in writing. The big advantage of it being in writing is that it then provides the memory itself; the recipient can show their family and friends. Especially as almost all written communications nowadays are electronic, a hand-written note can work particularly well. But as mobile company 3 have found, a text message can be effective within the sort of population for whom this is the communication norm. But whatever the medium this is what to aim for:

- Be genuine – if you don't mean it, then don't say it.
- Be timely – make it as close to the event as you can.
- Be personal – use the person's name.
- Make it specific – refer to exactly what they did.
- Be clear – explain why it is appreciated.
- Make it public – find a way to let others know.

You may not manage to hit all six of these factors every time, but keep them all in mind and aim for as many as you can. But the one you need to ensure every single time is the first – make it genuine. As Kouzes and Posner (2007) say, 'When people see a charlatan making noisy affectations, they turn away in disgust.'

Establish guidelines

If you want to start at the informal end of the recognition continuum, I suggest developing a simple set of guidelines for managers. It is also sensible to ensure that recognition is a value reflected in manager and leadership development and training. Rideau, based in Montreal, has demonstrated correlation between recognition and financial outcomes and has shown that coaching managers in recognition can have the greatest impact.

Here are some examples of the sort of things companies have used as part of their guidelines on recognition.

Southwest Airlines in the US have a simple guide to recognition which can be summarized in the following (Freiberg and Freiberg, 1996):

- Say 'thank you' often.

- Always celebrate people from the heart.

- Make heroes and heroines of employees who glorify your company's values.

- Find people who serve behind the scenes and celebrate their contributions.

- Create a celebration signature – balloons, photos, trophies.

- Celebrate at work like you do at home. Celebrate at home like Southwest does at work.

A major retailer summarized its approach in a set of 10 dos and don'ts, which formed part of a larger resource pack for managers:

Do:

- Relate to the culture of the business.

- Link to company values.

- Give responsibility to individuals and line managers.

- Learn from how people have used the tools.

- Make it simple to use and understand.

Don't:

- Assume everyone likes to be recognized in the same way.

- Assume everyone likes to be recognized at all.

- Assume it will solve all business challenges.

- Make it bureaucratic.

- Underestimate the power of a simple thank you.

Sky has developed a range of tips and advice primarily as guidance for new managers, which emphasizes four core elements.

Four Elements

Everyone wants to do a good job for their customers and their colleagues and wants to enjoy what they are doing. Everyone needs to be acknowledged and valued for their contributions, especially if they do something outstanding.

The key to effective recognition is to understand that recognition comes in many forms. Here are four key elements of recognition that really work:

Praise

- Keep it in proportion – don't go over the top, yet don't underplay it.

- Do it at the right time – don't wait, the sooner the better.

- Clear & simple – don't ramble, tell them what they did and what you appreciated about it.

Thanks

- Say Thanks – that's what it's all about.

- Be sincere – Say it like you mean it and find the right time to do it.

- Think about how you deliver it and vary from time to time eg in person, via e-mail.

Opportunity

- Constantly look for opportunities to recognize people – there's potential with every interaction eg emails, feedback, team meetings, delegating, one-to-ones.

- Also provide people with new opportunities – to contribute in new ways, learn new skills, to have more freedom in how they approach work.

Respect

- Recognize people not just for what they do – but who they are.

- Consider employee needs as you make decisions and you recognize employee value.

▶

One size doesn't fit all

One of the most important things to remember with recognition is that one size does not fit all! As you know what will truly engage one person may switch off another. By operating mass recognition with no appreciation of the individual needs and interests of your employees – at best they'll feel half acknowledged!

Some people like public recognition – others prefer a private thank you. Some like to engage in corporate schemes like Team Sky – others prefer things on more informal basis. So keep things fresh and continually review what you do.

Key tips for individual recognition:

- Identify how each individual contributes.

- Learn more about people around you and what's important to them.

- Recognize unique contributions with personalized recognition that takes interests into account.

What some great managers do:

- Great managers make recognition part of their day-to-day approach to leadership! They find ways to add employee recognition to every interaction.

- When you delegate – add a little praise.

- When you receive updates from your team – thank them for being so prompt, thorough or accurate.

- When you hold a team meeting talking about a new challenge – express confidence in your team's ability to meet that challenge.

Some techniques of great managers we found:

- 'I ensure I say good morning to every single person in the team – really simple but it creates a more positive environment.'

- 'I write a hand-written note to each direct report on the anniversary of their hire date – thanking them for their contribution and picking out key achievements.'

- 'I go to each member of the team at the end of the day and find out what went well for them that day.'

- 'Occasionally I'll ask a more senior manager to send a letter of acknowledgment to those that have made a significant contribution in my team.'

- 'I sometimes take time to stop and think about each member of my team in turn and when I last recognized them – then take action as required!'

- 'I make a conscious effort to ask for feedback as often as I can –
  I get some great insights and people appreciate getting a chance to
  air their views.'

Don't get caught out with some common recognition myths:

- Some people believe being paid is the only recognition that
  people need.

- Some managers believe that recognition takes us too much time.

- Some managers believe if they do too much recognition they'll be
  accused of playing favourites.

Non-cash – for recognition and incentives

I have so far emphasized the value of recognition. As I have said, recognition is all about the message, not the prize. However, within the continuum I gave in Figure 11.1, there is a place for some tangible awards. But they should not distract from the message – a recognition programme with high-value awards is almost certainly missing the point and may be destroying value.

Non-cash recognition can be very simple and low key and make a significant impact.

> 'If you want to acknowledge something straight away, it's easy to get the person a bunch of flowers or take them out for a meal. It's the little things, but things that are in control of the manager, so that it happens instantaneously and everyone knows why.'
>
> *Manager in Kent County Council Service Centre* (Brown and West 2006)

Non-cash tangible awards can also be used to complement or replace a financial incentive. I believe that non-cash can beat cash in a number of ways that I will explain here.

A study that offered either cash or non-cash incentives of an equivalent value found that the group who received non-cash awards performed twice as well as the group who received cash. But the cost was the same. Although when asked, those incentivized with non-cash, said they would have preferred cash (Jeffrey, 2004).

We all like to receive presents; there is something about receiving a tangible award that trumps cash. But there are four main reasons for using non-cash awards over cash particularly for recognition and incentive programmes:

- Differentiation – non-cash awards differentiate a recognition programme from pay. I was consulting with an organization that paid recognition awards through payroll. The managers' dominant view was that the important part of the process was the pay. The great majority of recipients, on the other hand, said that the most memorable and important part was receiving the letter of thanks recognizing what they had done.

- Memory value – the effect of non-cash awards is longer-lasting than cash. It is sometimes said that cash is a motivator for as long as it takes before it is spent. In contrast, every time a non-cash item is used or enjoyed the recipient may remember why and how they earned it.

- Perceived value – the perceived value of a non-cash award can be much higher than the actual cost, so that a non-cash award is valued more highly than cash of the same value. It may be that the organization can source an award much cheaper than the individual could. This may be because they are buying in bulk or can negotiate a better deal with a supplier or through a third party.

- More personal – a non-cash award can be tailored to the needs and interests of the recipient, showing a greater amount of thought than a simple cash sum would reflect. We only need to think about the difference between receiving a birthday present of a cheque or a really well-chosen gift.

Think for the moment of a highly-paid employee. I don't know what that would mean in your organization, but let's say on a salary of £250,000. What would happen if you gave someone like that a cash bonus of £150? I have known people on that sort of salary level claim to be insulted with a bonus of £50,000, so £150...? You would never do it. But think about replaying this.

How about if that individual received a hand-written note from the CEO thanking them specifically for something they have done plus a good bottle of champagne? Even grossed up for tax the cost of the champagne is about the same as the £150 we just considered. But the message is entirely different and appreciated.

Non-cash incentives

For a non-cash award to be, in any way, effective as an incentive it needs to be desirable. Where sales incentives use such awards they are typically something special such as an exclusive holiday or a very expensive watch. In a sales environment such awards are built into the budgets so that people who have sold enough will have generated the revenue that pays for the prize as well as their cash bonus. So they are entirely self-financing as you only qualify if you have met the clear financial targets.

Like any other non-cash award these can be talked about in a way that cash cannot. They allow people to demonstrate their achievement, meeting an ego need, often having been won through qualifying in a sales competition.

Prize draws

Where an organization wants to use non-cash as an incentive (or recognition), but wants to manage costs, they can use a prize draw approach. The prize will be desirable but perhaps not quite at the level described so far. When an individual achieves a certain level of target they can gain an additional opportunity to win a prize. So the highest achievers will have a better chance of winning a prize than those who were not so successful.

Prize draws rather than a single award can be considered in different situations other than sales. For example, small short-term competitions for teams or individuals who all achieve a similar level of achievement may each have an opportunity to win a prize. Not only does this make it easy to budget, but allows each to be a winner although only some will receive the award(s).

What to do

Here is a checklist of how you can add value by using recognition and non-cash awards for recognition and incentives (Rose, 2011):

Recognition

- Create a culture where you celebrate successes.
- Turn 'values' and 'behaviours' into stories.
- Consider carefully the impact and relationship between the new recognition programme(s) and existing HR programmes, such as reward, performance management and learning and development.
- Start with the day-to-day/informal low-key line manager-based programmes before bringing in any more formal programmes.

- Issue support and simple guidelines to managers, but do not use specific goals or measurable objectives as the criteria for recognition awards.
- Build recognition into your learning and development programmes for managers.
- Build on existing informal programmes that some line managers may already be running.
- Provide budget and infrastructure for a range of relatively low-value non-cash awards that can be matched to the person and the achievement.
- Try to make it as easy as possible for managers to source gifts and prizes, perhaps by using a third-party provider.
- Be very wary of simply buying an off-the-shelf recognition system.
- Encourage recognition to be delivered in an open and public way immediately after the event; it should be sincere and should match the award to the person and the achievement.
- Do not try to limit recognition to a budget or a quota.
- Avoid recognition programmes that are time bound, like employee of the month.
- Do not try to measure the success of a programme simply by the number of awards made but do monitor the trend of usage.
- Use engagement surveys and exit interviews over time to monitor the impact of recognition strategies.
- If you are going to have some form of panel, consider using previous winners, rather than senior managers, to make decisions on those to receive awards.

Incentives

- Look at how you can use non-cash to support your cash incentive programmes.
- Use non-cash for short-term competitions and targets.
- Remember the value of social recognition of achievement as part of the incentive design.

Both

- Monitor the programmes and expect to refresh them regularly.
- Ensure you cover the tax issues for non-cash awards.

Steps to introduce a recognition programme

- Review rationale for considering a recognition programme – survey evidence, exit interviews, management views etc.
- Research – visit other organizations with recognition programmes.
- Discuss outline ideas with key stakeholders in the organization; agree concept in principle.
- Form design and implementation project team.
- Define aims of the programme – medium-term aims and overall success; establish what success indicators will be.
- Consider how you will explain the relationship between the recognition programme and other HR programmes, particularly reward and performance management.
- Ensure that 'recognition' is reflected in management development and training.
- Establish an outline budget.
- Develop scheme structure – who can recognize who, level of awards etc.
- Review opportunity for sourcing awards – in-house or outsource using a third-party provider?
- Agree proposals with senior team as appropriate – timing, budget etc.
- Develop programme guidelines for manager.
- Develop guidelines for all employees if it is also peer-to-peer recognition.
- Launch.
- Review regularly; monitor both programme and success indicators. (Rose, 2011)

Summary

Recognition is all about the message – catching people out doing something right, rather than the reward. If you start from a reward perspective you are likely to get this wrong. But non-cash can help reinforce the message. Non-cash can be much more memorable and have a disproportionate impact for its cost if used in the right way. Non-cash awards can complement a cash plan.

Questions

- Do you have any evidence of the extent to which people feel adequately recognized?

- Do any of your programmes confuse recognition and incentive?

- What opportunities are there to enhance existing cash programmes with non-cash?

- Could you allocate a small proportion of your bonus budget or pay review budget to fund recognition?

- Should you discuss with your learning and development colleagues to investigate how a joint approach to recognition could add value?

CASE STUDY   HSBC

This case study illustrates the way in which an organization can develop an approach to recognition by keeping the emphasis where it should be – on the local message – but whilst providing a simple set of guidelines and infrastructure organized by HR. It shows how to get the balance right between control and local discretion.

HSBC's UK bank developed an approach to recognition anchored in new HSBC Group values which were core to repositioning the bank following the financial crisis. It gave maximum discretion to managers in how to recognize people, including local arrangements. It also provided an imaginative infrastructure within which managers could procure gifts and awards in a simple, flexible, but managed way.

Background

HSBC Holdings is one of the largest banking and financial services organizations in the world, serving 58m customers across 81 counties and territories. Operating through its four global businesses of Retail Banking & Wealth Management, Commercial Banking, Global Banking and Markets, and Global Private Banking, the bank employs over 250,000 people based in 6,600 offices around the world.

In the UK, close to 50,000 employees are located across 1,800 sites including the group's headquarters in Canary Wharf.

HSBC aims to be the world's leading international bank, taking advantage of its strong network of businesses in the markets most relevant to international trade and capital flows and where wealth is being created.

Banking crisis

The banking crisis of 2008 had a huge impact across the global economy and the financial services sector, including the much publicized collapse of some well-known global banks and UK government bailouts of Lloyds and RBS. Risky lending, inadequate reserves, complex products and ineffective governance were seen as core contributors to the financial crisis. Blame has been pointed in many directions, including the use of inappropriate reward systems common across the banking industry, which have been widely held to have encouraged excessive risk-taking and mis-selling of products. There was much criticism of the culture within banks that had allowed the situation to arise. Governments and regulators reacted to the crisis with a range of measures including even stronger regulation and a specific focus on change to reward policy and practices.

HSBC changes

Although widely regarded as having survived the financial crisis better than other banks, HSBC had suffered along with other major banks during the crisis and implemented far-reaching changes in a number of key areas, including reward.

A practical step was to review its reward policies including sales incentives and stop those that could encourage mis-selling. A more holistic issue was the need to take a completely different approach centred on shifting its culture to be successful in the future in light of the new world. The core of the change in culture has been an emphasis on values. This is not to pay lip service to empty values, but to make values central to the way in which everyone in the bank behaves. HSBC expresses this as follows:

> 'At HSBC we put great emphasis on our values. We want to ensure that our employees feel empowered to do the right thing and to act with courageous integrity. By doing so we will meet the expectations of society, customers, regulators and investors.'

The HSBC values are:

- dependable and do the right thing;
- open to different ideas and cultures;
- connected to customers, communities, regulators and each other.

These values are core to the way in which the bank operates and are built into learning and development. They are also a key part of every employee's performance review which reflects behaviours in terms of values as well as performance. Incentive payments which link to the performance rating, only trigger where minimum standards have been achieved in relation to measured satisfactory behaviour of values.

Recognition

Whilst the bank had a range of recognition programmes, there was historic confusion between what recognition was and what reward was, with little differentiation between the two. This meant plans that were notionally considered recognition (in practice non-cash awards) were often linked to cash-based incentives and so in some cases had become part of the problem.

HSBC now clearly differentiates between reward and recognition:

- Reward is fixed pay and variable *incentives* rewarding performance against objectives.

- Recognition is about saying thank you to colleagues who demonstrate outstanding behaviour of values in practice *after* the event.

Recognition is also used to help embed the values, not only for the individuals recognized, but also by communicating the most powerful recognition stories widely to help demonstrate what HSBC values mean in everyday practice.

HSBC's UK Bank has three strands to its recognition framework: Shine awards, National Champions awards, and business-specific awards. Each is covered below.

Shine awards

This programme was launched in 2009 and has been continually refined over recent years. The emphasis of Shine awards is the message from the manager to thank people for what they have done or, more typically, how they have done it in support of one or more of the values. HSBC ensures that Shine budgets are not used for sales or productivity incentive awards, for example campaigns or competitions.

HSBC wanted to make the line manager central to fostering a 'thank you' environment and to support them rather than control what they did. HSBC did not wish to be prescriptive about exactly how managers use Shine, but there are short guidelines which are shown below.

Recognition Guidelines for Shine cardholders, ie front-line managers and team leaders

Recognition toolkit

SHINE is for recognizing individuals and teams demonstrating outstanding examples of HSBC values and business principles in practice.

In everything we do we should act with courageous integrity, having the courage to make decisions based on doing the right thing for our people, our customers, our shareholders and the wider community. Individuals and teams working in the UK Bank are eligible to receive a SHINE award for role-model behaviour of our dependable, open, or connected values.

Good recognition is as much about how you say thank you as the supporting gift or award.

Please consider the following best practices when you are planning to give a recognition award:

Best Practice 1: Plan for success

Look back at recognition awards you may have made in the previous quarter and create a plan for the forthcoming quarter. In your plan include:

1 Specific behaviours you would like to recognize.

2 A good balance between individual and team awards.

3 A spread of awards across your business area and job roles.

4 When and where you plan to make the awards.

Best Practice 2: Be clear and specific

Awards that have the most impact on recipients are those that are clear and specific. These can include:

1 What behaviour is being recognized? For example, does the recipient show strong or role model behaviours supporting our values of dependable, open or connected?

2 Why the specific behaviour stands out as strong or role model behaviour?

3 What is the 'story' behind the awardees' achievement?

4 How the behaviour being recognized impacts on superior customer service, either internally or externally?

▶

◀

Best Practice 3: Know your colleague

When making an award, there are two key things to consider:

1 Whether you make the award in a public or private setting. Whilst a 'celebration' is most effective in a public setting and can motivate others to be recognized in future, you should be sensitive to the awardee's personality. Some colleagues may not seek the limelight and prefer a private recognition.

2 If you are supporting the recognition with a tangible award, what award will have the most impact? Some might consider a 'voucher' to represent a 'monetary' award. Others might prefer an item that has a more memorable and lasting impact. Or an award which has a personal relevance to the awardee's interests outside work, for example a CD of the awardee's favourite band. This is an opportunity for awarding managers to show they take a personal interest in the awardee's life outside work.

Best Practice 4: Get ready

Research shows colleagues value a personal thanks and in the following order:

1 face-to-face;

2 hand-written note;

3 phone call;

4 voice message;

5 e-mail message.

Best Practice 5: Timing is everything

Awards should be made as soon as possible after the strong or role model behaviour has been demonstrated, providing the maximum benefit in recognizing an individual's contribution. The supporting gift should have an appropriate value, and please remember little awards for little things done well are an important part of recognition.

In summary: Use the S.T.O.P. principle

- **Be Specific** – people need to know what you are recognizing and why, showing that you really know and value what the awardee(s) have done and providing context for others.

▶

- **Be Timely** – recognition should be timely to the action showing that that you are paying attention and that you care. By saying thank you in person, or by writing a personal note or a thank-you card, and by supporting this with an appropriate gift, you will maximize the impact of the recognition.

- **Do it Often** – by making recognition part of your day-to-day management style it will become natural. The more sincere the recognition, the more your team will feel valued and engaged.

- **Be Personal** – by knowing what motivates people, you can customize the way you say thank you, making a more memorable impact and experience for the awardees.

Around 2,000 managers and team leaders have been provided with a prepaid MasterCard that they can use to buy small gifts that are appropriate to reinforce the 'thank you' message. HSBC encourages managers to make frequent 'little and often' recognition awards as they have demonstrated that there is a link between award frequency and measured employee engagement. They know that the award is just a small part of the thank you; it is the recognition from the manager itself that is important and they want to encourage recognition touching as many people as possible.

The budget for the cards is held centrally and is based on £25 per year per person in the manager's team. To encourage the little and often approach, the card is loaded quarterly and any balance at the end of a quarter is lost. Guidelines on using the card state that the cardholders are responsible for:

- Ensuring HSBC values and saying 'thank you' becomes part of the culture in each business area.

- Ensuring card funding is used appropriately.

- Recording the awards made each quarter on an internal Shine Card Administration reporting system.

- Using Shine cards securely. HSBC Bank plc is the corporate sponsor of the programme and is liable for funding payments.

At the end of each quarter each cardholder completes a simple online schedule giving, for each award:

- the name of each recipient;
- the date;
- the value;
- why the award was given;
- the type of gift awarded.

This allows effective record keeping to ensure that any tax due is accounted for to HMRC, through the PAYE Settlement Agreement. Non-voucher and non-meals and entertainment awards of £10 or less can be excluded under HMRC's triviality guidelines, providing an individual employee does not receive more than four such awards during the tax year. Whilst Shine allows managers almost complete freedom in the nature of the supporting awards they procure via Shine prepaid cards, an online reporting and reconciliation system allows the programme managers in HR to monitor the level and quality of activity. In 2012 some 20,000 individual awards and 8,000 team awards were made through Shine.

Business-specific awards

Local award programmes can be developed within broad corporate guidelines, including regulatory guidelines on recognition arrangements. These will be funded locally and are to meet particular local needs. In 2013 there were six such local schemes in operation. Behaviours recognized must also demonstrate corporate values. The aim is to 'recognize colleagues who have made a significant impact in their business area or communities, showcasing our values'. The financial value may be greater than the Shine awards, but must still be appropriate to ensure that it remains a support to the message rather than any type of incentive. Award details are captured for compliance and tax purposes. Tax on any local awards is also settled though the PAYE Settlement Agreement.

National Champions awards

Launched in 2012 these awards are for 'recognizing the best of the best – colleagues who live, breathe and work our values'. In 2012 local management nominated around 400 people who had already been recognized through a Shine award or business-specific award. The nominations went to a panel made up of representatives from the business areas, HR and Organization Development. 120 winners received a letter of congratulations from the Head of UK Bank and an Olympics ticket package; 133 'runners-up' received a letter of congratulations from the head of HR and a further award. So 63 per cent of those nominated for the National Champion awards received further recognition and there was no one winner.

To help communicate what the values look like in practice, three of the most inspirational stories from the 120 winning stories were made into three-minute videos and were shown at the CEO annual conference. These stories help show what living the values actually looks like. So they help embed the values by lifting them off the page and turning them into meaningful stories.

HSBC continually reviews how best to manage its recognition programmes and at the time of writing it was reviewing to what extent, if at all, it would amend this plan.

Impact

HSBC believes that its approach to recognition is successful. In particular it has evidence that shows the success of the Shine awards. From a survey of cardholders it found that:

- 90 per cent agreed that Shine 'makes a positive impact on the ability of cardholders to source awards cost-effectively'.

- 86 per cent agreed that the programme awards 'make a positive impact on how valued colleagues feel'.

The bank undertakes regular employee surveys and these have found that receipt of a Shine award correlated with a higher engagement index score across the UK Bank. The average employee engagement index score was 87 for those who had received a Shine award and 83 for those who had not.

12 Long-term plans

Bonus plans, covered in Chapter 10, are contingent pay for a period of up to one year. In this chapter I cover long-term plans which provide potential financial value to the recipient over a period of more than one year. Typically, long-term plans deliver value in around three years.

Long-term plans aim to support retention and long-term performance as a balance to an annual plan that, by definition, rewards annual outcomes. There are two main categories of long-term plan: those paying out cash and those using company shares.

Role of long-term plans

There are many reasons why long-term plans are used for executives and employees which I will discuss. The main ones split by executives and employees are shown below:

Executives:

- To align the interests of the executives with the interests of the shareholders.
- To encourage focus on the longer-term success of the company.
- To provide some financial retention.

Employees:

- To share the longer-term financial success of the company.
- To be used to help communicate messages about the financial success of the company.
- To provide tax efficient value to employees.

If you are considering introducing one or more long-term plan you will need to build the business case with the costs and benefits. Whatever the rationale, which may be one or more of the points above, you will hope that the plan will have the desired effect. But one of the benefits of most long-term plans, particularly cash plans, is that they do not pay out unless the individual is employed when the plan vests. Therefore, one strategy you may wish to consider is moving money from short-term salary or bonus to long-term cash which only pays out if certain conditions have been met, including the individual still being employed. You should consider giving enough upside to the payout to offset the delay in payment over monthly salary or annual bonus.

Share plans

Overview

The particular type of share plans used will depend on the tax regime in the country. In the UK there are certain share-based plans that are approved by Her Majesty's Revenue & Customs (HMRC) and, so long as they are operated within HMRC rules, carry certain tax concessions. Some of the tax issues are highlighted in Chapter 7.

Whilst the detail of exactly how a particular share plan will operate will differ between plans, underpinning all plans are one of two basic types: share options and share grants. Each is described below.

Share options

This gives the recipient the right (option) to buy a certain number of shares in the company at a future date but at a predetermined price, so long as they are still employed. The option price may be the market price when the option is granted to the recipient or may be the market price discounted by, say, 10 per cent or 20 per cent. The recipient may need to save the money to pay for the shares or it may be that they are a nil-cost option, in which case they do not need to save any money. Here is a simple example.

> ## Example
>
> An employee is granted 6,000 share options on 1 March 2012 with an option price of £2.15. The option vests (when the employee may first exercise the option) after three years: 1 March 2015. The employee may exercise the option at any time from 1 March 2015 for a period of one year.
>
> In March 2015 the share price is £3.00. The total value is therefore £18,000 (£3.00 × 6,000). The employee decides to exercise the option and requests to sell enough shares to cover the cost of £12,900 (£2.15 × 6,000) that he has to pay.
>
> The employee sells 4,300 shares at £3.00 per share which produces the £12,900 needed and keeps the balance of 1,700 shares worth £5,100. He may have chosen to sell all the shares and received the £5,100 profit in cash. There may be tax due on the profit of £5,100 if held in shares or taken as cash. He may sell some more shares to pay the tax if required.
>
> Had the market price in March 2015 been £2.00, £0.15 lower than £2.15 ('underwater'), it would not have made sense to exercise the option as he would make a loss. However, as the employee has one year within which he may exercise the option, he can watch the share price and so may be able to exercise the option some time within that period and may still make a gain. The option would lapse with no value at the end of the year.

Stock grants (or restricted stock)

An executive may be provisionally granted shares that will not be owned by the executive until they vest. Typically, they must be held for two to five years, before they become owned by the executive and may be sold. In some plans the recipient is granted units that may be converted into shares on the vesting date. Like the options, above, the value would normally be lost if the individual left the company before the vesting date. There may also be some performance conditions that apply that increase or reduce the number of shares that vest. Relative or absolute performance conditions are common for executive plans, such as total shareholder return and earnings per share.

With a stock grant the value is always available on a specific date in the future – the vesting date. Contrast this with an option, which may have no value if the market price is lower than the option price, although there will normally be a period of some months or years during which the option may be exercised. Restricted stock holders may also receive value equivalent to the dividends paid before the vesting date, which is not available to shareholders.

> ### Example
>
> An employee is granted 6,000 share units on 1 March 2012. The grant vests 1 March 2015 when the units will be converted to 6,000 shares and become owned by the employee.
>
> On 1 March 2015 the share price is £3.00, so the total value of the shares he now holds is £18,000 (£3.00 × 6,000).
>
> There may be tax due on the profit of £18,000, so the employee may sell some share to pay the tax due.
>
> Had the market price in March 2015 been £2.00 the shares would still have been worth £12,000 (£2.00 × 6,000).

The further distinction between share plans is executive share plans and all-employee plans. Compared with cash plans, any form of share plan is complex and needs very effective communications regardless of the recipient. I have spent a considerable amount of time explaining their share plan to senior executives. So whilst the nature of the communications may be different, it is equally important for recipients of executive plans and all-employee plans.

Share plans are common for executives in quoted companies and can be very substantial. Whereas all-employee plans are less common and have a much lower potential value. I cover each below.

Executive plans

The senior executives of a company are accountable to the shareholders for the long-term success of the business. To reinforce this aim the majority of senior executives in large quoted companies will have some form of share plan. The M&S case study at the end of this chapter gives such an example. The simple aim is that normally this should align their interests with those of shareholders so that they gain or lose as do shareholders. Clearly this needs to be a significant part of their reward package if it is to achieve its aim. The size of grants for the most senior executives in the larger companies can be very high and executives can build very substantial value of company shares via options and grants.

According to PwC (2012), the number of companies that operate share option plans has dramatically decreased from 2006 levels where about two-thirds of companies had an option plan in place. By 2012 only 15 per cent of FTSE 350 companies operated an option plan. Performance share plans (restricted stock grants) have become the incentive vehicle of choice for the majority of companies replacing options for executives.

There are three main criticisms of share options, particularly for executives, which may have led to this:

- As the downside of an option is always the same (no value) but the upside can be considerable, options may encourage risk-taking behaviour.

- Option holders do not receive dividends, whilst shareholders do and may rely on them as income. So the leaders who determine, or strongly influence the dividend policy and who hold a considerable number of options may be influenced to reduce dividends and use the money in other ways to boost the share price from which they are likely to benefit.

- A much larger number of shares is needed as options to deliver a similar value to restricted stock, therefore options may dilute shareholders' value more than restricted stock.

KPMG (2012b) shows that chief executives of FTSE 100 companies received awards of performance shares as a percentage of salary as follows:

Upper quartile	338%
Median	203%
Lower quartile	187%

This sort of annual award can build very considerably and may dwarf salary and annual bonus. KPMG also shows the median total remuneration for chief executives of FTSE 100 companies for 2012, which I give as Table 12.1. Note that the vested shares column also contains other payments, but it is only the value of shares that vested in the year, not the total value of the grants held and yet to vest.

TABLE 12.1   Median total remuneration of FTSE 100 CEOs

Basic salary	Bonuses	Vested shares and misc. payments	Total earnings
£830,000	£990,000	£1,272,000	£3,092,000
27%	32%	41%	100%

Most executive share plans will have some form of performance conditions relating to key measures of corporate success. These will typically be measures that are to be delivered that will influence the number of shares that vest. Table 12.2 shows the performance conditions used in FTSE 350 companies (KPMG, 2012b).

TABLE 12.2   Performance conditions applied to new plans adopted during 2012

*TSR	15%	Net asset value	4%
TSR and #EPS	15%	Share price	4%
Profit	11%	Dividend payout	4%
EPS	8%	Return on capital employed	4%
EPS and other	8%	Return on equity	4%
Strategic	8%	Other	4%
TSR and other	7%	None	4%

* Total Shareholder return
# Earnings per share

Not only are executive share plans very common, but it is also common that companies require executives to hold a minimum value of shares at all times, such as one to three times their salary. This is to try to ensure that at least a reasonable proportion of their wealth is at risk in the same way as other shareholders. The majority of FTSE 350 executives actually have a shareholding in their company of over 200 per cent of salary. Fidelity (2012) state within their principles of ownership that they '… encourage management ownership of shares and over time we expect executive directors to build a shareholding in the company which is material in relation to their remuneration such that over time dividend income can become a meaningful component of their remuneration'.

Employee plans

Types of employee share plan

There are now two main types of all employee share plan approved by HMRC and which carry some tax advantages – either free of tax or subject to capital gains tax not income tax on any profit:

- Save as you earn share option scheme (SAYE) introduced in 1980 – the employee can save up to £250 a month for three or five years. At the end of that time they may use the money saved (plus any interest, which is set by the government) to exercise an option over company shares at an option price which was set at the start which may have been discounted by up to 20 per cent.

- Share Incentive Plan (SIP) introduced in 2000 – this is a more complex but flexible plan than the SAYE as it has four components:

  - Partnership shares: this is a savings plan similar to the SAYE, however shares are bought at market price rather than via an option. Employees can save a maximum of £125 per month from gross salary (before tax deductions, so they receive full tax relief on the savings). Company shares are bought by trustees, normally monthly and are held in trust. If they are held for five years (not sold by the employee within that time), they are free from tax and national insurance regardless of their value at the time.

  - Matching shares: this links to the partnership shares, where the employer can enhance the value of the shares purchased by the employee by matching the number of shares purchased by up to two matching shares for every one purchased.

  - Dividend shares: dividends paid on SIP shares can be re-invested in further shares known as dividend shares up to a maximum of £1,500 per participant for each tax year. There is no tax or national insurance due if the shares are kept for at least three years from the date of award.

  - Free shares: The company can give up to £3,000 of free shares to employees in each tax year on an equal basis. Tax and national insurance is payable if sold within five years.

Prevalence of employee share plans

Whilst executive share plans are common – all directors of the larger quoted companies will have some form of stock, they are a little less common for employees. Nevertheless, HMRC figures show that at the end of the 2012 tax year there were approximately 1,200 companies operating one or more all-employee share schemes. These companies operated 530 SAYE schemes and 840 SIPS:

- SAYE: 380,000 employees received an option grant in the year. The average value of shares over which options were granted was £3,800.
- SIP: 4,030,000 employees were awarded or purchased partnership shares; 2,620,000 received matching shares; 820,000 had dividend shares and 380,000 received free shares.

The number of companies providing an SAYE has reduced since the SIP was introduced in 2000.

Spreading risk

Senior executives may be required to hold a certain number of shares in the company to try to strongly align their interests with those of the shareholders. One of the factors analysts monitor is sales and purchases of shares by senior executives as it may be an indication of their view of the future of the business.

But most employees who may receive shares from an employee share plan should consider the extent to which it is appropriate to have a potentially significant part of their savings in the shares of one company, particularly their employer. They are unlikely to hold shares, or at least not a significant amount, in any other company. A financial adviser will emphasize the need to spread risk, or 'not putting all your eggs in one basket'. I do not think that employees who chose to sell shares as they are able to should be considered in any way disloyal or not committed to the company. Just that they are taking a sensible personal investment decision with their money.

Aim and impact of employee share plans

Employee share plans can be used to try and engage employees more with the overall success of the company and to take interest in the key financials that they can influence and the stock market will monitor. Share plans can help demonstrate the link between changes that may be being made within the company – such as pay freezes, reorganization, redundancies – with organizational performance which may be reflected in the share price. So they can help to communicate messages about the financial success of the company.

Where the company is successful with an increasing share price, an employee share plan will help directly give a financial benefit so that participants share in the longer-term financial success of the company.

Within the HMRC rules, an approved employee share plan can be very tax efficient, so whilst there remains a cost to the company they can provide tax efficient value to employees.

Research shows that employee share plans can have a positive effect on retention. McConville *et al* (2012) found that 50 per cent of employees thought they would stay longer because of their share plan participation compared to approximately 30 per cent who did not. The research also found that employees who really understood the share plan in which they participated reported higher levels of attitudinal and behavioural impact when compared to employees who felt they did not. This emphasizes the need to ensure you work hard to communicate the way the employee share plan works if you want it to have an impact.

The other main factor that will influence the impact an employee share plan will have is the extent to which it delivered against participants' expectations – primarily the expectation of a financial benefit from the plan. Employees whose expectations had been met were more likely to state that participating in the share plan had led them to feel:

- more likely to stay at the company longer;
- more integrated into the company;
- more committed to the company;
- happier to spend the rest of their career with the company;
- more likely to feel part of the family in the company;
- more motivated to work for the company;
- felt a greater sense of personal ownership for the company;
- more likely to produce better quality work;
- more likely to consider cost implications to the company of their actions;
- more likely to make suggestions concerning issues that affect the organization.

Cash plans

Reasons for using cash for long term

Long-term cash plans are typically used where shares are not available. This may be for a number of reasons:

- **No shares** – an organization with no shares – not-for-profit, public sector, private company with no shares outside the owners etc.

- **Share limit reached** – where shares may be used but are unavailable due to limits having been reached. Through shareholder approval there will be a maximum number of shares that may be used for executive and employee plans which may not be breached; for example 10 per cent of the issued shares.

- **Time or simplicity** – where time or the requirement for simplicity means cash may be more expedient. A share plan can take some months to set up and get approved whilst a cash plan can normally be set up very quickly. A cash plan has almost complete flexibility whereas a share plan will normally have to meet various compliance rules.

- **Tax issues** – for a global business in a country where share plans are taxed very heavily or in such a way as to make a share-based plan unworkable.

- **Set-up cost** – for a global business in a country where there may be only one or two participants and the set-up cost would be very high compared with cash.

- **Top-up** – to top up a share plan, for example because of an error in the original grant.

- **Underpin shares** – if you want to provide a minimum value for an existing share plan to aid retention you can use a cash plan that may pay at vesting of the share plan.

- **Retention** – for retention, only where certainty is required cash will be better than shares.

Phantom share plans

A phantom share plan is a cash plan that is designed to replicate the main elements of a share plan. It may be used for some of the reasons mentioned above. It is cash, so is taxable like any other cash payment. Phantom plans can be designed in many different ways. But a typical plan would look like this:

Example phantom share plan

Participants are granted a fixed number of units. There will be a set of plan rules issued explaining the plan, good and bad leaver provisions, how units are valued etc similar to the bonus plan rules covered in Chapter 10. To help reflect the value, being similar to a share plan, a certificate may be issued showing the number of units and the vesting date.

The units may be valued using a formula, for example based on the value of the company using a multiple of earnings or other measures. Where shares exist the unit price may be pegged to the market share price. Whatever method is used it will need to be stated in detail in the plan rules.

At the end of the term, say three years, the plan vests and a payment is made based on the value of the units multiplied by the number of units held. The payment will be made through payroll so that tax and national insurance is deducted correctly.

Retention plans

If the objective is retention, then the best model is to use a fixed cash amount payable at a given point in time in the future with no performance conditions. The amount payable needs to be greater the longer the period the recipient needs to wait. The term is likely to be two to four years; typically three years.

There is evidence that shows that executives will discount the value of a future payment (shares or cash) by over 20 per cent p.a. (PwC, 2011). This means that a deferred bonus (or share) award payable after three years will have perceived value of only around half the level of paying it immediately. The less certainty there is of the payment, for example because of performance conditions, the greater the discount individuals apply.

The balance between time and value is a matter of judgement of what seems reasonable. There is no point in making the amount too small as it will have no effect. As the PwC survey suggests, it generally needs to be a larger amount than you might first think. It is always best to consider the amount in terms of a percentage of salary. One way to look at this is to ask yourself what percentage of your own salary would you consider a significant amount that is likely to help retain you for between two and four years. My suggestion as a starter is:

TABLE 12.3   Cash retention value required over time

Term	per cent of salary
2 years	35–50
3 years	60–75
4 years	100–125

Nowadays, four years is a long time in an organization so I would not exceed three years. However, you may wish to provide a second grant 12 months after the first for an equal term or provide two grants initially – one for a smaller amount vesting in two years and one for a larger amount vesting in three.

An employer may lend an employee (not director) up to £10,000 interest free and there is no tax payable by the employee on the benefit. So one route, for smaller retention plans could be to provide such a loan and then write it off (grossing up for tax) at the end of a period. This may be worth considering for example for graduate trainees (see endowment effect in Appendix).

Whatever the detail, a cash retention plan will only have an effect where everything else is reasonable. A very disengaged employee will not stay whatever the amount.

Steps to develop a long-term cash plan

The steps you should take are very similar to those required to develop a shorter-term bonus plan covered in Chapter 10. You might find it helpful to refer back to that chapter in this context, but here is a summary of the key steps:

- **Aims and design principles** – you need to establish why you are developing this plan – what it is meant to do, what problems to help solve etc and agree this with the key stakeholders assuming that they are not potential beneficiaries. It may be the remuneration committee. If you are looking at a cash retention plan it is valuable to first develop some design principles that you can agree with the key stakeholders. Here are some simple principles that you may wish to develop for your own situation:

- Significant: to have real retention value the amount payable must be meaningful, particularly taking into account the time before payment
- Phased: to ensure there is always some value at risk and no cliff edge
- Simple: to be able to explain easily to participants
- Certain: to increase perceived value there needs to be guaranteed payment not dependent on performance measures

- **Target population** – who is the plan for. This is likely to be a much smaller population than a short-term bonus.
- **Alignment** – think through the relationship between existing short-term bonus and the long-term plan you are considering.
- **Measures** – what will drive any payout – corporate goals, share price retention only etc?
- **Term** – agree the term, typically two or three years.
- **Funding** – how is the plan to be funded? Agree with your finance colleagues and ensure that they know the details so that they can accrue for the plan each year.
- **Distribution** – is any sum guaranteed as long as the individual is employed when the plan vests or what variables are there?
- **Scenario testing** – look at range of scenarios including corporate changes such as takeovers, acquisitions, mergers, and decide if any would trigger payment.
- **Document** – draft plan rules and agree them.
- **Briefings** – ensure leaders are briefed.
- **Communication** – to the participants. This is likely to be lower key than an annual bonus that is open to a larger population.
- **Manage** – where there is a link to some measures, communicate the progress throughout the plan term to the participants.
- **Review** – and adjust for a further grant as appropriate.

Deferred bonus

Some annual bonus design provides for a percentage of the bonus to be deferred for one to three years before it will be paid out. There are two main reasons for doing this:

- To link the deferred part of the bonus to some longer-term performance factor. This issue came to the fore during the banking crisis, from around 2008. It became clear that annual bonuses had been paid out based on results in the year. However, the apparent value was short lived and what at the time was thought to be profitable business on which bonus had been paid, turned out to be loss making. Bonus deferral became more common to only pay out when the longer-term results are known.

- To help retention. Some organizations report a peak of resignations immediately after the annual bonus round. To help retention, deferring some bonus each year will mean that there is always something to lose on resigning.

Summary

Long-term plans can provide some incentive for the longer term to give some balance with an annual bonus, encourage retention, reward joint success and help communicate the issues in the business. There is an argument that there should be more weight to longer-term plans than annual plans for the leaders of the company to encourage focus on the long-term success of the business. You should consider what value tax efficient share plans can deliver if you are in a company where they can work. But even if not, a cash plan can fairly easily be developed to help reward and retain over a period of a few years.

Questions

- Do you have people in your organization who make an impact over a period of more than one year for whom you should consider some form of longer-term plan to counter short-term incentives?

- Should you consider moving some short-term reward to longer term?

- Do you have a reward statement or policy that makes reference to reward over the longer term? If not, should you consider adding something?

- If you are in a quoted company, should you consider if an approved employee share plan could add value?

CASE STUDY   Marks and Spencer plc.

This case study illustrates how a long-term commitment to employee and executive shares can become a reflection of the culture of the organization. The organization undertakes regular reviews of all its share plans to ensure that they are fit for purpose.

Marks and Spencer has used a range of share plans as a fundamental part of its reward strategy for senior managers and all employees over more than 30 years.

Background

Marks and Spencer (M&S) is a FTSE 100 company and one of the best known retailers in the UK. The group had a turnover of over £10 billion to March 2013. It operates in over 50 territories worldwide and employs almost 82,000 people. In the UK, M&S employs over 74,000 people of whom 69,000 are store based. M&S has about 766 stores across the UK and around 418 international stores. It also has a growing e-commerce business. For 2012/13, the UK turnover of just under £9 billion was split between food (54 per cent) and general merchandise (46 per cent).

M&S launched Plan A in January 2007. It currently has 180 commitments to achieve by 2015, with the ultimate goal of becoming the world's most sustainable major retailer. Through Plan A, M&S is working with its customers and suppliers to combat climate change, reduce waste, use sustainable raw materials, trade ethically, and help customers to lead healthier lifestyles.

Share plan philosophy

M&S has a long history of providing executive and all employee share plans. The company sees them as an important element in their reward packages. For executives and senior managers they are to provide incentive to achieve long-term business success and to help attract and retain leaders who are focused and motivated to deliver the business priorities which are aligned to shareholder interests.

Share schemes that are offered to all employees help encourage an interest in business success and foster engagement through sharing the success of the company. M&S's stated philosophy for this approach is as follows:

> *'Sharesave, the Company's Save As You Earn scheme (SAYE) is an integral part of the Total Reward package, encouraging and supporting our people in taking responsibility for their future financial security, and enabling them to invest in the future success of the business as a Marks & Spencer Shareholder.'*

Executive and management share plans

M&S operates three main share plans for their executives and senior managers. The first two are the Performance Share Plan and the Deferred Share Bonus Plan. The stated aims of these two plans are to:

- link individual reward with long-term company performance and align the recipients with shareholders' interests through long-term financial performance and delivery of business strategy.

In each case the value of the shares and dividends paid on vesting/exercise is subject to tax and National Insurance. Each of the three plans is described below.

Performance Share Plan (PSP)

This is the primary long-term incentive plan for approximately 100 of the most senior managers and executives in M&S. Discretionary awards may be offered based on a percentage of salary. The percentage by which any award vests after three years is determined by performance of key performance measures. For awards made in 2013/14, the performance metrics and targets are as shown in Table 12.4.

TABLE 12.4 Performance metrics and targets

Weighting	Performance metric	Commercial rationale	Basis of measurement
50%	Earnings per share (EPS)	Rewards focus on bottom-line performance	Based on annualized underlying EPS growth over three-year performance period
20%	Return on Capital Employed (ROCE)	Rewards efficient use of capital	Based on average ROCE % over three-year performance period against predetermined targets
30%	Revenue	Rewards top-line growth in line with business strategy	Based on strategic growth targets: 10% for each of UK, International and Multi-channel

For each of the metrics shown, there is a minimum threshold performance at which up to 20 per cent of the award vests and a maximum at which 100 per cent vests.

The remuneration committee regularly reviews the performance measures to ensure that they are correctly aligned to the business strategy and appropriately reflect the key drivers of shareholder value.

Deferred Share Bonus Plan (DSBP)

M&S provides an annual bonus opportunity for all employees in a range of plans. At the highest level the maximum annual bonus for executive directors is 200 per cent of salary for 'maximum' performance. For approximately 450 of the most senior managers and executive directors there is a compulsory deferral into shares of a percentage of any annual bonus. This was introduced in 2005. The deferral is 50 per cent of any bonus for the top 150 directors and senior managers and 33 per cent for the next 300 senior managers. There are no further performance conditions other than continued employment and the shares vest after three years so long as the recipient remains employed. In addition, the value of any dividends earned during the deferred period is paid on vesting.

Restricted Share Plan (RSP)

The purpose of this third plan is to help retain and recruit senior managers who are vital to the success of the business. Discretionary awards may be made at recruitment or as part of the review of an individual's reward package. Shares are held in trust for one to three years at which point they are released to the employee so long as they are still employed. In certain circumstances, the company may attach performance conditions to the award. The value of any dividends earned during the restricted period is also paid at the time of vesting.

All executive directors of M&S are required to hold shares equivalent in value to a minimum value of 200 per cent of salary for the CEO and 100 per cent of their salary for the other executive directors within five years from their date of appointment. For this purpose holdings include the net value of all unexercised awards under the Deferred Share Bonus Plan and Restricted Share Plan.

Executive Share Option Scheme (ESOS)

M&S also has an approved ESOS which was used annually up until 2005. At that time the remuneration committee reviewed the executive share plans (as it does regularly) and concluded that the aims of the business would be better met by the combination of the PSP and DSBP as described above, rather than using share options. Therefore, since then no options have been granted under the scheme.

Employee share ownership – Sharesave

M&S has operated an approved Sharesave plan continuously since 1981, the first time they became available. Whilst there is no explicit link made between business performance and the share plan, the company believes that the scheme encourages participants to take a keener interest in the business performance, particularly around the quarterly trading statements and annual results. M&S also believes that an employee share ownership scheme allows participants to directly share from the success of the business.

M&S considered if the new SIP would be a suitable alternative when it was introduced, but concluded that the Sharesave was a better fit for their population. This was because they believed that the SIP five-year holding period to benefit from the tax advantages was too long, there was a greater risk profile than the Sharesave, and finally it would mean providing it to all including the more senior people already receiving shares.

Plan outline

The plan allows employees to save any amount between £5 and £250 each month for three years. At the end of three years they can get their money back or use it to buy shares at a 20 per cent discounted price. The price at which options are offered is 80 per cent of the average mid-market price for three consecutive dealing days preceding the offer date. Sharesave launches each year in October and is open for all employees who started working for M&S before 1 July in that year.

Take-up

Around one third of employees participate in Sharesave at any one time. This is a high percentage for the retail sector. Currently there are around 25,000 people participating with a total of around 45,000 accounts. There will always be more accounts as employees may participate in a three-year Sharesave each year so long as their aggregate monthly savings do not exceed the HMRC maximum of £250. The average saving is £112 pm with around £32m pa being saved in total.

Changes over time

The basic model of allowing saving in the full range allowed by HMRC (£5 – £250 pm) and the maximum 20 per cent discount have remained unchanged since 1981. However, for many years M&S offered Sharesave with the full range of saving options allowed by HMRC – three, five or seven years. During the regular annual review in 2003 it found that the seven-year option was rarely selected and so it was dropped. The five-year option was dropped in 2008, when M&S found that fewer than 15 per cent of participants chose this saving period.

The Sharesave that matured in January 2008 was the first for several years for M&S where the option price was below the market price – it was underwater. Whilst the participants were free, as they always are, to just take the cash savings rather than exercise the option, M&S wanted to do something more. It recognized that participants were in the plan to become shareholders. It therefore set up a special share-dealing service where employees who had funds maturing could use their savings (from a minimum of £150 up to their total savings) to buy shares, which was all undertaken on a specified day. This was simple and employees could benefit from lower dealing charges than if they bought shares as individuals. Over the three years where the option price has been underwater at maturity, about 2,000 people have used this service.

Communications

M&S does not recognize a union, but it has an extensive system of employee involvement through the Business Involvement Groups (BIG). Representatives from each location (store, distribution centre, head office etc) are elected to represent their colleagues. There will be between two and 25 representatives depending on the number of people at the location. From the location level there is then a regional, divisional and national structure, and then up to a European works council.

M&S discusses proposals for changes to Sharesave with the appropriate BIG representatives. For example, it discussed with them the proposal to move to three-year savings only and the way to handle the underwater issue in 2008.

M&S recognizes the criticality of effective employee communications to promote Sharesave. Each year it runs a one-day high-level planning session, including BIG representatives, to review what worked or did not work the previous year and consider how best to communicate that year's Sharesave launch. It works with the scheme administrators to review communications concepts that are refined to get to the final design.

It tries to keep the messages focused and as simple as possible, avoiding jargon. For example, rather than using 'option price' it uses 'discount price'. M&S realized that there was little benefit in spending considerable time detailing the options and process at maturity at the point of launch as this just overcomplicated the communications. So it explains simply that at the end of the three years the participants can get their savings back or buy discounted shares. It then leaves the detail to when it is needed – at maturity.

Communication materials are high quality, to the same standard that M&S uses for customer merchandising and promotions, and reflect the 'look and feel' for the launch. The company balances out the need to keep in line with Plan A and the focus on reducing paper and the needs of its employees, the majority of whom do not have internet access at work. Therefore, the key communication method is a brochure sent to the employee at home. However, all employees are encouraged to apply online, by text or phone.

Individuals receive a targeted invitation that differs between those currently saving and those who are not. Existing savers receive a separate section in their brochure giving details of their current Sharesave schemes.

A wide range of supporting materials are used to help maximize awareness in the 'backstage' areas of stores and to try to create a buzz about Sharesave. These include:

- 6ft-high pop-up displays
- Coffee table brochures
- Posters that change weekly during the Sharesave enrolment period
- Bunting
- Features in *People Quarterly* and *Your M&S*
- Intranet

There are regular store team briefings and M&S and the administrators run surgeries where employees can ask questions about the scheme. Communications include some short quotes from named individual participants and simple examples such as the following:

> The table below shows how your savings build up and ideas of what you could do with that money.
>
> ## TABLE 12.X
>
> | Monthly saving | Saving after 3 years | What you could do with your savings |
> | --- | --- | --- |
> | £10 | £360 | Get a laptop computer |
> | £20 | £720 | Buy a new TV |
> | £50 | £1,800 | Help pay off your student loan |
> | £100 | £3,600 | Have a dream holiday |
> | £200 | £7,200 | Drive a new car |
> | £250 | £9,000 | Put down a deposit on a new home |
>
> But if you decide to buy some M&S shares with the exclusive discount your savings could be worth a great deal more!

Impact

Having a Sharesave scheme for over 30 years has become a part of the culture of the business. It is seen to have been very successful in fostering employee engagement, encourages a real interest in the performance of the business and allows employees to share success.

M&S has undertaken research that shows a correlation between levels of Sharesave participation, staff turnover and levels of employee engagement. As shown in Table 12.5 (comparing two M&S stores), M&S has one of the lowest employee turnover rates in the retail sector and about half of the employees have been with the company for more than five years.

TABLE 12.5   Comparison between two M&S stores

	Store A	Store B
Sharesave participation (%)	30	7
Staff turnover (%)	8	39
Employee engagement (%)	88	62

Benefits

Benefits are the non-cash parts of reward that are provided by the employer either to all employees or differentiated by level. Benefits can be a significant part of reward, but even when they are, they are generally poorly understood.

Which benefits to offer and why

Analysing your benefits

Most organizations have a range of benefits that may have been built up over years, often with little strategic intent. I believe that it is worth standing back and questioning quite why we have each of the benefits we do in our organizations. Other than for a legal requirement, such as paid holidays, I suggest that there are only five reasons why an organization chooses to provide particular benefits to its employees:

1 Market need: a benefit is needed to compete effectively in a particular market; eg executive stock.

2 Tax efficiency: a benefit that has tax and/or national insurance savings over cash; eg pension.

3 Organization provision: a benefit that the organization can provide much cheaper than can an individual; eg private medical insurance.

4 Moral: the employer believes that they have a moral responsibility; they may also consider a reputational risk if the benefit is absent; eg life assurance.

5 Organization value: there is a direct value to the organization as well as to the employee; eg company car.

I recommend that as part of a review of benefits you analyse your existing benefits against these five criteria on a table as illustrated in Table 13.1 below. The table is completed for some of the benefits for an organization using ticks and crosses. You may want slightly more fine tuning by using, high, medium and low.

TABLE 13.1   Five criteria for providing benefit

Benefit	Market need	Tax efficient	Organization provision	Moral/ reputation	Organization value
Private medical insurance			✓	✗	✓
Employee assistance programme	✗	✓	✓	✓	✓
Company car	✗	✗	✗	✗	✓
Life assurance			✓	✓	✗

One way or another these criteria are about delivering value to the employee and the organization that cash does not. We always need a balance between taking a total reward approach – to maximize overall value – and distinguishing between the separate elements of reward which are there to do different things.

There is no simple answer to the question of which benefits you should offer. There are statutory benefits such as a minimum of 20 days paid holiday a year and the requirement to offer a pension with automatic enrolment. But other than these you could choose to offer no benefits. However, looking at the rationale above, there is a case to be made for offering benefits that can deliver more value to the employee than the cost to the employer. So even smaller organizations should look at the opportunities that may be available.

Provision of benefits

The 2013 CIPD Reward Management survey gave a list of 71 benefits provided by participating organizations (up from 57 the previous year). Table 13.2 shows the top 10 and bottom three by provision to all employees.

One interesting point from this survey is that benefits are mostly provided on a common basis, (single status) to all employees rather than by seniority.

TABLE 13.2 Most and least common benefits provided

Benefit	Provide to all employees %	Provision dependent on grade/seniority %
Top ten:		
Paid leave for bereavement	92.9	0.9
Pension scheme	83.8	4.9
25 days and over paid leave (excluding public holidays)	73.0	19.7
Life assurance	68.7	6.3
Christmas party/lunch	66.9	2.1
Tea/coffee/cold drinks – free	66.7	2.8
Childcare vouchers	63.3	1.4
Eye-care vouchers	62.9	2.8
On-site car parking	59.6	15.9
Allow internet purchases to be delivered at work	59.5	3.4
Employee assistance programme	56.2	1.4
Bottom three:		
Company car	0.2	37.6
Mobile phone (salary sacrifice)	1.0	7.2
First-home deposit	1.0	0

There were only five benefits in the survey where more than 25 per cent of organizations based provision by seniority:

- car allowance 51.6%
- company car 37.6%
- mobile phone 37.1%
- relocation assistance 32.8%
- flexible time/homeworking 32.3%

There is no doubt from the data that the majority of employers have a single status approach to benefits other than where there is clear market practice otherwise, and the number with status driven benefits is dropping. This has been the trend for many years – to minimize differences in benefit provision. This reflects the cultural trend in most organizations to try to minimize artificial hierarchy and encourage engagement and involvement.

Benefit policy

To provide the framework within which benefits may be provided I recommend developing a simple benefit policy which should be part of the reward policy and should address the following questions:

- Based on the five points above, why are you providing the benefits you are?
- What are benefits meant to do as part of the reward package?
- Will you state broadly how you will position benefits against the market?
- Will benefits be single status or hierarchical?
- How much choice there should be for employees?

When you have developed a policy you can discuss and agree a final version with your key stakeholders.

Moog Inc operates in 27 countries with over 11,000 employees. In some countries the local market may have relatively low levels of benefits eg China where paid annual leave is often set at the statutory minimum of five days. As a global employer, Moog decided that it should provide at least a minimum level of certain key benefits as a minimum standard regardless of the local market. It therefore set minimum standards globally for the following benefits as a part of its benefit policy:

- retirement income saving;
- paid vacation time;
- paid sickness absence;
- medical insurance;
- life assurance.

Some organizations group their benefits into a few categories each of which reflect the core aims of the overall benefit provision. Groupings may be, for example:

- health and well-being;
- your time and flexible working;
- security for your family;
- financial and savings.

The main reason to do this is to help clarify the rationale for benefits and to aid understanding and the value of benefits. It is easier to explain the connections of a relatively large number of benefits if they are shown in a smaller number of groups.

Value

Of all the elements of reward, benefits are, without doubt, the least understood and appreciated. In many cases employees do not even remember that they have a particular benefit that may be costing the employer a substantial amount. There is clearly little point in the company spending large amounts of money on a benefit that is unappreciated; the employer is getting no value from it.

Where benefits are not understood it is up to the organization to do something about it. It is a waste of time setting up a suite of benefits and not spending considerable time communicating them very well. This is the main driver in the use of reward statements which are discussed in Chapter 6 on communications.

Key benefits

The benefits that employers offer will vary considerably, but in this section I discuss some of the main ones.

Insured benefits

A number of benefits are insured. That is to say, the organization, and maybe the employee, pay a premium to a third party insurer to provide the benefit and cover the risk. The employer normally uses a broker to find the most appropriate cover. The policies usually renew annually. Typical insured benefits are:

- Life assurance – commonly four times salary paid out on death in service.

- Permanent health insurance – providing an income of 50 per cent to 75 per cent of normal earnings if the employee is unable to work long term due to sickness or injury.
- Critical illness insurance – providing a lump sum payment on diagnosis of specified illnesses.
- Personal accident insurance – paying a lump sum following an accident. The sum will vary according to the severity of the injury.
- Private medical insurance – paying the cost of private hospital in-patient and out-patient treatment.
- Travel insurance – paying for certain losses while travelling abroad.

Pensions

Pensions are a specialist part of benefits and are subject to a whole set of legislation including the requirement for automatic enrolment into a pension scheme. The Kingfisher case study at the end of this chapter is on its approach to pensions and summarizes some of the main changes it has made. Although there are some hybrid schemes, pension plans fall into one of two types – defined benefits (DB) and defined contribution or money purchase (DC). In both cases their names help describe their differences.

Defined benefit pensions

The pension benefit is defined in a formula and the employer has to contribute enough into the pension scheme to enable the benefits to be paid. A typical DB pension may allow participants to accrue benefits at $1/60^{th}$ of final pensionable salary per year of service. If the individual was a member of the organization's DB pension scheme for 40 years they would be able to retire on a pension of $40/60^{ths}$ or two-thirds of their salary when they retire. It is irrelevant that they may have been on a low salary in the past; it is the salary at retirement (normally defined by a simple formula) that counts.

The pension is payable for life of the member and may continue, usually reduced, for a surviving spouse. The employer will have had to fund the pension scheme to ensure that the pensions can be paid no matter how long the retired member (and spouse) live. This means that as life expectancy has been increasing, the cost of funding DB pensions has also increased. According to the Office for National Statistics, between 1960 and 2010 the average life span in the UK has increased by about 10 years for a man and eight years for a woman.

DB pensions are set up under a trust so that their assets are ring-fenced from those of the employer. The trustees have a legal obligation to run the pension scheme in the best interests of the members. The members will be in one of three groups:

- **Active members** – employees who are accruing benefits eg 60[ths].

- **Deferred members** – former employees who have left the organization but have some accrued benefits that will be payable when they retire. They are not accruing benefits, but the value of the benefits they have accrued is normally increased by inflation.

- **Pensioners** – members who have retired and are now drawing a pension. They may have retired from active service or may have retired from being a deferred member.

DB pensions are clearly a very long-term commitment for an employer. They will need to be contributing whilst benefits are accruing and for the pensions being paid. A DB pension is the one benefit that will still be costing the employer money long after the employee has stopped working.

The risk is almost all with the employer as, whatever happens to life expectancy, annuity rates or the rate of return on investments, the company has to provide enough money to fund the scheme. The value of the assets and liabilities can move very considerably even in the short term, and this volatility makes it very difficult for an employer to budget for the costs of funding the scheme.

An increase in pensionable salary will have a knock-on effect to a pension and the additional funding cost to the employer. This is often not understood. I have seen line managers increase the salary of someone in a DB scheme close to retirement as they think that the cost is small as their salary costs will stop at retirement. But as you see from the following example, the costs to the employer can be substantial.

An employee has 30 years' service in a 60[ths] DB scheme. Therefore, they have already accrued pension benefits of 50 per cent of salary at retirement. With a current pensionable salary of £40,000 this is worth about £20,000 pa as pension. The capital sum required to be funded to provide this is around £450,000.

Let's say this person is promoted and given a salary increase of £10,000 to a new salary of £50,000. Pension goes up to approximately £25,000 and the capital sum required goes up to approximately £563,000. The additional £113,000 becomes an additional liability on the pension scheme and pushes up the funding cost for the employer. The cost of each year's future service also increases considerably.

The huge increase in costs of running a DB pension has meant that the majority of companies no longer offer them for new employees. An increasing number have also stopped providing them for existing employees and have replaced them with DC pensions. It is only in the public sector where this very expensive benefit is still commonly available.

Legislation relating to pensions has changed very frequently, in particular reducing the tax-free limits available. This means that with the current limits on annual contributions and total values, many executives are more likely to look to building stock to provide wealth for future income in retirement rather than pensions.

Defined Contribution pension

This is almost the opposite of a DB scheme. The employer and, almost always, the employee save money into a DC pension scheme each month. The contributions are almost always defined as a percentage of salary. Each individual's saving pot is defined and it increases with the contributions made and by the increase in the investments. When the individual wants to retire, they have a pot of money that they can use to provide an income, within certain limits.

A DC scheme may be set up under a trust or may be run by an insurance company, typically as a Group Personal Pension Plan.

The risk profile is very different from a DB scheme. The longevity risk, annuity risk and investment risk are now with the employee and not the employer. The employer can easily budget for the cost of the scheme as their obligation is only to make the contributions they have stated.

Private medical insurance

Private medical insurance (PMI) covers the cost of private medical treatment; normally consultations, tests, and in- and out-patient procedures. It is a benefit that can be of value both to the employee and the employer, in terms of effective use of time and potentially being able to be back at work more quickly.

Where the employer is paying some or all of the premium, then the employee is liable to tax on that as a 'benefit-in-kind'. There is, therefore, some common interest in keeping the premiums low as it reduces the cost to the employer and reduces the tax for the employee. The cost of PMI is relatively high and the typical increase in annual premium is around 10 per cent. Employers have therefore been taking different actions to try to keep costs down.

For example, introducing or increasing the excess. An excess is the first part of a claim up to a limit, paid by the employee. It normally applies to each individual covered for each year, not per condition. Typical excess levels are

£100–£200. They can have quite a significant impact in reducing the premium. This is because they reduce the amount that the insurer has to pay and also tend to deter employees from making small claims. A £150 excess can reduce the annual premium by around 3 per cent and an excess of £200 can reduce it by around 5 per cent.

Voluntary benefits

Voluntary benefits are facilitated by the employer, sometimes by paying a fee to a third party, but the costs of any benefits are borne by the employee. Voluntary benefits may be some of the insured benefits mentioned above. For example, travel insurance may be part of voluntary benefits where the employer collects the premiums from salary from those employees who want the cover. More common are voluntary benefits such as discount arrangements from a wide range of retailers and service providers. Retail gift vouchers with discounts of 5–10 per cent are often part of the arrangement. This is one of the benefits used in the Guideposts case study at the end of this chapter.

Voluntary benefits can deliver reasonable value to employees for a very low, or nil, cost to the employer so are worth considering.

Flexible benefits

Flexible benefits (flex) is a system whereby individual employees can choose different benefits and different levels of benefits within a given menu to meet their lifestyle but at a neutral cost to the employer. It is normally run through an online system allowing an annual selection of benefits for the following 12 months. A part of flexible benefits is the use of 'salary sacrifice' which is covered in Chapter 7.

The 2013 CIPD Reward Management survey found that just over 20 per cent of the participating organizations operated a flex plan. However, flex was more common in larger organizations:

SME (<250)	12.4%
Large (250–9,999)	23.5%
Very large (10,000+)	44.1%

I believe that flex should be considered by any organization other than the very smallest. Whilst flex was in the past disproportionately expensive for smaller employers, due to the set-up costs, there are now systems that target businesses which were previously too small to make flex a sensible option. An online system requires access to a computer, which would not be available to everyone at work. However, now the expansion of home computers and smartphones mean that even if employees do not have regular access to a PC for their work, they are likely to have access at home.

I have written this section using the format of needing to write a business case to introduce flex. Within this I have, by implication, outlined the main issues that you need to take into account.

Building the business case for flexible benefits

Firstly, you will need to be very clear about why you believe that flex should be introduced.

Research

As part of any consideration on introducing flex it is important to get both external and internal information.

External information

There is a considerable amount of information available on flex. There are four main sources:

- Internet and publications – There are frequent articles and case studies in the HR press and online, particularly *Employee Benefits Magazine* and e-reward.

- Conferences – Flex is now the subject of many conferences. For example, *Employee Benefits* holds an exhibition and conference each year in London. There are also a number of flex providers exhibiting. The CIPD conference held annually in Manchester occasionally has a speaker on flex. But again, there are always exhibitors in the field. Some professional advisers run open conferences on flex.

- Case studies – Look for organizations that have implemented flex. Use your network and consider organizations that have a business relationship with your own – customers and suppliers. Most people will be happy to talk about their experiences and the practical issues they faced.

- Professional advisers – When you get to implementation you are likely to need professional help. But you may also wish to discuss the feasibility of implementing flex early with an adviser. Of course, you are likely to start to incur fees so you will need to budget appropriately.

Internal Information

What information do you already have that can help you in considering the need for flex?

Exit, or termination, interviews may give you some information on how people feel about the benefits you provide and the significance of the benefits provided by a new organization.

Staff engagement/attitude surveys can also give you an understanding of what people think of the benefits on offer. Most engagement surveys have very little in detail on benefits; there is unlikely to be more than one question. So you might want to run an internal survey specifically on benefits. You can run short simple surveys online with easily available software designed for the purpose. Some organizations can run surveys as part of their intranet. They do not need to have more than a dozen questions. The aim is to find out what people already know about the benefits you provide, their value and how they work. Typically, understanding is poor so a survey can show you which benefits employees already value and which ones they do not even remember; what sort of benefits are they interested in and how much flexibility they would like. It is, of course, important to manage expectations in this process.

Suggested outline of a business case

You need to be clear about who exactly are the decision makers and who are the influencers. It is unlikely that a leadership team will make a decision on something like introducing flex without them knowing that it has support within the organization. So you may well need to lobby the people who will influence the decision makers in advance.

The decision-making process will differ between organizations, but you will probably have to draft some form of paper and possibly present to the decision making group, such as the board of directors. Notwithstanding the particular approach you take to build and present the business case, I consider below what such a business case might look like. You should be able to deal with every section if you want to be successful.

Introduction

Explain the purpose of the paper and any relevant background information so that it is clear exactly what it is you are asking to be decided.

What is flex?

It is helpful to ensure that all the readers understand what you mean by flex. You may wish to draw on some of the descriptions from external sources.

Do not go into the detailed design of what you propose, but give a fairly high-level overview of flex. You may wish to give a couple of examples so that the benefits in the next section can be assessed.

Competitor analysis

If this is an important issue you may wish to give a summary of which of your main competitors, or the employment market in general, have flex.

The business benefits

Here you will need to explain under the appropriate number of sections exactly what benefits will flex give you. Some of the main reasons why organizations consider flex:

- **Reinforce culture** – if you empower people in the organization to make decisions more quickly for customers, you may think that flex, which empowers people to make choices over their benefits, will help you reinforce that culture. Benefits set by the employer can seem quite paternalistic compared with flex.

- **Maximize the value of benefits** – many organizations spend a considerable amount of their pay bill on benefits, but employees do not always recognize or understand their value. Reward statements can help improve this understanding, but flex engages people in having to actually do something.

- **Control costs** – benefits are often administered and accounted for separately. The cost of a benefit may not be particularly visible to managers. Flex can help give more transparency to benefit costs and make decision makers more aware of the costs of benefits. Flex can give a framework to cost benefits.

- **Reduce costs** – this would need to be looked at carefully. Although there may be some direct savings from flex, such as employers' National Insurance, flex is not really about saving money.

- **Improve recruitment** – flex can give a competitive edge in recruitment. It can be quite powerful to explain the flex choices to a prospective employee. The perceived value can be very high particularly from someone with fixed benefits. It can also say a lot about the sort the organization you are.

However, you need to present your own organizational benefits. Example sub headings you may wish to use could be:

- harmonizing benefits;
- cultural change – empowerment, reduce status barriers, flexibility;

- diversity of workforce;
- recruitment;
- retention;
- market leading/following;
- employee engagement;
- maximize value of existing benefits to employees;
- help bring together elements of reward towards a total reward position;
- framework to easily expand range of benefits;
- national insurance savings.

Costs and savings

Explain the various direct and indirect costs of implementing flex. Direct costs should cover the cost of technology – purchase/license of software, development costs to existing systems such as HRIS and payroll, external consultancy and advisors fees, administration costs such as running a telephone helpline internally or outsourced communications for launch. You will need to determine with your finance colleagues how some of these costs will be treated in the accounts and will probably need to show the cost over, say, three years. In addition to the set-up costs, remember development and communications costs in subsequent years. You will probably need to be clear in which financial years expenditure will be incurred.

Direct savings are likely to be in National Insurance, consolidation of providers and salary savings through buying holiday being more popular than selling.

Indirect savings are usually more difficult to demonstrate. However, if you expect that flex will help in recruitment what would the financial benefit of an improved acceptance to offer ratio? Support in cultural change, for example, with empowerment and helping to improve customer service may be important. If you have data you may draw on this to illustrate what effect you expect flex to have.

Plan outline

Give enough information about each benefit that you propose to put in the plan for the first year. Also outline plans or ideas for future years.

Timetable

Explain the proposed effective date for benefit choices and the timetable to get there.

Communications

Decision-making groups will need assurance that a flex plan can be communicated and understood so that it will be effective in delivering its objectives. Summarize the communications plans including media and timing.

Summary

Benefits can be a valuable part of the reward package, but only if you are clear on why you have them and you ensure that employees understand how they work, what they cost and their value to them. Flexible benefits are now available even to SMEs and are well worth considering.

Questions

- Why do you offer the benefits you do?
- Should you review all of your benefits against the five points suggested at the start of this chapter?
- Would it be helpful to repackage benefits in themed groups – lifestyle etc?
- Do you know if your employees understand the benefits you provide and their value?
- Should you do some work on the potential opportunities you may have to introduce flex?

Case studies

I have included two very different case studies for this chapter. The first is a charity, Guideposts, and the second is a FTSE 100 company, Kingfisher plc.

Kingfisher has made considerable strategic changes to completely reposition its UK pension arrangements since 2004 including closing its Defined Benefit (DB) pension scheme to 5,000 active members, enhancing its Defined Contribution (DC) scheme which has increased by 19,000 members and planning its long-term pension strategy over 30 years. The case study illustrates the complexity and long-term nature of pensions as well as the need to take a considered strategic approach.

The charity, Guideposts, relaunched its pension plan and introduced two new benefits with the aim of maximizing value to employees whilst containing costs. This was the first step in making other cost effective changes to its benefits over the longer term. The case study shows how a small organization can seek to maximize value from their overall spend on reward through effective use of benefits.

CASE STUDY   Guideposts Trust Limited

Guideposts Trust is an independent charity that helps people with mental health issues, dementia, learning disabilities, physical impairments, and their carers and families to make the best possible choices for quality care services. In some cases their projects aim to help people to live more independent lives. In all cases they aim to reduce social exclusion and isolation and promote equal opportunities, well-being and quality of life for all of their service users.

Services and support include: a 24-hour national dementia helpline and website and a range of community-based services including carer's support services, children's services, mental health services, employment training and day and leisure services.

The head office is in Witney, Oxfordshire, and it has regional offices in Hertfordshire, Warwickshire, Gloucestershire, Suffolk and Essex. There are around 250 people who work for Guideposts and over 200 volunteers. Its turnover is about £10 million per annum.

Issues

In early 2012 Guideposts established its five-year plan. One part of the plan was related to staff: to recruit and retain the people needed to ensure optimal staffing for the services Guideposts ran and wanted to develop. One part of the people proposition was to ensure there was an attractive reward package, but within the context of a charity.

Whilst Guideposts had a pension plan, where the charity matched a 3 per cent contribution from employees with 6 per cent, the take-up was poor. Only 35 out of 250 (14 per cent) were members of the pension plan. There were no other non-statutory benefits. Guideposts felt that improvements to benefits could help enhance the package. It wanted to increase membership of the pension plan and look at other benefits that could be introduced at little or no cost. They were also conscious that they would need to introduce automatic enrolment from February 2014.

Changes made

In the summer of 2012 Guideposts put the management of pension out to tender, which resulted in it appointing a new adviser. Its initial brief was to improve the take-up of pensions and advise on other benefits that could be introduced in the short term at low cost. Guideposts also wanted to take a longer-term view and consider other benefits that may be introduced over the following years. It was important that the charity was able to maximize value to their employees for a low cost for the organization. The initial proposals were to:

- amend the pension plan to make it more attractive;

- introduce discounted shopping voluntary benefits;

- introduce childcare vouchers.

Group personal pension

A new Group Personal Pension was to be introduced via a new provider. It would maintain the simple matching contribution plan, so that if the employee contributed 3 per cent of basic salary, Guideposts would contribute 6 per cent. But it also introduced the option of operating this via salary exchange (salary sacrifice, see Chapter 7 on tax issues). The way in which Guideposts decided to operate this was that the whole of the employer and employee National Insurance saving was reinvested into pension. This made the pension even more attractive for no cost to the charity. This is illustrated under 'Communications' below.

Childcare vouchers

Childcare vouchers would be introduced using salary sacrifice, within the statutory limits. With the majority of employees being relatively low paid, and so basic rate tax payers, this would offer good value to employees at no cost to Guideposts. Employees could exchange salary that was subject to tax and national insurance for vouchers that were free of tax and National Insurance, to help towards paying for childcare. Guideposts would make a direct saving by incurring lower national insurance contributions. Although any savings were planned to be used to offset the administration and other costs associated with the benefit changes.

Voluntary benefits

This was an online shopping and discount arrangement that employees could access at home, by smart phone or in the office. It included retail vouchers with a wide selection of shops with discounts of up to 10 per cent. There would be a modest annual cost to Guideposts of £10 per year per employee.

Communications

After discussion with senior managers, a communications plan was agreed. Firstly, in October 2012, the changes were featured in the staff newsletter. This was followed by a simple desk drop and posters that summarized each of the three benefits in one paragraph. Employees were also invited to a roadshow in November (prior to implementation on 1 December) run by the benefit advisers and with an HR adviser attending. More than 100 employees attended the roadshows.

The roadshow presentation used a simple set of slides. For example, it used a simple example to illustrate the pensions savings:

Non-salary exchange

£80	–	Contribution
£20	–	20% tax relief
£100	–	**invested**

Salary exchange

£80	–	Contribution
£20	–	20% tax relief
£25.80	–	Enhancement from NI savings
£125.80	–	**Invested**

The additional £25.80 was made up of 13.8 per cent employers NI saving and 12 per cent employees NI saving.

Impact

Pension membership increased from 35 (14 per cent) to over 80 (33 per cent) on the implementation on 1 December 2012 – 90 per cent of these selected salary exchange.

From introduction in December 2012 to June 2013, one-third of employees had regularly used the discount shopping site.

The take-up of childcare vouchers was disappointing and analysis was being undertaken to understand why and make changes as appropriate.

Future plans

Guideposts made these initial benefit changes to help improve the employee reward package but at a modest cost to the charity. This was only the first step and it plans to review the effectiveness of these benefits and consider other benefit opportunities in the same way – high value to employees at a modest cost to the organization. At the time of writing, Guideposts was looking to promote the benefits further in the second half of 2013. Guideposts was keen to encourage employees to join the pension plan in advance of automatic enrolment it was required to introduce in February 2014.

CASE STUDY   Kingfisher plc

Background

Kingfisher is Europe's largest home improvement retailer with over 1,000 stores in nine countries and a turnover of more than £10 billion. It is a FTSE 100 company and the second largest UK listed retailer, after Tesco. It employs globally 78,000 people and nearly 6 million customers shop in its stores every week. In the UK it trades under a number of brands such as B&Q and Screwfix. In 2001/2 Kingfisher made a strategic decision to concentrate on the home improvement sector and it disposed of a number of subsidiaries such as Woolworths, Superdrug and Comet.

Closing defined benefits scheme to new members

The pensions landscape in Kingfisher was complex due to the history of the UK businesses. By 2004, Kingfisher had over 34,000 deferred members and pensioners in its main DB pension scheme as well as over 13,500 active members. At that time it decided to close the DB scheme to new joiners. It also made changes to the future accrual. The DB scheme had an accrual rate of 1/60th per year of service and the active members were required to contribute 5 per cent of salary. The accrual rate was reduced to $1/80^{th}$ per year of service for service after April 2004 with the contribution rate remaining at 5 per cent. However, employees had a choice at that time to retain the 60th rate of accrual but for a higher contribution rate of 7 per cent.

Defined contribution scheme

In 2004, Kingfisher introduced a new DC pension scheme where the company matched employee contributions. For managers, the company matched employee contributions of between 5 per cent and 8 per cent. For those below manager level, it was a match of between 3 per cent and 5 per cent; this group also had to have 12 months' completed service to be able to join the scheme. Both groups only became eligible for the higher levels of matching after five years of service. At that five-year service date, the onus was on the individual to request to make a higher contribution, and hence receive the higher matched contribution from the company. There was no default fund and the scheme was not being actively promoted by the company.

2005–09 changes

In addition to closing the DB scheme to new joiners in 2004, over the next few years the company also worked with the trustees to de-risk the DB section of the scheme by moving the assets from equities to gilts. The company and trustees were planning ahead for the following 20–30 years.

In 2009, and ahead of automatic enrolment, Kingfisher decided to improve the DC pension scheme. It introduced the following changes:

- Adopted a 'white labelled' approach for the investment funds on offer to the membership.

- Changed fund managers and the external DC administration provider.

- Rationalized (previously 16 funds) and introduced a new choice of nine funds, including a diversified return fund, a money market fund (rather than cash), an ethical fund and a sharia fund.

- Introduced a new 'lifestyle' default fund option.

Strategic principles

In 2011 Kingfisher established a set of strategic principles to frame its UK approach to retirement provision as follows:

- To offer a retirement package that helps support the recruitment, retention and engagement of its UK colleagues which:
  - aims to deliver for colleagues a quality and acceptable level of retirement provision as part of the choices the member makes for their long-term savings;
  - allows for a holistic approach based on fairness and consistency;
  - is competitive (eg average to upper quartile) when compared to other UK retailers;
  - supports employee communications that are transparent, accessible and easily understood by colleagues and members;
  - promotes excellent education of colleagues, allowing for individuals to make suitable and informed investment choices which fit to their lifestyle;
  - ensures a smooth and informed transition for colleagues from active membership into retirement (eg annuity purchase and/or income drawdown);
  - results in a benefit design and provision that is more compatible with the concept of flexible retirement (eg recent legislative removal of default retirement age, annuity revision and wider ability to draw down income from savings).
- Has integrity ie from a governance and regulation viewpoint.
- Is affordable to the businesses, but also moves pension provision away from being purely a 'hygiene' factor to a genuine enabling approach aligned with the Kingfisher corporate culture of engaging employees.

Closing DB scheme and enhancing DC

In February 2012 the company and trustees began consultation with the active membership regarding the closure of the DB scheme to future accrual. The driver of the proposals was to reduce liabilities and volatility rather than to reduce costs. The closure was implemented on 30 June 2012. This meant that the existing active members who had been accruing benefits under the scheme would accrue no further benefits in the DB Scheme, but would be offered membership of the DC scheme for future service from 1 July 2012. At the time there were approximately 4,800 active DB members – about two-thirds of whom were contributing 7 per cent and accruing benefits at 1/60th and 1/3rd contributing 5 per cent and accruing benefits at an 80th.

A wide range of communications was used to help in the consultation process: regular newsletters, videos, a dedicated website and telephone helpline, posters, table stands, pension clinics, presentations, seminars and literature explaining the outcome and decisions the members were required to make. A social media page was created where individuals could voice their opinions, comment and question either anonymously or publicly.

Recognizing that the closure was not driven by saving money, Kingfisher redirected some savings to increase the attractiveness of the DC scheme to all employees. The design of the scheme was reviewed and the decision was made to offer substantially enhanced employer contribution rates, from 1 July 2012, which match or exceed those made by the member. Salary sacrifice (SMART) was also introduced to further enhance the tax-efficiency of the members' contributions. DC pension now became single status with all employees treated the same with equal access to the new pension. The new contribution rates for all were:

TABLE 13.3 DC contribution rates

Employee contribution (%)	Company matched contribution (%)
3	3
4	4
5	5
6	6
7	10
8	14

This change moved the DC scheme from bottom quartile for the sector to upper quartile.

During the consultation with DB members on the closure of the DB scheme, the company and trustee also had to explain to the affected members about the DC scheme. This was a 'step change' for those employees as they had not previously had to actively make decisions in terms of contribution levels, investment options, optional incapacity benefits etc.

A range of new literature was created to educate the membership about the DC plan: member guides and individual and lifestyle fund fact sheets. In addition, a SMART pension calculator was created that allowed individuals to see how much they could potentially save by contributing into the scheme via SMART.

In June 2012, at the time of the DB closure, there were approximately 2,200 DC section active members. An additional 4,800 ex-DB members joined the DC scheme. Nine months later in March 2013 a further 14,000 joined the DC scheme with automatic enrolment. So within nine months the membership of the DC scheme went from 2,200 to 21,000.

The trustee website (**www.kingfisherpensions.com**) was relaunched in September 2012 to improve engagement with members. The website underwent a huge makeover to bring it more in line with the Kingfisher Group branding and to also improve the navigation and purpose.

From March 2013 with automatic enrolment a new first tier was added to the DC contributions where a 1 per cent employee contribution was matched with 2 per cent from the company.

Kingfisher has found that the numbers opting out of pension at automatic enrolment has been very low at around 6 per cent.

Impact

As part of an internal post-implementation review, feedback from the retail HR community is that members find the scheme communications engaging, simple and concise. Visits to the trustee website have increased by several thousand per month.

In 2011 the scheme received the UK SIF Responsible Pension Leader gold award and in May 2012 received the NAPF Pension Quality Mark Plus award for its DC section.

Conclusions

Reward is important as it can cost up to 75 per cent of the total costs of the organization and it carries strong messages. It can play an important part in the engagement of people in the business. But this can only be where it is aligned with the culture and strategy of the business.

Reward may be proactive and seek to help drive business strategy. However, very great care needs to be taken to avoid unintended consequences. Evidence suggests that reward can have positive impact in the short term but may have limited impact in sustaining change in the long term. Financial retention can help but not in the face of other negatives. A determined competitor can almost always offer more to an individual they really want to recruit.

Whatever the reward strategy you are going to establish, you need to agree some clear statements on reward philosophy and strategy with your leadership team and other stakeholders. Invest some time in this stage and, along with whatever corporate values etc there are, you should have the framework to develop changes to reward in the organization. But you need to monitor the internal and external environment to ensure that you spot the issues that either give an opportunity for changes or require changes to be made.

Effective reward management is about both the individual elements of reward and the total cost and value. The different parts of reward may be for different purposes, make impact in different ways and carry different messages but they all cost money to provide, so the organization needs to look at the total as well as the separate elements. There may be trade-offs available between them that may deliver better value. Figure 14.1 summaries the relationship between the main elements of reward, their drivers and associated issues, their relationship with total reward and where they should make impact.

You need to question why you have the reward programmes you do and what they are for. For example, benefits have often developed with little strategic intent, but you can review what they are meant to be doing collectively and individually. Benefits are commonly misunderstood and undervalued. Where this is the case you are wasting money and need to do something about it – change the benefits or communicate them much better.

FIGURE 14.1   Holistic reward model

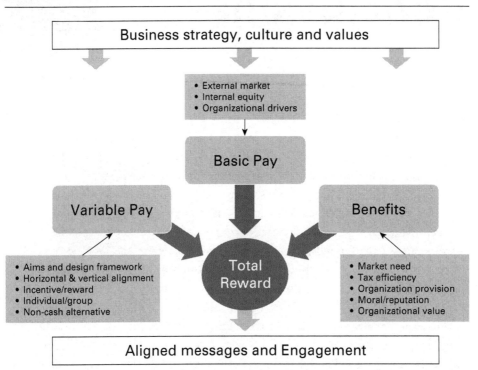

To the extent to which pay must compete in the external market there is likely to be reducing marginal value from increasing salary much above the median. Pay is always one element of the employee proposition but only one of many. Unless you get everything else right, pay will do little to engage people.

Internal equity is a more significant demotivator than absolute pay levels. You need to be clear about what you are paying for and be able to explain it to employees. Whilst pay structures and similar systems may help, ultimately success is likely to be down to managers being consistent in their approach.

Looking through a 'reward filter' you can too easily see reward as the solution rather than in some circumstances the message being core and some element of reward providing tangible reinforcement. Recognition and the thoughtful use of non-cash can have a significant sustained impact over incentives. Maximizing the effectiveness of recognition and performance management require a joint approach with learning and development colleagues.

To meet the challenges of the strategic reward agenda requires a new skill-set for the reward professional including emphasis on communications and change management and using evidence based on relevant academic research. Both depth of reward expertise and breadth of understanding of the wider HR relationships and business understanding are now critical.

What of the future? Here are seven themes to consider:

- **Employee engagement** – reward needs to be considered in terms of its impact on engagement – align reward to values, make reward solutions part of the whole of the 'joined up' employee value proposition, challenge assumptions on extrinsic reward, use qualitative not just quantitative measures.

- **Millennium generation** – want to be seen to make a difference and receive great feedback, want freedom and their own time but a good salary. In reward, you will need to:
  - Find ways to give people more control over time; use different contracts.
  - Concentrate on the outputs, not the inputs.
  - Develop new and even more flexible benefit plans.
  - Ensure better feedback mechanisms and communicate pay messages clearly.

- **Social networking** – Information can no longer be controlled by companies as it used to be. You can find out what it is like to work for a particular organization through social media sites. People will be even better informed about your organization including pay and benefit levels with exchanges of pay data. Therefore, rethink what is 'confidential'. As data will be exchanged anyway outside the organization, look at introducing forums and internal social media sites such as Yammer. Get the performance management system in shape as it will be scrutinized even more.

- **Life expectancy** – continues to increase. Across Europe state retirement pension ages have increased and will continue to do so. Defined benefit pension plans are mostly closed to new employees and are closing rapidly to existing employees. There will be further moves from state to company pension schemes. DB schemes will be closed to all employees and new tax-effective savings vehicles will develop.

- **Environment issues** – are mainstream and employees expect to see their companies implement changes to save energy. We will move to considering the 'whole carbon footprint' of products and of people: home, travel, work. Reward related issues will be:

- Bonuses will need to reflect environmental impact.
- There will be a radical change to cars and a reduction in conventional company cars and no company-provided fuel.
- Greener options will be the norm in flexible benefits plans.
- Greater need to communicate change with low environmental impact – recycled or ideally no paper: electronic only.

● **Shareholder pressure** – Over the last few years there has been an increase in shareholders objecting to companies' executive reward policies. Shareholders, reinforced by further corporate governance legislation, will want to see an appropriate level of reward that reflects company performance. Greater care will be needed in designing executive compensation working with the remuneration committee taking a longer-term view of what company success looks like and the appropriate levels of reward and the potential reputational issues in designing termination terms in executive contracts.

● **Pace of change** – will continue to increase. Reward programmes will need constant review to ensure that they are fit for purpose. This means greater flexibility in reward and perhaps some new thinking on the relationship between common corporate-wide programmes and more discretion to meet the needs of parts of the organization that have changed.

However you view reward, look for those things that will work best for your organization, what will fit with your agenda and not the so called 'best practice' that might be doing the rounds. Critically review the opportunities available against your desired culture, aims and values.

APPENDIX

Relevant research based models and theories

The following models and theories are relevant to an understanding of different elements of reward and engagement and how reward fits into the totality of HR interventions. Whilst an overemphasis on theories does not play well for most managers in organizations, I believe that they can be helpful. For each theory presented I indicate the elements of reward, or reward-related programmes to which I believe they are most relevant. I do not endorse all of the theories as appropriate to the modern organization, in particular neither Principal-Agent theory nor Labour market theory.

Whilst you can find more details on these models and theories from many sources, Perkins and White (2008) cover many of them in some detail.

Endowment effect

Endowment effect, also known as 'status quo bias', is the phenomenon in which most people put a considerably higher price for a product that they own than they would be prepared to pay for it. People tend to try to avoid what they see as a loss (Thaler, 1980).

Relevance – retention plans, incentive plans, reward communications

Equity theory

Equity theory assumes that employees seek to maintain an equitable ratio between the inputs they bring to the employee relationship and the outcomes they receive from it. So this is about an employee's perception of what they receive as an employee for what they have to give. But it does not just apply to the employer–employee relationship. Of critical importance is the way in which employees evaluate their own input/output ratios based on their comparison with the input/outcome ratios of other employees. In other words, an individual may be demotivated if their perception is that they are paid less than someone else doing a similar role.

Inputs in this context include the employee's time, expertise, qualifications, experience, intangible personal qualities such as drive and ambition, and interpersonal skills. Outcomes include reward and flexible work arrangements. Employees who perceive inequity or injustice will seek to reduce it, either by distorting inputs and/or outcomes in their own minds ('cognitive distortion'), directly altering inputs and/or outcomes, or leaving the organization.

Relevance – pay structures, pay review mechanisms, performance-related pay, engagement

Expectancy theory

Vroom's expectancy theory (1964) says that the strength of any motivation will vary according to:

- the desires for a particular outcome;
- the expectancy that action will lead to the outcome; and
- the likelihood that the goal can be achieved.

It is the consequences of attaining a goal that is significant rather than the intrinsic value of the goal itself. The theory is based on a rational cognitive approach, which assumes that a person will, in effect, weigh up the value to them of an outcome in terms of its consequences as well as the likelihood of it happening. So, according to the theory, people will pursue that level of performance that they believe will maximize their overall best interest. This would then predict that a reward given that was not contingent on behaviour, or was not expected to be contingent, would have no effect on the choices that an individual makes.

Relevance – incentive bonus plans

Hierarchy of needs

Maslow considers that there is a hierarchy of needs that is a fundamental part of motivation as illustrated in the figure below.

In Maslow's model it is only when a lower order need has been satisfied that a need higher up the hierarchy may become a cause of motivation. A criticism of this 'ordered approach' is that it implies that everyone requires a similar amount of the basic needs (Hertzberg, 1968).

In most western countries the basic needs are met to a great extent for most people in work; food, water, shelter, security, freedom from fear and

APPENDIX 1   Maslow's Hierarchy of Needs

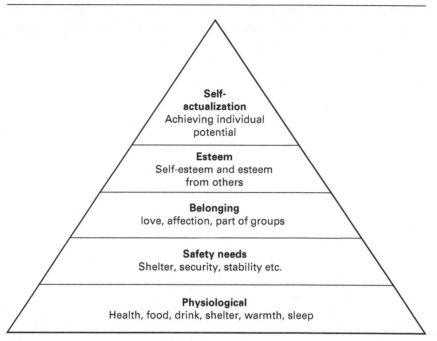

anxiety and chaos, and are taken for granted. These needs may be perceived in terms of salary providing the income necessary to meet basic needs of food and shelter. Benefits such as pension, life assurance and medical insurance meet some part of the safety need. The contractual terms may provide security of tenure and belonging needs may be met by group membership. The state is also likely to provide some form of welfare benefits if needed to meet at least the basic needs.

Relevance – recognition plans, benefits, engagement

Labour market theory

This 'classical' labour market theory considers the market for labour to be a rational market where the relationship between supply and demand will determine the price of labour. The underlying assumptions are that workers can choose between work and leisure and employers can choose to hire or not. The theory follows the same economic model of supply and demand where demand increases the price until supply increases to meet it at a point of equilibrium.

This overly pure model does not reflect the modern understanding of behaviours – as reflected now in behavioural economics, where a number of Nobel prize winners for economics have been psychologists. However, it is important in our understanding of market pressures on salary levels.

Relevance – pay market

Operant conditioning

Skinner developed the model of 'Operant conditioning' from work primarily on animals. This research found that an animal that responded voluntarily to a stimulus (for example a lever in the box) and was rewarded by food as a consequence of its voluntary action tended to repeat the behaviour. The voluntary behaviour was being reinforced by the food. This positive reinforcement was a core element of Skinner's operant theory of motivation. 'A positive reinforcer is a stimulus which, when added to a situation, strengthens the probability of an operant response' (Skinner, 1953).

The opposite of this positive reinforcement is 'extinction' where under repeated non-reinforcement the behaviour decreases and eventually disappears. In the context of pay this may suggest that the expectation and regular delivery of monthly or weekly pay means that it will have little or no motivation effect.

Skinner's theory would argue that '... the only tool needed for worker motivation is the presence or absence of positive reinforcement. In other words, managers do not, as a general rule, need to use punishment in order to control behaviour' (Steers and Porter, 1991).

Relevance – recognition

Organizational citizenship

Organ (1988) defines organizational citizenship as, 'individual behaviour that is discretionary, not directly or explicitly recognized by the formal reward system, and that in the aggregate promotes the effective functioning of the organization'. Organ's definition includes three critical elements of organizational citizenship behaviours (OCBs):

- OCBs are thought of as discretionary behaviours, which are not part of the job description, and are performed by the employee as a result of personal choice.

- OCBs go above and beyond that which is an enforceable requirement of the job description.
- OCBs contribute positively to overall organizational effectiveness.

A simple way of thinking about organizational citizenship is that it is the extent to which an employee's voluntary support contributes to their employer's success. If treated well by their employer, the employee wants to reciprocate by doing their best.

Relevance – engagement, recognition

Principal-agent theory (Agency theory)

Agency theory was developed as an economic theory. In employment terms it centres around aligning what it sees as the otherwise divergent interests of the agent (employee) and the principal (employer). Agency theory says that the principal must use schemes that helps align the interest of the agents with the principal's own interests, such as merit pay, stock-option schemes, profit sharing and incentives. These are the agency cost and are the means by which the employer seeks to ensure that the employee does what the employer wishes. The theory also suggests the need to set objectives and monitor performance. The theory emphasizes the need for extrinsic motivators and reflects the thinking in McGregor's theory X.

Relevance – incentives, contingent reward

Psychological contract

This is normally seen as the unwritten contract that exists between employer and employee. It has been defined as, 'a set of beliefs about what each party is entitled to receive, and obligated to give in exchange for another party's contributions' (Perkins and White, 2008). These will typically be values such as fairness and trust and to a large extent will reflect the culture within the organization.

Relevance – reward philosophy and strategy, communications, engagement

Theory X and Theory Y

McGregor's theory X assumes that people are inherently lazy and therefore must be motivated by outside incentives. Their natural goals are counter-productive with those of the organization, therefore they must be controlled by external forces to get them to work towards the goals of the organization; people are basically incapable of self-discipline and self-control. Theory Y assumes that human motives fall within a hierarchy, from the most basic through to self-actualization (similar to Maslow's theory). People are primarily self-motivated and self-controlled; there is no inherent conflict between the goals of the individual and more effective organizational performance; employees will integrate their own goals with those of the organization (McGregor, 1960 quoted in Schein, 1980).

Theory X would take a rational-economic perspective and advocate the need for extrinsic reinforcement within an assumption that people are primarily motivated by economic incentives and will do whatever gives them the greatest economic gain. Theory Y would argue for the dominance of intrinsic reward.

Relevance – incentives, engagement

Two-factor theory

Hertzberg's research of accountants and engineers in the 1950s asked the subjects to recall examples of situations where they had positive and negative feelings about the job (Hertzberg *et al*, 1959). Based on the responses, Hertzberg's theory is that there are factors which are satisfiers that can change behaviour positively as 'motivators' relating to job content – achievement, recognition, work itself, responsibility and advancement. There are also 'hygiene factors', which act as dissatisfiers, relating to job context – company policy and administration, supervision, salary, interpersonal relations and working conditions. Although these are commonly the main source of dissatisfaction they do not become a source of motivation if 'reversed'.

Hertzberg criticises Maslow's hierarchy concept that suggests an order of need (Hertzberg *et al*, 1959). However, he describes a study undertaken by Fantz where Maslow's three lower level needs were equated to the hygiene factors and the three higher needs represented the motivators. Hertzberg seems to accept this relationship between the two models of motivation (Hertzberg, 1968).

Relevance – recognition, engagement

Utility theory

Primarily a theory in economics and investment that although it is impossible to measure the utility derived from a good or service, it is usually possible to rank the alternatives in their order of preference to the consumer. The principle of expected utility maximization states that a rational investor, when faced with a choice among a set of competing feasible investment alternatives, acts to select an investment that maximizes his expected utility of wealth.

In our terms utility theory is interested in people's preferences or values. The simple point of interest is that different people will have different preferences, getting greater utility from some parts of their reward and terms and conditions than others.

Relevance – benefits, flexible benefits, employee communications

REFERENCES

Anik, L *et al* (2013) Prosocial bonuses increase employee satisfaction and team performance, working paper, Harvard Business School

Aon Hewitt, Total Rewards Survey, 2012

Armstrong, M and Murlis, H (2004) *Reward Management*, Kogan Page, London

Ascent Group Inc (2009) Reward & Recognition Program Profiles & Best Practices

Blanchard, K and Johnson, S (1993) *The One Minute Manager*, HarperCollins, London

Brown, D (2001) *Reward Strategies: From intent to impact*, CIPD, London

Brown, D and West, M A (2006) Pride and groom, *People Management* (January 26), pp 16–17

Caudron, S (1995) The top 20 ways to motivate employees, *Industry Week*, **244** (7) (April 3)

CIPD (2005) *How to develop a reward strategy*

CIPD (2012) Annual survey report, Reward risks (October)

CIPD (2006) *Working Life: Employee attitudes and engagement research Report*

Civil Service People Survey (2012) [online] http://www.civilservice.gov.uk/wp-content/uploads/2013/01/csps2012_summary-of-findings_final.pdf

Deloitte (2013) *Resetting Horizons Human Capital Trends* [online] https://www.deloitte.com/view/en_GX/global/services/consulting/human-capital/81e324da20d0e310VgnVCM1000003256f70aRCRD.htm#.UlQWYdJJOSo

Fidelity (2012) *Principles of Ownership* (December) [online] https://www.fidelity.co.uk/static/pdf/common/footer/principles.pdf

Freiberg, K, and Freiberg, J (1996) *Nuts! Southwest Airlines' crazy recipe for business and personal success*, Bard Press, Austin

FSA (2013) Final guidance: risks to customers from financial incentives (January) [online] http://www.fsa.gov.uk/library/policy/final_guides/2013/fg1301

Glucksberg, S (1962) The influence of strength of drive on functional fixedness and perceptual recognition, *Journal of Experimental Psychology*, **63** (1), pp 36–41

Handy, C (1994) *The Empty Raincoat*, Random House, London

Hay Group Guide Chart – Profile method of job evaluation, Hay Group (www.haygroup.com) [online] http://www.haygroup.com/downloads/au/Guide_Chart-Profile_Method_of_Job_Evaluation_Brochure_web.pdf

Hertzberg, F (1968) *Work and the Nature of Man*, Granada, London

Hertzberg, F, Mausner, B and Snyderman, B B (1959) *The Motivation to Work*, John Wiley & Sons, New York

Hoffmann, C, Lesser, E and Ringo, T (2012) *Calculating Success*, Harvard Business School, Boston

Institute of Leadership and Management (2013) Beyond the Bonus: Driving employee performance

Jacquart, P and Armstrong, J S (2013) Are top executives paid enough? The Wharton School, University of Pennsylvania

Jeffrey, S (2004) Right Answer, Wrong Question, University of Chicago

Juran, J (2003) *Juran on Leadership For Quality*, Simon & Schuster, New York

Kenexa (2013) Perception is Reality: The importance of pay fairness to employees and organizations

Kohn, A (1993) Why incentive plans cannot work, *Harvard Business Review* (Sept–Oct)

Kouzes, J M and Posner, B Z (2007) *The Leadership Challenge*, Jossey-Bass, San Francisco

KPMG (2012a) Rethinking human resources in a changing world [online] http://www.kpmg.com/Global/en/IssuesAndInsights/ArticlesPublications/hr-transformations-survey/Documents/hr-transformations-survey-full-report.pdf

KPMG (2012b) Guide to Directors' Remuneration [online] http://www.kpmg.com/uk/en/issuesandinsights/articlespublications/pages/kpmgs-guide-to-directors-remuneration.aspx

La Motta, T (1995) *Recognition The Quality Way*, Quality Resources, New York

MacLeod, D and Clark, N (2009) Engaging for success: enhancing performance through employee engagement. A report to government, Department for Business, Innovation and Skills [online] http://www.bis.gov.uk/files/file52215.pdf

McConville, D, Smith, A and Arnold, J (2012) *The Human and Organisational Impact of Employee Share Ownership*, Loughborough University

McKinsey Quarterly (2009) Motivating people: getting beyond money (November) [online] http://www.mckinsey.com/insights/organization/motivating_people_getting_beyond_money

McLean, B and Elkind, P (2004) *The Smartest Guys in the Room*, Penguin, London

Maslow, A H (1970) *Motivation and Personality*, Harper & Row, New York

Mercer (2011) What's Working survey

Nelson, B (1996) Dump the cash, load on the praise, *Personnel Journal*, 75 (7), pp 65–70

Organ, D W (1988) *Organizational Citizenship Behavior: The good soldier syndrome*, Lexington Books, Lanham, MD

Oosterbeek, H, Sloof, R and Van de Kuilen, G (2003) Cultural differences in ultimatum game experiments: evidence from a meta-analysis, University of Amsterdam

Perkins, S J and White, G (2008) *Employee Reward*, CIPD, London

Pink, D (2010) *Drive*, Canongate Books, New York

Pink, D (2013) Don't tell me what to do, *People Management* (May), pp 38–40

PwC (2011) Making executive pay work: the psychology of incentives

PwC (2012) Getting the balance of executive pay right, executive reward survey

PwC (2013) NextGen: a global generational study

Rath, T and Clifton, D O (2004) *How Full is Your Bucket?* Gallup Press, New York

Roffey Park Management Institute (2007) The Management Agenda

Rose, M (2001) *Recognising Performance*, CIPD, London

Rose, M (2011) *A Guide to Non-cash Reward*, Kogan Page, London

Schein, F H (1980) *Organizational Psychology*, Prentice-Hall, Englewood Cliffs, New Jersey

Skinner, B F (1953) *Science and Human Behavior*, Macmillan, New York

Steers, R M and Porter, L W (1991) *Motivation and Work Behavior*, McGraw-Hill, New York

Thaler, R (1980) Toward a positive theory of consumer choice, *Journal of Economic Behaviour and Organization*, **1** (1), pp 39–60

Towers Watson (2010) Creating a sustainable rewards and talent management model

Tyson, S (1995) *Human Resource Strategy*, Pitman, London

Vartiainen, M *et al* (2008) *Reward Management – Facts and Trends in Europe*, PABST Science Publishers, Lengerich

Vroom, V H (1964) *Work and Motivation*, Wiley, New York

Workspan (2012) Beyond spreadsheets (December)

Workspan (2013) Beyond the survey: how to increase engagement (June)

Further resources

www.e-reward.co.uk – register to gain access to this excellent site with a huge number of resources on reward.

www.cipd.co.uk – the CIPD publishes an annual rewards management survey, normally in May, but also has other free resources.

www.employeebenefits.co.uk – this is the website for the monthly magazine that focuses on benefit-related issues but also covers other aspects of reward.

www.worldatwork.org/waw/home/html/home.jsp – this is the US professional reward body which is a membership organization. Little is available on the site without joining.

www.employeeengagement.ning.com – an international forum for people with an interest in employee engagement. Free to join.

http://theirf.org – The Incentive Research Foundation, which is a not-for-profit research organization with some excellent research on motivation, incentive and reward

www.hmrc.gov.uk/index.htm – the HMRC site for all UK tax issues

INDEX

(*italics* indicate a figure or table in the text)